CEREMONIAL COSTUME

By Phillis Cunnington and Alan Mansfield:
English Costume for Sports and Outdoor Recreation

Her Majesty Queen Elizabeth II, Sovereign of the Most Honourable Order of the Bath, wearing the Mantle and Insignia (From the Portrait by Leonard Boden, R.P., F.R.S.A., painted for The Royal Military Academy Sandhurst. Photo by courtesy of the Colchester Searchlight Tattoo).

CEREMONIAL COSTUME

Court, civil and civic costume
from 1660 to the present day

ALAN MANSFIELD

'. . . clothed not only in wool
but with Dignity and a
Mystic Dominion . . .'
Carlyle: *Sartor Resartus*

ADAM & CHARLES BLACK · LONDON

First published 1980
A & C Black (Publishers) Limited
35 Bedford Row, London WC1R 4JH

© 1980 A & C Black (Publishers) Limited
ISBN 0 7136 2083 8

Mansfield, Alan
  Cermonial costume.
    1. Courts and courtiers – Costume
    2. Uniforms, Civil – Great Britain
    3. Great Britain – Court and courtiers
    I. Title
    391'.8   GT1755.G7

    ISBN 0–7136–2083–8

Text set in 11/12 pt Photon Baskerville, printed and bound
in Great Britain at The Pitman Press, Bath

CONTENTS

LIST OF ILLUSTRATIONS

PLATES

ACKNOWLEDGEMENTS

Major Mansfield completed his manuscript before his death in 1979 but
was unable to oversee all the stages of production leading to publication.

Publisher's note

The author's thanks and gratitude are extended to the following institutions and individuals who have given invaluable direct or indirect
assistance in the preparation of this work:

Army & Navy Stores Ltd., Army Dept. Public Relations, John
Bensusan-Butt Esq., City of Birmingham, Major J. D. Braisby R.A., City
of Bristol, British Library, British Museum, C. N. Bullivant Esq., Miss
Bridget Chamberlain, Central Chancery of the Order of Knighthood, Lt.
Col. R. W. Charlton, Chief Constable of Essex, Miss Pamela Clabburn, D.
T-D. Clarke Esq., C. F. Clifton Esq., Lt. Col. Peter Clifton, H. S. Cobb
Esq., Dame Elizabeth Coker, Colchester Borough Council, Colchester
Library, Colchester Museums, College of Arms, *Country Life*, Courtauld
Institute, P. Coverly Esq., Martin Dean, Esq., Messrs Ede & Ravenscroft
Ltd., Essex Archaeological Society Library, Essex County Library, Essex
County Newspapers, Essex Record Office, Jeremy Farrell Esq., Roy
Farthing, Esq., Worshipful Company of Feltmakers, Gallery of English
Costume, Manchester, Mrs Madelaine Ginsburg, Miss Elisabeth Grant
and Mrs Grant, V. W. Gray Esq., Guildhall Library and Museum, *Gunner*
Magazine, Miss Zillah Halls, Wm. Heinemann Ltd., House of Commons,
House of Lords, *Illustrated London News*, City of Kingston-upon-Hull,
Royal Borough of Kingston-upon-Thames, London Museum, Lord
Chamberlain's Office, Mrs J. Mcfie, Miss Malley, Dean and Chapter of
Manchester Cathedral, National Army Museum, National Portrait
Gallery, Nottingham Museums, Order of St John, Press Association,
Public Record Office, *Punch*, G. Pyman Esq., Sir John Ruggles-Brise
Bart., Scottish National Portrait Gallery, City of Sheffield, City of
Southampton, Town Serjeant Spong, Colchester, Sjt. Steele (Essex
Police), David Swanston Esq., *Tailor & Cutter*, Corporation of Trinity
House, Miss V. Vaughan, Victoria and Albert Museum, Major N. S.
Watkin-Williams, Peter Watson Esq., Miss Anne Watts, D. Webb Esq.,
City of York. Many of the illustrations are from photographs by Roy
Farthing of Mersea Island.

Especial thanks are due to Aubrey Bowden Esq. and Philip Mansel Esq. for generously making available their researches as yet unpublished, and to J. L. Nevinson Esq. for his great help and encouragement, and again, generous provision from his works. Major General P. B. Gillett, Secretary of the Central Chancery of the Orders of Knighthood has been most forbearing and helpful in replying to the many letters with which I bombarded him.

The contributions of A. & C. Black, Susan Luckham and Valerie Mansfield are acknowledged in the Introduction.

Finally, this book is dedicated to the late Phillis Cunnington and the late Catherine Lucas whose enthusiasm, advice and scholarship encouraged the author over many years, in this and other aspects of the History of Costume.

Quotations from "The King" by Roger Fulford contained in *Edwardian England* edited by Simon Nowell-Smith are copyright of the Oxford University Press 1964 and used by their permission.

Extracts from the various editions of *Dress Worn at Court* are by permission of the Lord Chamberlain and Messrs Harrison & Sons Ltd.

Several illustrations have been used from *English Costume* by George Clinch, published by Methuen & Co. Ltd., 1909.

The Editor of *The Connoisseur* has given permission for the extracts from "Windsor Uniform" by Sir Owen Morshead, 1935, and "Order of the Garter" by J. L. Nevinson, 1937.

The author hopes that no one has been omitted from these acknowledgements; if so, they are assured that it is only by regrettable mischance, and their indulgence is craved.

To the memory of
Phillis Cunnington
and
Catherine Lucas

INTRODUCTION

The year 1660 may seem an arbitrary starting point for this survey, but it appears to me to mark in various ways the starting point of much of the dress, general and specialised, which is, or was, worn on occasions of ceremony by both men and women. Much, of course, of the state dress of 1660 was inherited from before the Interregnum, and in some cases I refer briefly to earlier history, but also we see introduced reforms and variations and in some cases an up-dating of costume, for example, Charles II's "Persian" dress, perhaps the first attempt to introduce a court costume for ordinary men not entitled to any distinguishing mantles or robes.

Again, many of our now cherished sartorial institutions were introduced during the eighteenth and nineteenth centuries: cocked hats, buckled shoes, wigs and knee-breeches to name a few.

The Restoration of the Monarchy, and the re-constitution of the Court, now significantly different from its Tudor and medieval counterparts, gave an impetus and uplift to life and society in general and regenerated many customs and costumes of the past that had fallen into desuetude.

This book deals, not, I confess, as deeply as I should like, with civil costume omitting those specialised branches of ecclesiastical, legal and academic dress. Even omitting these branches the subject is a vast one, and the line had to be drawn somewhere: I hope I have drawn it in more or less the right place. Omissions such as the Queen's Bargemaster, the Royal Band, the Deputy of Brightlingsea, and many more, are deliberate. Military uniforms are also omitted, except in the case of such quasi-military bodies and individuals as The Yeomen of the Guard and Lord-Lieutenants.

The reader may think some of the information skimpy, in other cases that I have been too prolix. I would say in my defence that information is very patchy: some areas have deep and easily accessible mines of it, others have few and scattered deposits. Some institutions are surprisingly ignorant of their customs and their past; much relevant information is only recorded in manuscript in such places as the Public Record Office and the Record Offices of Counties and Cities: some queries seem to have no answers. Time in large quantities, and corresponding financial support is required by the researcher who will, one day I hope, fill in the many existing gaps.

Actual garments exist up and down the country; some are illustrated in this book. The finest collection is that of the old London Museum now incorporated in the Museum of London. All the work I did at the London Museum and all the help I received from the staff of the Costume Department was centred on Kensington Palace.

The Bibliography will point the way to the most common relevant works, contemporary and modern, and many additional details are there available to the keen student; for instance he (or she) will find in *Dress and Insignia to be Worn at Court*, 1929 edition, that civil uniform is to be worn by, among many others occupying twenty-three pages, The Chief Inspector of Alkali Works (Ministry of Health) and the Director of Kew Gardens.

We now have Lady Peers, appropriately clad in parliamentary robes as are the men, Lady Mayors (for many years past now) also adopting the male plumage, but Lady Deputy Lord-Lieutenants and Privy Councillors are without any suitable official garb, as is still, I believe, a lady taking the Speaker's chair in the House of Commons and Deputy Chairman of Ways and Means. I feel most strongly that these anomalies should be put right.

I acknowledge and thank in preceding pages the many kindnesses and great help I have received from individuals, institutions and other bodies, but I wish in this Introduction to say especial thanks to my wife for coping for years with the book, and acting (in addition to her normal daily round) as secretary, illustrator and nurse: to Mrs Ralph Luckham for deciphering my handwriting and producing an orderly and correct typescript in one go, and last but not least to Messrs A. & C. Black for their patience and forbearance in waiting for this book – which I hope will prove worthwhile.

West Mersea   Alan Mansfield
December 1978

CHAPTER I

Peers and Parliament

THE PEERAGE

The House of Lords is constituted of the Lords Spiritual, being the two Archbishops and twenty-one senior Diocesan Bishops of the Church of England, and the Lords Temporal, being the hereditary degrees of Duke, Marquess, Earl, Viscount and Baron of the United Kingdom, certain elected Scottish Peers and of Life Peers, generally of Baron's rank. The House is presided over by the Lord Chancellor, a political appointment, who is also a Cabinet Minister and the head of the Judiciary. The Lord Chancellor is not of necessity a peer himself.

In considering the dress of the peerage the Lords Spiritual and the Lord Chancellor in his legal capacity are not included.

In 1649 the Commonwealth abolished the House of Lords, and although in 1657 a nominated Upper House – known at least to Cromwell as "the Lords" – was created, it was not until the Restoration in 1660 that the ancient pattern of Parliament was fully re-established as Monarch, Peers and People assembled together.

The custom of wearing a robe or mantle, often fur-lined, on ceremonial occasions by knights and members of the nobility appears to have been established in the early Middle Ages. Sometimes it was bestowed by the monarch or feudal lord as a mark of honour (in 1397 Richard II had bestowed a robe of honour on the newly created Earl of Somerset): later, the mantle, now in the form of a "gown", was also appropriated by the learned and dignified professions and guilds and awarded by the regulating bodies of these professions and companies.

It seems that a distinctive official costume for the peerage originated some time in the later fifteenth century, in the form of a robe or mantle

with an ermine cape resembling the ecclesiastical almuce. Before the
use of robes, however, it had been customary for newly created dukes
to be invested with a cap of estate, which may have been encircled with
a coronet: marquesses received a "chaplet" or gold circle for the head.

During the sixteenth century it becomes evident that for some classes
of peers there are two sets of robes; the "investiture" or "coronation"
robe or robe of estate, and the parliamentary robe. The first was worn
only for coronations and at the investiture of new peers: the second
was to be worn on parliamentary and other occasions when such a
mark of dignity and position was required. The original peers' robes,
whatever their form, appear to have been of the category of
"parliamentary" robes and in the earlier sixteenth century only dukes,
marquesses and earls had coronation investiture robes as well:
viscounts received theirs under Elizabeth I, but the barons had to wait
almost a century longer for theirs, until 1685.

1. Henry Montague, First
Earl of Manchester in parlia-
ment robe, *c* 1600. (From a
reproduction in Manchester,
*Court and Society . . . from the
Papers at Kimbolton*, 1864)

2. Parliament robes of a viscount, 1614. (From Planché after Seldon, *Titles of Honor*, 1614)

By the seventeenth century peers' robes were established in much the form that they are today; Seldon in his *Titles of Honor* published in 1614, illustrated the degrees of nobility in their robes. Parliamentary or parliament robes consisted of a mantle, kirtle and hood. The mantle was of circular cut, open from the shoulder on the right hand side and with a short slit at the front of the neck. (Planché's reproduction of the figures from Vincent MS 151 in the College of Arms seems to indicate also a slit up the front from the hem.) From illustrations it appears that the mantle may have been fur faced or lined sometimes. From centre front to centre back of the mantle, across the right shoulder and side were miniver "guards", consisting of bars of white fur with a gold lace edging above each bar.

The kirtle, worn under the mantle, was a long, loose, open-fronted garment, girdled at the waist; the hood, worn over the kirtle and under the mantle, a type of shoulder cape with a small hood proper as an appendage at the back. When the mantle was put on over kirtle and hood, this small hood proper was pulled out from underneath, behind the head, to hang down the back of the mantle. The parliament robes were all of scarlet cloth, as they are today. "My Lordes scarlett Parliament Robbes being in three severall peeces . . ." (*Easton Lodge Inventory* 1637 ed. F. W. Steer, 1952).

In 1621 the investiture of new peers by the sovereign was replaced by "introducing" the newly created peer to the House of Lords by two members of his own degree, as is still done today. Up to that time, in the reign of James I, for investiture by the sovereign dukes, marquesses, earls and viscounts wore the crimson velvet coronation or investiture robes, as they also did at the coronation of a new monarch. Barons, then having only parliament robes presumably wore them on these occasions.

From the earliest references to peers' robes in the late Middle Ages the distinction between "parliament" and "investiture" or "coronation" is somewhat confused. The sixteenth century monarchs proceeding to their coronations are described as going in parliament robes of crimson velvet, and returning in their purple "robes of estate". This custom has persisted from that time so that the monarch's parliament robe is of crimson velvet, corresponding in fact to the coronation robe of the peerage generally today.

In his *Cyclopaedia of Costume*, Planché states that earls, marquesses and dukes up to James I's time were "invested with robes of purple velvet, the mantles having capes or tippets of ermine, the degrees being marked by rows of black tails in lieu of bars of miniver on the right shoulder. . . ." Unfortunately Planché does not quote any direct evidence to support his statement: indeed what evidence there is seems

3. Coronation robes of an earl. Worn at investitures until 1621, since then only at coronations. The sword suspended from the neck was part of the investiture ceremony. (From Planché after Seldon, *Titles of Honor*, 1614)

to contradict it. A description of a duke's "manteau" during Edward IV's reign (B. M. Lansdown MS 285 f 205 v) gives it as of crimson velvet, and Harleian MS 6064 art. 35, probably dating from the 1570s or 80s, says an earl has a mantle of "crymson velvett". Planché may have been muddled by the changes in the colour of the garter robes about this time.

The coronation or investiture mantle was more cloak-like than the parliament robe and had a front opening only, fastening at the neck. Instead of miniver guards it did indeed, and still does, have a cape of white ermine with rows of black tails equating with the bars of miniver on the parliament robe to indicate rank. This is known as "doubling" or "a doublet" of ermine. The robe or mantle was worn over a long sleeveless velvet kirtle or surcoat, tied at the waist with a silk sash. Again, like the parliament robe, the mantle may have at times been fur lined or faced: today the front opening is edged with white fur.

The indications of rank or degree on both types of mantle, that is guards of miniver or doublets of ermine, were:

> For a Duke, four rows
> For a Marquess, three and a half rows
> For an Earl, three rows
> For a Viscount, two and a half rows
> For a Baron, two rows,

and these distinctions are the same today. (Royal dukes have six rows of ermine, two more on the collar and ermine on the front fur edging.) The surcoat also appears to have had a shoulder cape, the edges of which, together with the opening front, were trimmed with white fur.

Robes were often passed from father to son: in 1694 when William, Earl of Bedford was created Duke, he had his parliament robe, apparently originally his father's, altered. Five years previously for William and Mary's coronation he had had his father's investiture mantle refurbished with new miniver (Scott-Tomson, *Life in a Noble Household*, 1965).

During the eighteenth century the surcoat of the investiture robe becomes smaller and eventually disappears, although for the coronation of George IV in 1821, Lord Braybrooke bought a coronation mantle and surcoat. As will be seen later, George IV's coronation was a somewhat fancy-dress affair.

In 1788 according to *The Pocket Peerage*, "the mantle and surcoat which a Duke wears at the coronation . . . is of crimson velvet lined with white taffeta, and the mantle is doubled from the neck to below the elbow with ermine having four rows of spots on each shoulder." By

4. Earl's coronation robe and surcoat. Collar and garter of the Garter.
Coronet with cap of maintenance. White Wand of Household Officer. (1st
Earl Rochester, by Godfrey Kneller, 1688. National Portrait Gallery)

5. Charles Montague, First
Duke of Manchester in cor-
onation or investiture robes.
The coronet has not caught
up, it is an earl's. (From
reproduction in Manchester,
*Court and Society . . . from the
Papers at Kimbolton*, 1864)

this time a white fur turn-down collar had been added to the ermine
cape.

The *Pocket Peerage* goes on to describe a duke's parliamentary robes
"of fine scarlet cloth, lined with white taffeta, and is doubled with four
guards of ermine [sic] at equal distances with gold lace above each
guard and is tied up to the left shoulder by a black riband". There is
also a white fur turn-down collar, replacing the earlier separate hood,
which survives as a small triangular strip of red cloth at the back of the
neck, emerging below the fur collar.

The parliamentary mantle is worn without the former kirtle and is
shown as trained and open up both sides, tied with black ribbon on the
left, as noted above. However, the mantle in Nottingham Museum of
Costume belonging to the 3rd Duke of Portland (1762–1809) is open
on the right side only, the left side being so arranged as to be drawn up
by a cord inside to allow it to drape over the left arm. From the front of
the neck down the breast is a vertical slit about twenty inches long,
guarded with fur and gold lace and tied at the neck with a white
ribbon.

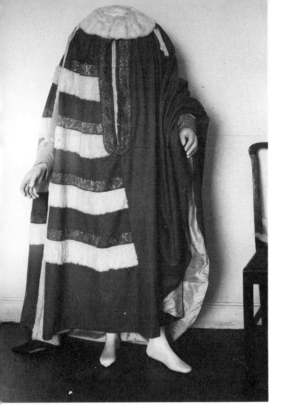

6. Parliament robe of the Third Duke of Portland. Note appearance of guarded neck slit and that the guards of ermine and gold now extend almost down to the hem. Late eighteenth century. (Courtesy of Museum of Costume and Textiles, Nottingham)

7. Side view of 6. Vestigial hood at back can just be seen. (Courtesy of Museum of Costume and Textiles, Nottingham)

Underneath the parliamentary mantle plain clothes were worn, ". . . the peers, their scarlet mantles negligently thrown over their ordinary dress . . ." noted Prince Puckler-Muskau in 1826 (Butler, *A Regency Visitor*).

With the coronation robes the surcoat, as noted above, also became obsolescent during the eighteenth century, and eventually disappeared. Not, however, before the coronation of George IV in 1821 when the "Peers being very sumptuous all with crimson velvet mantles" worn over surcoats of the same, most of knee-length only, but some, according to contemporary illustrations, calf-length. The mantles and surcoats were worn over fanciful sixteenth century garments, in which all the male participants in the ceremony were garbed, including doublets and trunk-hose. To quote a Mrs Murray Smith, who was there, "you are to understand that all the dresses were of the time of Queen Elizabeth; consequently all the men had ruffs of various sizes" ("Annals of Westminster Abbey" *Sphere*, 1911).

So it came about that the Lord Braybrooke mentioned above bought not only mantle and surcoat, but also a doublet, "pantaloons" (trunk hose?) and underdrawers as well as knee and shoe "roseates", inter alia, according to his bill from William Webb of Holywell Street, London (Essex Record Office). Apart from this extravagance the peerage wore normal civil dress or uniform under its robes. Some members of the aristocracy seem to have let the splendour of the coronation go to their heads: Princess Lieven records on 11 April 1822 a visit to a certain Lady Stewart: "she showed me her bedroom . . . above the bed is a baron's coronet . . . red velvet, ermine, everything that goes with it". In addition the bed curtains were "held up by four large gilt figures of Hercules, nude and fashioned exactly like real men".

At Queen Victoria's coronation in 1838 the peers attended wearing coronation robes over court dress or uniform, surcoats not being in evidence.

Debretts Peerage of 1845 describes both coronation and parliamentary robes much as above, but states that the parliamentary robes are tied at the left shoulder with white ribbon, instead of black. But in 1877 black bows are in evidence again. The white ribbon is mentioned again in the 1917 edition of *Whittaker's Peerage*, but pictures of 1910 and 1911 show black ribbon ties.

The official publication *Dress Worn at Court*, which was produced by the Lord Chamberlain's office and appeared in various editions from 1898, although referring in later editions to the robes of the peerage, makes only brief mention and does not go into details of design or methods of securing. The 1912 edition says "The Peer's Robe of scarlet cloth (known as the 'Parliamentary Robe') is of scarlet superfine cloth with ermine and gold lace, and is trimmed according to rank". Later twentieth-century illustrations of the parliament robe, however, all show black ribbon ties, at the front neck and on the left shoulder, as they have today. The parliament robe is now lined with white silk with miniver guards and edging to the right hand opening, and is worn over uniform or ordinary day dress on occasions of ceremony in the House of Lords and when the peers attend in a body at a church service or other solemn or formal event outside the House.

The coronation or investiture robe had by the twentieth century become known generally as the state robe or mantle. Since the abolition of investiture by the monarch, in the seventeenth century, this

8. Parliamentary robe of a baron, early nineteenth century. (Lord Colchester, by James Lonsdale, 1817. Courtesy of Colchester Borough and Colchester Castle Museum)

9. Peers in coronation robes and a variety of underdress at the Coronation of H.M. the Queen. Royal Peers in foreground showing their additional doublings of ermine, 1953. (Press Association)

robe has become confined to wear at coronations, when it is worn over uniform or court dress. It has become standardised as a crimson velvet cloak, slightly trained, lined with white silk and edged with miniver, the collar and cape also of miniver, the cape powdered with bars or rows of ermine according to rank. The ermine, originally the black-tipped tail of that animal, has for a long time past been replaced by pieces of black fur cut out with special steel punch. A vestigial hood, similar to that on the parliamentary mantle, of crimson silk, is attached at the neck at the back of the cape.

CORONETS AND CAPS

As we have seen it had long been the custom to dignify peers upon their creation or promotion by bestowing a chaplet or coronet, even before the general introduction of distinguishing robes.

The original chaplet may well have been a wreath or garland, but became a gold circle, sometimes jewelled and often ornamented in the shape of flowers. The coronet proper, a more crown-like headdress, is seen from the fourteenth century; but the name appears to date from the late fifteenth. At first the granting of coronets was confined to dukes and earls. A somewhat more elaborate one is seen in some representations of Princes of Wales. In 1385 when the degree of marquess was established a coronet was awarded. Viscounts are credited with being granted a coronet by James I but the evidence is conflicting (see St John Hope, "The Cap of Maintenance", W. H. St John Hope appx. to *English Coronation Reccords*, 1902).

Barons acquired a coronet in 1661 from Charles II: Evelyn records for 22 April that year that the King created "six Earls, and as many Barons" and that "they were then rob'd, their coronets and collars put on by his Majestie . . . but the Barons [later] put off their caps and circles and held them in their hands, the Earles keeping on their coronets as cousins to the King." Again there is some confusion, St John Hope quotes a source, not published until 1820, stating that it was caps of maintenance (or estate) only that the barons received in April, the coronet not being accorded to them until the August of that year. According to Planché quoting a manuscript in the College of Arms the barons already had a plain gold circle or chaplet, which they had changed for the coronet. However whether April or August, and whether or not there was a previous chaplet, by 1661 all ranks of the peerage had coronets.

The coronets varied in decoration according to degree: each was a headband or circlet with devices as follows raised above the upper edge:

Duke: eight gold strawberry leaves
Marquess: four gold strawberry leaves alternating with four silver balls ("pearls") on points or spikes
Earl: eight silver balls raised on tall points or spikes with gold strawberry leaves between the points
Viscount: sixteen small silver balls around the top edge
Baron: six larger silver balls around the top edge

Up to 1661 the circlets of ranks above viscount were chased or engraved, the viscount's was plain. When the barons were given the coronet, however, the viscounts became engraved also and the barons succeeded to the plain circlet. In 1665 the Scottish and Irish peers were authorised to wear coronets similar to those of the English peerage.

Originally coronets of all degrees were probably of gold, but today, and for a long time past, they are of silver gilt. No significant change has taken place in the form or ornament of coronets since the seventeenth century, or even earlier, except that modern rules forbid the use of real or artificial pearls or precious stones in coronets, a regulation that seems first to have appeared for the coronation of King George II in 1727. "It is His Majesty's pleasure that all and every the Peers and Peeresses who shall attend the said coronation do forbear to set or use any jewels or precious stones in their coronets." (Earl Marshal's Regulations, 22 September 1727.) Certainly in previous times jewels had been used to ornament some coronets although the practice seems to have been dying out even during the seventeenth century.

Whether the designation "pearls" referring to the silver balls decorating the rims of coronets ever signified the use of real pearls is open to question. The *Shorter Oxford Dictionary* attributes the use of "pearl" in this sense to 1688, but it also gives the use of the word to represent white or silver (argent) when blazoning arms with jewels as dating from 1500. Medieval representations of coronets, however, would point to the use of metal balls, unless the size of real pearls, if used, was greatly exaggerated.

The modern coronet looks as if it is lined with crimson velvet and bordered with ermine; this is officially described as a "crimson velvet cap turned up with ermine, with a gold tassel in the centre" (Trendall, *Dress Worn at His Majesty's Court*). This represents the cap of maintenance, originally a separate article; and still so treated in the case of the monarch.

The cap of maintenance, or cap of estate, apparently occurs in England from the early fourteenth century and at first was restricted to the king, and his sons as royal dukes; later in the century it was also bestowed upon lesser peers when they were promoted to dukedoms. This ducal cap was probably encircled by a coronet. By the end of the fifteenth century the distinction had been extended to marquesses by Edward IV; and later to earls by Edward VI, who on 16 February, 1546–7 issued letters patent creating the Earls of Warwick and Southampton, in each case with "unam capam honoris et dignitatis atque circulum aureum. . . ."

Viscounts appear to have achieved the cap of estate under James I – certainly they had them at the coronation of Charles I. Barons were to wait for the Restoration for their caps, as they did for their coronets. In 1631 Seldon shows the caps of dukes, marquesses and earls as turned up with ermine, and viscounts with plain fur. A 1661 figure in a

Patent Roll (13, Charles II) depicts the barons' new cap as a plain red silk with no fur. Today all ranks are turned up with ermine. The gold tassel surmounting the cap is apparently of Elizabethan origin. At the coronation of 1953 the cap of estate alone was sanctioned to be worn by baron's only, if they did not possess a coronet.

HATS

Although coronets would appear to have been worn with both coronation and parliament robes, from the seventeenth century the practice of wearing hats with parliamentary robes seems to have developed. Viscount Brackly, who was Lord High Chancellor from 1596 to 1617 was painted in parliament robes and a broad-brimmed high crowned hat.

The three-cornered cocked hat appeared in the late seventeenth century and became the regulation wear with parliamentary robes and survived at trials of impeachment and of fellow peers (the last trial of impeachment was in 1806 and the right of peers to be tried by the House of Lords instead of by the courts was abolished in 1936), for Royal Commissions, and at the introduction of new peers, which had taken the place of installation by the monarch.

The fore-and-aft cocked hat which became popular at the beginning of the nineteenth century replaced the three-cornered hat for wear with parliamentary robes: the Lord Chancellor, however, remained faithful to the older style.

FEMALE PEERS

Lady peers – as opposed to peeresses, the wives of male peers – are members of the House of Lords on equal terms with the men. The first creations were in 1958 under the Life Peerage Act, and these were followed by the admission of hereditary female peers under an Act of 1963. However, hereditary female peers – those ladies whose title could descend in the female line, not solely by tail male – have long attended coronations in their own right, and thus worn a peeress's coronation robe and coronet.

Now both types of lady peer are eligible to wear parliament robes of the same design and on the same occasions as their male counterparts over ordinary day dress, or evening dress, at the opening of Parliament. On introduction they wear a small round black hat with a gold cockade on the left side. Presumably for future coronations they will wear robes as now ordained for peeresses generally. Whether or not, in view of their equality with male peers, they will be entitled to a full size

10. Life baroness in parliamentary robes and round black hat being introduced to the House by two peers of equal rank carrying cocked hats, 1971. (Press Association)

coronet is a matter not yet known, but perhaps the precedent of the peeresses in their own right at past coronations will be followed.

PEERESSES

Peeresses are not members of the Upper House, and therefore possess no parliamentary robes (but see p. 22).

The coronation robe, like the men's, is of crimson velvet, but its style is quite different and during most of the period we are considering it formed an integral part of the dress: an open robe or kirtle with bodice closed in front with a stomacher and a trained overskirt, worn open over a contrasting petticoat or underskirt. A separate train, topped with a cape of miniver powdered with rows of ermine according to rank, fell from the shoulders of the bodice, where it could be, apparently, either sewn or attached by cords. The short sleeves and open edges of the overskirt were cut scalloped. Borders of the neckline, sleeves, train and overskirt were of miniver or ermine, as was the stomacher. A heavy silver or gilt cord girdle around the waist was knotted in front, the ends falling below the knee, where they ended in large tassels. Gold lace and galloon often ornamented the bodice and in eighteenth century portraits rosettes and tassels occur in the scallops of the overskirt. The stomacher, and sometimes the neckline, was ornamented with paste jewels or pearls. In some eighteenth century portraits the sleeves have, in addition to the scalloped miniver edging, two plain bands of miniver above, and strips of miniver running from the shoulder to the upper hand. A white silk lining to kirtle and train was usual.

The petticoat or underskirt was according to the wearer's choice, and in some cases may have consisted of an inferior base with a rich front-panel where it was exposed by the open overskirt. Such a petticoat is among the robes worn by the Duchess of Richmond and Lennox at the coronation of Queen Anne in 1702 and it now adorns her

11. Peeress at the Coronation of James II, 1685. (Planché after Francis Sandford, *A History of the Coronation of James II*, 1685)

effigy in Westminster Abbey. However, according to Mr J. L. Nevinson, this may have been made up especially to dress the effigy. The design reflects the fashion of the late seventeenth century, and, indeed, was fixed as a "sealed pattern" for James II's coronation in 1687.

As noted above, the powderings of ermine on the cape denoted rank, but in addition the length of the train also indicates their rank, as does the width of the miniver borders or edging (see end of Chapter I).

That untiring and enquiring traveller, Celia Fiennes, gives a splendid description of peeresses' robes at the coronation of Queen Anne in 1702:

> ... in crimson velvet robes lined with earmine, and cut waved in a long traine lined with white sarsnet, the sleeves were open to the shoulder, tyed up there with silver cords and tassells hanging down to the wast, the sleeves being fringed with silver, under which fine point or lace sleeves and ruffles, with gloves laced or with ribbon gold and white, their peticoates were white, some tissue laced with gold or silver, and their stomachers some were all diamonds; over all they had mantles of the same crimson velvet lined with earmine and fastened to the shoulder, on which there was a broad earmine like a cape reaching to the waste powder'd with rowes according to their degree ... these all having long traines suitable to their robes and were in length as their degree.

The baronesses had their trains two and a quarter yards long drawing on the ground, the viscountesses two and a half yards, the marchionesses two and three-quarter yards, the duchesses three yards. As can be seen from the table at the end of this chapter, these figures are about twice the present length, which is said to have been the same as in the time of William and Mary (*The Gentlewoman*, Coronation Number 1902). Certainly the illustrations to Charles II's and James II's coronation processions do not indicate the longer lengths, and I wonder if Celia Fiennes's figures are at fault, although she got her rows of ermine right.

This pattern of robe, with minor variations, remained unchanged until the present century. At William IV's and Queen Victoria's coronations in 1831 and 1838 it is shown as extremely decolletée and cut to expose the shoulders completely, in the fashion of the evening dresses of that time. A strange garment is portrayed by Sir Thomas Lawrence in his portrait of the 4th Duchess of Newcastle (attributed *c* 1807). She stands clad in the simple, high waisted, low cut dress of the day over which is negligently worn an open coat or cloak with long close fitting sleeves. Sleeves and front edges and neck of the coat or cloak are edged with miniver, spotted with ermine. However, as about

12. Peeress in robe, jewelled stomacher, mid eighteenth century. (From portrait of Lady Ann Compton, by Allan Ramsay)

a century earlier Queen Anne's Duchess Sarah was painted seated with an amorphous ermine lined and edged garment draped partially over her, it is, I think, artistic licence pressed into service to provide a mark of the rank and importance of the sitter.

The long reign of Queen Victoria meant that the robes of peeresses did not again see the light of day until the twentieth century, at King Edward VII's coronation in 1902. Presumably some peeresses were able to make use of family robes, with appropriate alterations to fit, but new creations would require new robes and so did some of the members of the older nobility. The Earl Marshal's instructions referred to "robes or mantles" of peeresses and directed them to be "worn over the usual full Court dress". By royal command all the dresses and all new robes were to be made of British silk.

The term "mantle" indicates the one piece open robe as described below, as does the order to wear them over a separate dress, but the earlier type also persisted. For instance the Museum of London possess among others, the robes of the Countess of Moray worn at King Edward VII's coronation. These take the form of a crimson velvet dress of separate bodice and skirt (the usual fashion of the time) each with a centre front section of white corded silk, decorated with embroidery in

13. Augusta, Princess of Wales in Robe of State. Although more elaborate
and with a longer train, the picture shows the general style of a peeress's robe
with the court petticoat, or skirt, exposed in front, 1756. (Engraving by Baron
after J. B. Vanloo. Crown copyright, Victoria and Albert Museum)

gold and silver, pearls, and diamanté. The dress has ermine edgings, as has the train, which also has an ermine shoulder cape powdered with three rows and with gold cords and tassels.

In 1911, for George V's coronation, similar robes were in evidence: again the Museum of London has examples with separate skirt and stomacher panels, but with the velvet robe in one piece, not a separate bodice and skirt. Petticoats or underdresses had to be white or cream, with embroidery in silver or gold.

Sleeve edges were scalloped or vandyked at both times, but the miniver border to the robe (or kirtle as it is sometimes called) shows variations of scallops or is plain and straight.

Many of the 1902 and 1911 examples were re-used both in 1937, at George VI's coronation, and again in 1953 for the crowning of Elizabeth II. Most of these show signs of alteration, generally aimed at simplifying them. The robe or kirtle now takes the form of a one piece gown, open its full length down the centre front, edged with miniver, either plain or scalloped. The gown is shaped to the waist, where it can be secured by a clasp or gold cord girdle or left unfastened. The short sleeves have in general two miniver bands and a scalloped miniver edging.

In one photograph of 1953 the sleeves have only one band in addition to the edging, but miniver strips from the shoulders to the edge. It is understood this robe was also worn at King Edward VII's coronation.

14. Peeress's robes at the Coronation of George V, 1911. One piece robe worn over embroidered under-dress. (*Girls' Own Annual,* 1911)

15. Left, the new style sleeveless open robe designed by Norman Hartnell as an alternative to the traditional style (right). The new robe has no separate train and the deep fur collar is powdered with ermine front and back. The cap of estate is an alternative to the coronet; as is the similar cap (centre) for some peers. 1953. (Courtesy of Radio Times Hulton Picture Library)

The train with attached shoulder cape powdered as formerly with the ermine doublets of distinction has ornamental gold cords and tassels at the shoulders and is attached at the neckline of the kirtle. Beneath was worn a close fitting, low necked dress, white or silver or gold and white, often embroidered down the front, where the kirtle is open, the rest of the dress being plain.

In the seventeenth-century illustrations, and in some of the eighteenth and nineteenth century, there appear below the short sleeves of the kirtle what seem to be the chemise sleeves, or frilled linen undersleeves. In the eighteenth century, other pictures and Celia Fiennes's description show one or more wide lace ruffles, as in the prevailing fashion, and these persisted up to the present century, being, however, much less in evidence at the coronation of Queen Elizabeth II. In the present century, at least, long white kid gloves were also worn.

In connection with the coronation of Elizabeth II, authority was given in 1952 for a simplified design for peeresses not possessing inherited robes. The new style was designed by Norman Hartnell in association with the Earl Marshal. Instead of separate kirtle and train there is only a trained open robe or gown, sleeveless, with an all round cape collar of white fur, powdered with ermine according to rank. The robe is of crimson velvet, lined with white silk and with the traditional white fur border. For ladies below the rank of countess there is an alternative to the coronet in the form of matching round cap of estate, trimmed with gold braid.

CORONETS AND CAPS

The coronets and caps of peeresses are similar to those of their husbands, but are smaller, not encircling the head, but designed to be worn upon the intricacies of the female hair style already topped by a tiara, and previously also by a veil.

As the peeresses at a coronation do not put on their coronets until the queen is crowned (as the peers only put on theirs at the crowning of the king) the tiara and veil were originally prescribed following the command of St Paul that women's heads should be covered at times of prayer. Thus the coronet in their case was small enough (the average size is about five inches diameter) to place inside the tiara or other headdress without disturbing it or the coiffure.

Again Celia Fiennes gives a vivid description in 1702: "Their heads were dressed with much hair and long locks full of diamonds . . . their heads so dress'd as a space left for their coronets to be set, all the rest is filled with hair, jewells and gold, and white small ribbon, or gold thinn lace. . . ."

The small size of the coronets necessitated some kind of pinning to the hair to secure them, and in some examples built in sliding hatpin-like prongs are permanently attached to the rim. In 1911 a fashion writer said the hair styles were: "fluffed out full and softly at the sides," so that the "coronet rests comfortably and prettily on the head, and forms a really becoming finish". (*Girl's Own Annual*, 1911.)

In 1937 the *Woman's Pictorial* noted "peeresses are busy now experimenting in order to find the best way of arranging their hair under their coronet. A centre parting is necessary in nearly every case, a style recently adopted by the Duchess of Kent when wearing a tiara. The Duchess kept her hair smooth on top with a mass of little curls at the back."

THE LORD CHANCELLOR

As chairman of the House of Lords the Lord Chancellor today presides
clad in a black silk gown and a full-bottomed wig, much the same as

16. Edward Hyde, Earl of Clarendon, Lord Chancellor 1658–67. Gold
guarded black gown, plain square-cut falling-band as neckwear. The pattern
and arrangement of the gold lace varies between this and the next two
illustrations. (Engraving by J. Cochrane after Lely)

the Speaker of the House of Commons. He is accompanied not only by a mace, as is the Speaker, but also by the Purse, which theoretically contains the Great Seal, and with the mace, remains in the House throughout its sessions.

The gown is descended from the medieval gown which was worn for warmth indoors and out and which survived into the later sixteenth century, when it was replaced generally by a variety of other clothes, being retained, however, by the elderly and as a mark of dignity by the learned. By the seventeenth century it had thus acquired connotations of professional status among lawyers, doctors, academics and state and civil dignitaries. It is in the seventeenth century that it appears as a mark of office for the Chancellor in the form of a black damask state robe, slightly trained and richly guarded and trimmed with gold lace. Similar gowns were worn also by the Speaker and possibly by Privy Councillors generally. It still exists as coronation wear for the Chancellor of the Exchequer and Mytens portrait of Lionel, Earl of Middlesex, Lord Treasurer to James I, shows him in a gold laced gown and holding a white wand of office. In view of the gold lacing and guarding of such gowns at this time it is interesting to note that this Earl of Middlesex had started life as a retailer of gold lace. A portrait of Thomas Sackville, Earl of Dorset, painted about 1600 shows him in a less richly decorated gown which it has been suggested is that of Chancellor of Oxford University, but he is also holding a white wand, possibly as Lord High Treasurer.

Originally this damask and gold gown, now worn only on great state occasions, appears to have been normal wear; the plain silk version being a later work-a-day addition.

Before the adoption of the gown the Lord Chancellor seems to have worn his peer's robe, as shown in the portrait of Viscount Brackley who held office from 1596 to 1617, and this form of dress has been seen in subsequent times as an alternative to the gown. The Earl of Eldon wore the coronation robe of his degree at the coronation of George IV, as did the Chancellor at the coronation in 1911 of George V. Parliamentary robes are shown on the Lord Chancellor who is presenting the speech form the Throne to Queen Victoria on 1 February 1849. At the 1937 coronation he was depicted in both the state robe and a peer's coronation mantle.

From what records there are it seems that until quite recently peer's robes were worn on certain occasions at the choice of the Chancellor. As the present century advanced fewer new peers acquired robes and today the black damask gown is accepted as correct wear for great ceremonies of state.

17. John, Lord Somers, Lord High Chancellor 1693–1701; the lace cravat became standard neckwear. (Engraving in Clinch, *English Costume*, 1909)

The gown at the end of the seventeenth and early in the eighteenth centuries is seen in pictures of Lord Somers and Robert Walpole. The pattern of the gold lace has remained unaltered from the eighteenth century to the present day.

18. Robert Walpole as Chancellor. Black and gold gown worn over ordinary contemporary clothes and riband of the Garter, *c* 1740. (J. B. Vanloo. National Portrait Gallery)

Peers' robes or a black gown were originally worn over the normal dress of the day which gradually became stylised as a court suit. In *Dress Worn by Gentlemen at Her Majesty's Court* 1898, the Lord Chancellor's dress at courts and drawing rooms is laid down as

State Robe of Black Damask, trimmed with gold; Lace Bands and Ruffles; Full Dress Coat, lined with silk; Cloth of Gold Waistcoat; Black Breeches, hose, shoes with gilt buckles, Full Bottomed Wig, and Purse, Beaver Hat etc.

At Levées – The Black Silk Gown with train over a Full Dress Court Suit of Black; steel Buckles on Shoes; Cambric Bands; Full Bottomed Wig and Silk Hat.

Ten years later, in 1908, the prescribed dress is a black velvet suit with black velvet waistcoat, and gilt buckles on breeches and shoes, black damask gold trimmed state robe and full bottomed wig. The purse is carried and white gloves are worn. At levees, a cloth suit, steel buckles and a black silk gown with train are worn; at courts, lace bands; at levees, cambric. In 1908 no mention is made of a hat, and in 1912 it is flatly stated, "No hat".

19. Lord Chancellor's black and gold robe worn over court dress and with now stylised wig, 1897. (From a contemporary photograph)

The current manual of dress is *Dress and Insignia Worn at H.M.'s. Court*, edited by G. A. Titman, 1937, and this confirms the detail of the earlier edition. In addition to "bands", references are also made to "lace frill and ruffles". In 1937 the "frill" is defined as a "soft Stock of pleated lawn or batiste with lace at the ends". Over the years pictures show an increasing width of white lace across the chancellorial bosom, completely obscuring any bands that might be worn beneath.

For court mourning, lace is replaced by a "broad-hemmed frill and ruffles"; gilt by black buckles, and at levees a black paramatta gown, instead of a silk one. "Weepers" of white lawn (defined in 1937 as "covers on the cuffs of the coat") are worn also. Court dress as above is worn under the state robe on occasions of great ceremony – normally the black silk robe and a cloth court suit is worn.

The Chancellor's headwear shows some interesting variations. Originally, until the end of the seventeenth century, a normal contemporary hat or cap was worn. By the beginning of the eighteenth century the most common type of hat was the three-cornered cocked hat, which was christened the "tricorn" in the nineteenth century. Like the gown, this has remained the official headdress of the Lord Chancellor. At the end of the seventeenth century the periwig was adopted and again this remained, as it did on the heads of the bench and bar generally. Gradually the tricorn became less and less worn, the wig alone becoming the normal headwear for them. Pictures often show a small black circle on the top of the wig: this represents the skull cap

20. Lord Chancellor in peer's robe presenting Speech from the Throne, opening of Parliament, 1849. (After drawing in *Illustrated London News*)

21. Lord High Chancellor (Earl of Eldon) attended by his page at the Coronation of George IV. Peer's robe and coronet, but Chancellor's wig. 1821. (After picture in Naylor, *Coronation of George IV*, 1824–39)

22. King William III opening Parliament in an "imaginary" House of Lords. Chancellor on Woolsack, judges, bishops, clerks etc. in centre. The artist was not noted for his accuracy, and there is no key existing to the numbered figures and groups. 1689. (Engraving by Romeyn de Hooghe, National Portrait Gallery)

23. H.M. the Queen opening Parliament. Chancellor and Law Lords, Bishops and peers in centre. Other peers, members of the Diplomatic Corps and peeresses in evening dress at sides. Officers of Arms, State and Household officials to each side of Throne. Cap of Maintenance and Sword of State, Ladies in Waiting and Page of Honour on steps of Throne, 1958. (Press Association)

and coif worn in previous days by the judges. The hat is now reserved for such events as at the introduction of a new peer or when the Chancellor presides in the Lords over a Royal Commission.

For coronations, however, those Chancellors who were peers always assumed their coronets with the rest when the monarch was crowned; this was commented upon by John Constable, the painter, at William IV's coronation. Lord Brougham was Chancellor, and of him Constable wrote, "a sight than which nothing could be more ridiculous, for his coronet was perched on top of an enormous wig". (C. P. Leslie, *Memorial of the Life of John Constable*, 1843).

Wig and gown alike are removed, as the Chancellor leaves the Woolsack, when the House goes into committee.

GENTLEMAN USHER OF THE BLACK ROD; SERJEANT-AT-ARMS; CLERK OF THE PARLIAMENTS AND OTHER CLERKS; MESSENGERS, ATTENDANTS, etc.

Black Rod

The ancient office of Black Rod was created in the reign of Edward III as an officer of the Order of the Garter, later, as Ashmole puts it: "as Garter was declared the Principal Officer of Arms, so was the Black Rod (for the honor of the Order) appointed the Chief Usher in the Kingdom. . . ." (*The Institution of the Garter*, 1672.) Today, of his three duties, First Usher of the Court and Kingdom, Principal Usher of the Order of the Garter, and Official of the House of Lords, the last is by far the most important and onerous.

In all capacities he derives his authority from his rod or staff, which also symbolises that authority. The staff, wand, or rod has, from very ancient times, been regarded and even venerated as the outward and visible sign of an inward and a spiritual grace, or at least of corporal power. It is seen in various guises – black and white rods, silver sticks, maces, sceptres, or the Field Marshal's baton.

The original Black Rod seems to have been designated "hostiarius", (doorkeeper, from the Latin *ostiarius*), of the Royal Chapel at Windsor, but before long he is also known as the Bearer of the Wand or Rod and Black-rod Bearer. The black rod, topped with the lion of England, was appointed to be his "ensign" by Edward III on his first creation. "This Rod serves instead of a mace . . ."

Also bestowed on Black Rod is a gold garter badge worn on a gold chain "before his breast" as Ashmole puts it, also stating that Queen

Elizabeth I conferred the badge and chain. (Black Rod's dress as an officer of the Order of the Garter will be described in Chapter II.)

As an Officer of the House of Lords (in which capacity he is to maintain order, which includes the power to arrest a peer for offences noticed by the House, and serve as messenger from the Lords to the Commons), he appears, from the seventeenth century at least, to have worn plain contemporary clothes with the addition of his staff and badge and chain.

With the emergence of an official court dress at the end of the eighteenth century he appeared in the House and at Court functions so dressed. Although not mentioned in the original *Dress Worn at Court*, in the 1908 edition he is ordered to wear in the House a black cloth court suit without the black rod or chain of office, but these are added when he summons the House of Commons to the Lords chamber, and on other ceremonial occasions. At the opening of Parliament, also at court functions, he may wear, if he is entitled to, service or civil uniform, if not, a velvet court suit. These instructions still apply today.

The Serjeant-at-Arms

The Serjeant-at-Arms is the holder of another ancient office. He was originally attached to the monarch, but later the office and its holder multiplied and we find Serjeants-at-Arms, or Serjeants at Mace attending on the Lord Chancellor, the Speaker, the Lord Mayor, and provincial mayors. All these officials had powers of arrest in certain cases and their sign of authority was a mace.

In the seventeenth and eighteenth centuries the Serjeants-at-Arms generally are depicted in plain clothes, bearing maces and sometimes wearing a chain of office. Hats appear to have been optional.

For the Lords the chain is a silver collar of Ss denoting his status as one of the Royal Serjeants at Arms. A black cloth court suit is now worn in the House of Lords, with a sword. The collar of Ss is only worn on special occasions, such as the opening of Parliament.

The collar of Ss is thought to have been introduced by Henry IV and was bestowed as a mark of royal favour or authority on men (and apparently women) of all degrees of rank. It carried no title but was a definite sign of office for judges and government officials. Today it is restricted to the Lord Chief Justice, Kings of Arms, heralds and Serjeants-at-Arms. The chain of office of the Lord Mayor of London is also a collar of Ss (see Chapter VIII). The collar has varied slightly over the centuries but the devices that made it up were flowers, knots and the letter S, or the letter S alone, which is its present form. The initial is inexplicable, although various theories such as its standing for "soverain" or "spiritus sanctus" have been put forward.

At Court functions as an alternative to the black cloth suit, the Serjeant at Arms, if so entitled, may wear service or civil uniform. In 1971 the office was amalgamated with that of Black Rod.

The Clerk of the Parliaments

The Clerk of the Parliaments and his various assistants are entitled to wear, at Court functions, civil uniform according to their grade, as do the Permanent Secretary and Private Secretary of the Lord Chancellor. In earlier days there seems to have been no particular form of dress. Various Dutch engravings of the late seventeenth century show the clerks either in plain clothes or in some form of gown, and sometimes a hat, but the accuracy of the representation is doubtful.

The Attendants or Messengers

The attendants or messengers of the House of Lords wore, as with the generality of private upper servants, normal clothes of the time. By the mid-nineteenth century this had settled down to a black evening dress suit, and this is still worn, with a black waistcoat and a silver neck badge. There is very little recorded about the uniform or its provision. Details of appointments in the eighteenth century and later are not given. However, a letter appointing a temporary messenger in 1915 states "the pay is 38/– a week and you will have to provide yourself with a suit of black evening dress clothes". (*Black Rod's Letter Book*, 1897–1935.) It is not until 1929 that a uniform allowance of £10 was recommended to be given to doorkeepers on appointment, and in 1932 it is recorded that that sum was refunded to one F. C. Bell, "expended on dress clothes".

One exception to the above is the doorkeeper known as Red Coat, whose livery is scarlet, the royal colour. Tradition has it that the original holder of this office was a servant of Charles I who was lent to the House, and that the position was not taken over by Black Rod until about seventy years ago.

HOUSE OF COMMONS

No special costume, ceremonial or otherwise, has been associated with the Commons House, except as has been mentioned earlier, the possibility that those members who were Privy Councillors may have worn a gown similar to that of the Lord Chancellor. This supposition is given some support by the existence of such a gown for the use of the Chancellor of the Exchequer today, although now its use is apparently confined to coronations and so its appearance has been limited to four occasions this century. That this was not always the case, and that it was worn at other times seems evidenced by a story told of Disraeli and recorded in *The Notebooks of a Spinster Lady*, 1878–1903:

> "When I was Chancellor of the Exchequer," said Disraeli, "I found the robes of office were handed on from one Chancellor to another. By the time they came to me they were half worn out, and by the time I went out

24. Gentleman Usher of the Black Rod summoning the Commons to the House of Lords for the State Opening of Parliament, wearing velvet court dress and chain and badge and carrying the black rod. Speaker in gold and black robe and full bottomed wig; clerks in gowns and short wigs; doorkeeper in evening dress and with silver badge. 1974. (Press Association)

of office they were nearly falling to pieces. I thought I should like to keep the old robes as a matter of curiosity. So I had some new ones made at my own expense, and nobly presenting them to my successor carried off the old ones myself."

Disraeli was Chancellor of the Exchequer for the first time in 1852. Young William Pitt who was at the Exchequer some seventy years earlier was painted by Gainsborough leaning nonchalantly against a chair over which is thrown the gold guarded gown.

With the introduction of civil uniform in the early nineteenth century, Cabinet Ministers as ex-officio Privy Councillors became entitled to its use. Although the 1898 issue of *Dress Worn at Court* did not specify who was so entitled, confining itself to stating that this had "been arranged from time to time by Her Majesty's Command", by 1908 they are mentioned as entitled to 1st class civil uniform, and between the 1912 and 1937 edition, which is still valid, they are upgraded to Privy Councillor's uniform, with half an inch more gold braid than the 1st class (see Chapter V).

But for most MPs the normal court suit was all they had to wear if presented at a levee, with no distinctions between them and their constituents. Before the advent of a settled court dress, on occasions of ceremony normal "full dress" seems to have been worn. Mrs Papendiek, writing in 1789 of the Thanksgiving Service at St Paul's for King George III's recovery, mentions "the Commons also in full dress"; here is meant the equivalent of a morning coat, or today even a lounge suit, as proper to a public ceremony.

At some special solemnities MPs were equipped with mourning gowns. The practice of distributing mourning gowns and hoods to those attending state and some private funerals was long established, and when Queen Mary II died in 1694 as William III still reigned, parliament, which up to then had expired with the sovereign, continued, and both Houses followed the Queen's body, the Commons clad in black cloaks, the Lords in their parliament robes. "The Queen dying while Parliament sate", wrote Celia Fiennes, "the King gave mourning to them (500) and cloakes". Evelyn, who also saw the procession recorded, "Never was so universal a mourning, all the Parliament men had cloaks given them, and 400 poore women."

At Lord Chatham's funeral in 1778, which was at the public expense, Members of Parliament were present and "cloaks, scarves, hatbands and gloves were sent from the Wardrobe and distributed under the Direction of the Officers of Arms". But apart from these melancholy occasions we can only see, to quote Puckler-Muskau in 1826 (Butler, *A*

Regency Visitor), "the Members of the Lower House, in the common dress of our day".

This common dress for many years included a hat, and hats were indifferently worn, or not worn, in the House; except when raising a point of order during a Division when the member had, and still has, to remain seated and wear a hat. Gladstone was once caught out without his hat near by at such a time and borrowed the Solicitor General's, which was much too small. Today I understand a hat is skulling around the Chamber in case such a point of order has to be raised.

In one instance at least freedom of choice was not confined to the hat: in the late nineteenth century it is said that a nameless Conservative member used to remove his boots and sit in an apparently dirty

25. The Speaker's reception. Court dress and ambassadorial uniforms. 1857. (After picture in *Illustrated London News*)

26. The Speaker wearing hat, wig, and gold and black robe in the House of Commons. Mid eighteenth century. (From an engraving after Hogarth)

pair of grey woollen socks. He was cured of this habit one night when a brother member managed to smuggle the boots out of the Chamber. A Division being called the offending one had to hop along the ventilating gratings in the floor to the lobby. His boots were later returned anonymously in a parcel via an attendant. After this incident he followed the advice of Montaigne always to have one's boots on and be ready to go.

Another reminder of the "common dress" of previous days is the red braid loops attached to the coat hangers in the Commons cloakroom. These are to hang swords in.

What seems to have been an unofficial occasion to wear some kind of official dress was, in the nineteenth century, the Speaker's custom of entertaining members of the House, and others, annually. This was known as the Speaker's levee and court dress or uniform worn by those attending.

THE SPEAKER, SERJEANT AT ARMS, AND HOUSE OF COMMONS STAFF

The Speaker

The dress of the Speaker is similar to that of the Lord Chancellor in his capacity of chairman of the House of Lords. In the seventeenth century a gown and hat were worn in the House: by the early eighteenth century the gown and the contemporary periwig are shown. In a picture of the House of Commons by Peter Tillemans of about 1710, the Speaker is shown in a dark full bottomed periwig, whereas the majority of members are wearing lighter coloured versions.

On normal days a black silk trained gown is worn over a black cloth court suit, with white bands, full bottomed wig and three cornered hat. On state occasions, such as the Opening of Parliament, the damask state robe with gold lace guarding, as for the Chancellor, is worn over a velvet court suit. Lace edged cravat (known as a "jabot") and lace ruffles or cuffs are added, and the three cornered hat and wig, as before, with the addition to the dress of white gloves.

For court mourning a black paramatta gown is worn on normal days with white "weepers" on the cuffs. Black buckles on shoes and at the knees replace the normal bright metal ones. In 1898 *Dress Worn at Court* lays down the dress for court or drawing rooms as black full dress court suit, "state robe of black satin damask trimmed with gold; gilt buckles; lace bands and ruffles; beaver hat and full bottomed wig." At levees a black velvet court suit, steel or silver buckles, "sword etc." are prescribed. Ten years later the 1908 edition gives more detail: for courts, levees, etc. the Speaker is now to wear "old style velvet court suit", but not the state robe for courts, as previously, or "Civil uniform, First Class". This was changed by the 1937 edition to "Privy Councillor's uniform". (The Speaker is ex officio a Privy Councillor.)

The wearing of the state robe is confined to "occasions when attending upon His Majesty *with the House of Commons*". The 1908 edition also details the House of Commons dress. His hat is always mentioned.

At the beginning of the twentieth century the Speaker loses his gold-guarded gown from his court dress but the Chancellor retains his and the plain silk gown for levees. The distinction here, I think, lies in the Chancellor's other function as head of the judiciary.

Today, in *Official Dress worn in the House of Commons*, by Lt. Col. Peter Thorne, everyday neckwear for the Speaker is given as "white linen bands and a stiff white linen evening dress collar". *Dress Worn at Court* provides for the alternative of a "white cambric necktie" for wear in the House, and this can be seen in some nineteenth century pictures also. Previous to this, bands were worn in the eighteenth century.

Although carried, the three cornered hat is nowadays rarely worn; one instance is when the Speaker is rebuking a Member at the Bar of the House. In the case of a new speaker, between his election by the Commons and approval by the monarch, the Speaker Elect wears a black cloth court suit and a short wig like the Clerk of the House, but no gown.

27. The Speaker in plain black trained gown as worn for normal occasions, wig and three-cornered hat. Train bearer in cloth court suit, hat and sword. 1890s. (Maxwell, *Sixty Years a Queen*)

The Serjeant-at-Arms

As in the Lords, the Serjeant-at-Arms in the Commons seems to have developed a uniform dress during the nineteenth century and it is substantially the same: cloth court suit, and sword. On certain state occasions lace and a collar of Ss are added. His deputy and assistant wear the same, except that they are not entitled to the collar. For court wear service or civil uniform may be worn, if entitled.

28. Serjeant-at-Arms escorting a
Member out of the House after his
refusal to leave when "named" by the
Speaker. 1881. (After contemporary
engraving reproduced in Bott, *Our
Fathers*, 1931)

29. The House of Commons in 1860. Speaker in plain black gown and wig.
Clerks in short wigs and gowns. All with court coats beneath. Some Members
wearing hats. (Photograph of painting by J. Phillips, R.A.)

Clerks, Doorkeepers and Messengers

Clerks are shown in eighteenth and nineteenth centuries wearing gowns, bands, and short wigs. In modern days these features persist, worn with a court dress suit and waistcoat, but trousers instead of the usual breeches. Breeches are worn by the Clerk of the House at the opening of Parliament, however. At court functions the clerks wear civil uniforms according to their grades. Doorkeepers and messengers wear evening dress with black waistcoat and a silver badge suspended from the neck.

Distinguishing marks of Degree displayed on the Robes of the Peerage

(Based on *Dress Worn at Court* and *Whittaker's Peerage*)

Peers	Robes	Coronets	
	Rows of Ermine Spots on Coronation Robe and Bars of Ermine and Gold lace on Parliamentary Robe	Strawberry Leaves	Silver Balls
Duke	4	8	—
Marquis	$3\frac{1}{2}$	4	4 on short "points"
Earl	3	8	8 on tall "points"
Viscount	$2\frac{1}{2}$	—	16
Baron	2	—	6

Peeresses	Coronation Robe Rows of Ermine Spots	Miniver Border	Train
Duchess	4	5 inches	2 yards
Marchioness	$3\frac{1}{2}$	4 inches	$1\frac{3}{4}$ yards
Countess	3	3 inches	$1\frac{1}{2}$ yards
Viscountess	$2\frac{1}{2}$	$2\frac{1}{2}$ inches	$1\frac{1}{4}$ yards
Baroness	2	2 inches	1 yard

Lady Peers and Peeresses with seats in the House have a Parliamentary Robe as for male Peers.

Peeresses' coronets, though smaller, are distinguished in the same manner as those of the Peers.

CHAPTER II

Knights and the Orders of Chivalry

KNIGHTS BACHELOR AND BARONETS

Although the origins and early history of knighthood generally are obscure, and early historians unreliable and even fanciful, it may be safely accepted that the Golden Age of Chivalry was from the end of the eleventh century to the beginning of the fifteenth.

Knighthood was said to be the first of all military dignitaries and the foundation of all later honours. Originally it was confined to fighting men of gentle blood who had spent their boyhood and youth serving some great lord as page and esquire. Knighthood appears to have, on occasion, been bestowed by other knights, lords, even priests and bishops, but mainly by kings and princes and eventually it was the sovereign alone, "the fount of honour" by whose hand the title and degree could be awarded. Elias Ashmole in 1672 wrote:

> Kings and Princes have in no age limited themselves, or confined their bestowing of this Dignity to martialists alone, who prefers Arms, and give themselves to the exercise of Military Virtue, as it was in its original Institution, viz. a Military employment, inasmuch as men of the long Robe [Lawyers] and such as have dedicated themselves to the managery of Civil Affairs, through their great worth and desert in that kind, have so well merited of their Prince and country, as to be thought worthy to share with those of the short Robe, in having this Honor conferred upon them.

However, William Shaw, in his *The Knights of England* considers that Ashmole's own day really saw the opening up of the ranks to the civilian:

> from the days of the Restoration, there began the sole and simple conception of knighthood as a personal dignity conferred by the ceremony of dubbing by the Sovereign or his deputy and, when this change had been effected, it became a recognised custom to confer upon civilians also what had originated as a purely military dignity.

The only exceptions were ecclesiastics, for from the very beginning of the ideas of knighthood "men of God" being exempt from bearing arms and protected by their cloth (at least in theory) from attack were clearly ineligible for inclusion in an order of men dedicated to the use of arms. Even today if senior clerics receive appointments in any of the orders of chivalry they are never dubbed knight with the sword.

Knighthood in the Middle Ages was really a military guild or brotherhood and this association was in many cases strengthened by the formation of orders of knighthood or chivalry. These were mostly national orders, but some, with a religious connotation, such as the Knights of St John of Jerusalem, were international, and acquired property and estates in their own right.

The Church, over the ages, kept an eye on knighthood and at times managed to inject into its code – that is the code of chivalry – the Christian ideals of service to God and man, faith, charity and humility. Religious rites became included in the ceremonies of conferring knighthood. These two elements, religious and military, flourished together more especially during the age of the crusades, but today the military element of knighthood is no longer paramount, and it is to the annual services held in the chapels of the great orders that public attention is most drawn. In the Middle Ages two methods of conferring knighthood arose, simple dubbing with a sword, and presentation of robes, arms, and insignia with secular and religious ceremonies.

Today the creation of a simple knight bachelor, that is knighthood unconnected with an order of chivalry, is carried out by the monarch dubbing by laying the blade of a sword on each shoulder of the recipient, an action known as the "accolade", and by the issuing of letters patent. During the dubbing ceremony no words are spoken. In the case of investiture as a knight into an order, the insignia are formally presented by the sovereign after the act of dubbing has first been performed.

In the reign of Charles I it was suggested that a riband and badge should be worn by knights bachelor, but the idea was rejected. In 1926

King George V authorised the wearing of a badge; an oval three inches by two inches, of gilt and vermilion colour bearing a sword and spurs surrounded by a belt. This is worn on the left breast, as is the star of an order. The badge is not presented, but may be purchased by the new knight.

Although knighthood was never hereditary, James I in 1611 created the degree of baronet, which new honour conferred the title of "Sir" by dubbing as a knight, and also the privilege of the title descending in the family through the eldest son, as in the peerage. Today new baronets are not automatically given the accolade, but are styled "Sir", with the suffix "Bt." after their name. The original baronets were created with the object of obtaining reinforcements for the army in Ireland "chiefly", as Ashmole puts it, "to secure the Plantation in the Province of Ulster". To this end each baronet had to maintain thirty foot soldiers in Ireland for three years, and also had to be, among other things, in receipt of an income of at least a thousand pounds a year part of which no doubt found its way into the government coffers.

Later, Irish baronets were created and in 1625 King Charles I created Baronets of Nova Scotia "for the planting of that Country by Scotch Colonies", according to Ashmole. In 1629 the King granted these Scotch baronets, who were said to have each been given eighteen square miles of Nova Scotian territory upon their creation, a badge, "to wear and carry about their necks in all time coming, an orange tawnie silk ribbon, whereon shall hang pendant in a scutcheon argent a saltiers azure thereon an inescutcheon of the arms of Scotland with an Imperial Crown above the escutcheon. . . ." (Warrant of 17 November, quoted by Berry in *Encyclopedia Heraldica*).

This badge appears to have been short lived – it probably did not survive the Commonwealth. In any event no Scottish baronets were created after 1707 and the existing ones became baronets of the United Kingdom and were granted the addition of the Red Hand of Ulster to their arms. The creation of Irish baronets ceased in 1801.

In 1835 the baronets petitioned for the re-grant of a badge, but this was refused. In 1929 King George V authorised the present badge, the arms of Ulster, the Red Hand, on a silver shield, surmounted by the imperial crown, all surrounded by an oval border of roses, shamrocks and thistles as a wreath. This badge, like that of the knights bachelor, is not presented, but can be purchased. It is worn around the neck, as the neck-badge of an order, on a one-and-three-quarter inch ribbon, orange with narrow blue borders.

THE ORDERS OF CHIVALRY

Up to the early years of the last century it was rare for persons who were neither of high rank in the armed services nor members of noble families to be appointed to the English orders of chivalry. The enlargements of the Order of the Bath in 1815 and 1847, the institution of the Order of St Michael and St George in 1818 and of the Order of the British Empire in 1917 accommodated and allowed for the vast increase of honours bestowed upon varied and sundry subjects in the last century and a half. Furthermore it was practically unknown for anyone other than a royal personage to hold more than one British order: in 1813 the Duke of Wellington resigned the Bath when he was awarded the Garter (although he was re-appointed as Knight Grand Cross when the Bath was enlarged two years later.) Today the various orders may be, and are, held in plurality.

The enlargement of the older and the creation of the new orders was to cope not only with increased numbers of military and diplomatic awards, but to enable such honours to be bestowed upon classes hitherto unrewarded – civic, literary, artistic and scientific leaders. It is interesting to note that George III had proposed a new order – that of Minerva, for writers and scientists, but the suggestion was not taken up, nor was a further attempt in 1834, when Sir Robert Peel opposing the proposal hoped that no order of chivalry to cater for scientists etc. would be created, as, he said: "I cannot think that it would raise the character of science in this country to establish a new system of reward and I deprecate the institution of a new Order for them."

In order of seniority there are today (1977) the following six official British orders of chivalry:

> The Most Noble Order of the Garter
> The Most Ancient and Most Noble Order of the Thistle
> The Most Honourable Order of the Bath
> The Most Distinguished Order of St Michael and St George
> The Royal Victorian Order
> The Most Excellent Order of the British Empire

In addition there are three obsolete orders: The Most Illustrious Order of St Patrick, The Most Exalted Order of the Star of India and The Most Eminent Order of the Indian Empire.

Of these orders, the Garter, the Thistle and the R.V.O. are bestowed only upon recipients personally selected by the sovereign. There are, and have been, also a number of orders, such as the Order of Merit, which do not convey any degree of knighthood and in which no robes are worn; they do not, therefore, come within the scope of this book.

THE MOST NOBLE ORDER OF THE GARTER

Ashmole, quoting Seldon, affirms that this Noble Order "hath precedency of antiquity, before the eldest rank of honor of that kind anywhere established"; and "that it exceeds in Majesty, Honor, and Fame, all chivalrous Orders in the world".

The order was founded by King Edward III and there has long been debate as to the exact year and circumstances in which it was first instituted. Modern opinion inclines to the date 1348 when to celebrate victory in the Hundred Years War the King, acting upon ideas he seems to have had for some years, refounded the Chapel at Windsor as a collegiate establishment of canons and "milites pauperes" or "valient men" who "hapned to fall in decay", and also created a new body of knights chivalrous, perhaps as Froissart suggests in emulation of "King Alfred" (sic) who "had founded that round table whence so many Knights had issued forth" (Froissart, *Chronicles*). This year of 1348 was confirmed when King George VI gave orders that 1948 was to be treated as the sexcentenary of the order's foundation. During this time, unlike some orders, the Garter has never fallen into desuetude or suspended animation, although it declined in numbers, naturally, under the Commonwealth; and after 1688 for a time both exiled Stuarts and Hanoverians seem to have made appointments to the order. In 1948 King George VI revived the ancient ceremonies of investiture and installation at St George's Chapel, Windsor.

As a result of the Commonwealth there was a dearth of both Knights Companion and of robes of the order at the time of the Restoration. Charles II acknowledged these facts in a dispensation issued in March 1661 allowing Chapters to be held up to 15 April of that year "to deliberate with the ancient Knights of the Order, who are neither in number sufficient to make up a Chapter, or all of them provided with Robes by reason of the late troubles". (Ashmole Appx. XVII.)

Six years later what Pepys (26 April 1667) describes as "a most scandalous thing" took place. In 1667 the Feast of St George was kept at Whitehall Palace. Pepys was told that

> our King and Knights of the Garter the other day, who, whereas heretofore their robes were only to be worn during their ceremonies and services, these, as proud of their coats, did wear them all day till night, and then rode into the Park with them on. Nay . . . my Lord Oxford and Duke of Monmouth in a hackney coach with two footmen in the Park, with their robes on . . . so as all gravity may be said to be lost among us.

Soon after the foundation it became the custom for queens consort, wives of certain of the knights and other great ladies to receive from the sovereign robes decorated with embroidered garters and fur lined to be worn during the annual celebrations of the feast of St George at Windsor. Garters also seem to have been presented, to be worn on the left arm; and several monumental figures in churches and cathedrals show the garter so positioned.

This custom of appointing Ladies of the Garter appears to have died out by the reign of Henry VIII and was not revived until 1902 when Queen Alexandra was appointed by King Edward VII on his coronation: King George V and King George VI followed this precedent, and in 1948 Princess Elizabeth, our present Queen, was also installed with her husband, the Duke of Edinburgh. George VI also honoured Queen Wilhelmina of the Netherlands in 1944, and her daughter, Queen Juliana, was admitted by Queen Elizabeth II in 1958. Queens regnant have, of course, always taken their place as Sovereigns of the Order.

30. Garter robes and insignia at the time of the Restoration. (Ashmole, *The Institution, Laws and Ceremonies of the Most Noble Order of the Garter*, 1672)

The dress and insignia of the order has consisted, or consists, of the following items:

> The Garter itself
> The Mantle
> The Surcoat
> The Hood
> The Cap, or hat
> The Collar
> The "George"
> The Riband
> The "Lesser George"
> The Star
> The Underdress

Of these the first four were the original insignia, the other items being added by successive sovereigns during the succeeding centuries.

The Garter

Traditionally, the original garter was of light blue, possibly silk, embroidered in gold with the motto of the order "Honi soit qui mal y pense", and worn on the leg, below the knee. The garter was, and is, the first of the insignia to be placed upon newly made knights at their installation.

Later, garters presented to foreign rulers were jewel-encrusted and heavily gold mounted, and those of our own kings became increasingly resplendent. King Charles II's garter contained two hundred and fifty diamonds with his miniature worked in the gold of the buckle. William, later 1st Duke of Bedford, paid £144 for two garters of diamonds and pearls and £12 for a plain gold and enamelled one in 1672. (Scott-Tomson, *Life in a Noble Household*.)

These elaborate and costly garters purchased by Knights Companion were, of course, their own property and were retained in the family after the death of the holder. Those garters presented by the sovereign, together with the other insignia, were, from an unknown date, usually returned to the sovereign upon the death of a Knight Companion, although in earlier times, in some instances as late as the sixteenth century, this was not always so. Today the garter, collar and George are returned to the Central Chancery of the order; the badge and star are returned to the sovereign personally by the nearest male relative of the dead Knight. In rare cases the sovereign has permitted some of the insignia to be retained in the family. As for the privately bought jewelled garter, as far as is known, none has been made for the last forty years or so.

With the coming of the Hanoverian line the garter colour was changed to a dark blue, and the modern version is of very dark blue velvet, about one inch wide, with the motto in letters of pure sheet gold, gold decorations, buckle and tab.

At first the garter was always worn, but with armour or riding boots this could be difficult, so Henry V decreed that a knight so dressed could substitute a piece of plain blue ribbon, "en signifiance du Jartier". This statute was repeated by Henry VIII and the blue ribbon "for convenience in travelling" is mentioned by Berry (*Encyclopedia Heraldica*), but he is somewhat ambiguous as to whether the custom still held in his day. Certainly the garter, together with star and ribbon was worn non-ceremonially in the early nineteenth century.

Ladies wore, and wear, the garter on the left arm, a practice apparently not known by the young Queen Victoria, who when she first realised she would have to wear it sent for the Duke of Norfolk and asked "... my Lord Duke, where *shall* I wear the Garter?" Norfolk referred her to a portrait of Queen Anne and accordingly we later read that at her first levee she appeared "black as a raven from head to foot ... but she wore the Ribbon of the Garter with the Star on her left arm"; and again, she prorogued Parliament a few days later "the garter round her arm...." (*The Early Court of Queen Victoria*, Clare Jerrold.)

As a younger woman Queen Victoria is frequently pictured with the garter on the arm, worn rather high, and often almost concealed by the flounces of sleeve or bertha falling over it. *The Times* of 2 May 1851, reporting the opening of the Great Exhibition on the previous day noted: "Her Majesty wore the Riband and George of the Order of the Garter and the Garter of the order as an armlet". In later years she did not wear more than the ribbon and star on most occasions.

Later Ladies of the Garter, for example, Queen Mary, seem to have worn it nearer the elbow than the shoulder.

The Mantle

The mantle was originally made of fine woollen cloth, but by the sixteenth century this had changed to velvet lined with white silk, which by the seventeenth century was a "taffaty".

From earliest times the mantle has been blue, except during the reigns of Edward VI to Charles I when it was purple (as, for example, that of King Christian IV of Denmark, in Copenhagen, which dates from 1603). But in about 1637 Charles I reverted to "a rich celestial blue", and according to Ashmole the knights provided themselves with new mantles (at 37/– a yard, velvet) "and the first time these Mantles were worn was to honour the installation of the present Sovereign

[Charles II]". Later, when new knights companion were installed by Charles II, he ordered "special good velvets of skie-colour" for making the new mantles.

During the later seventeenth and eighteenth centuries the blue seems to have varied, examples of actual mantles or paintings showing ultramarine, pale greenish-blue, sky-colour, violet (a written description), dark blue, and royal blue. Today it is of very dark blue velvet, which in some modern examples I have seen is, alas, of nylon (though these are considerably less weighty than the older pure silk velvet examples). The lining is white taffeta.

The sovereign's mantle, and those of other rulers and princes who were admitted to the order were trained, as is the case today. King Charles II had a two yard long train and his mantle contained some twenty yards of velvet. "Knights subject" did not have the train, and in 1672 the Earl of Bedford's mantle comprised some fifteen yards of velvet and a similar amount of white taffeta for the lining.

From the institution of the order it was ordained that the Knights should wear upon the left of the mantle, breast high, the badge of the order, being a white shield bearing St George's cross, surrounded by a garter with the motto. This is embroidered on the mantle in gold, silver, and silk; although in past times, like the garter itself, it was often embellished with gold plate, jewels and pearls. The Queen does not wear the badge on her mantle; its place is taken by a Georgian pattern (see p. 58) star. King George V and King George VI both also wore the star in place of the badge, although the former has been painted in garter robes with a normal badge.

Attached to the front of the neck are two long and imposing blue and gold cords, ending in massive tassels; these are described variously as "cordons", "robe-strings" or "laces". A gold hook and eye at the neck can reinforce the cords. Although not mentioned by Ashmole, some seventeenth- and eighteenth-century portraits show white ribbon bows on the shoulders, to support the collar of the order. Today these take the form of flat bows of wide white ribbon with vandyked ends.

In some portraits of the seventeenth and eighteenth centuries the mantle is shown as split down the right hand side, similar to the parliament robe of peers.

The mantle was, in earlier days, supplied from the Royal Wardrobe; in 1672 the Earl of Bedford received fifteen yards of blue velvet and a similar amount of white taffeta (Scott-Tomson, *Life in a Noble Household*).

31. King Charles II in Garter robes. (Ashmole, *The Institution . . . of the Garter*, 1672)

The Surcoat and Hood

Originally, like the mantle, the surcoat was of wool, lined with fur, and decorated with embroidered garters of a number according to the wearer's rank. Its colour changed annually and the discarded surcoats "disposed of for the use of the Colledge" (Ashmole).

During the sixteenth century, apparently, the fabric was changed to velvet, crimson in colour and lined with white silk. When this change was made the embroidered garters seem to have been discontinued and the surcoat was quite plain.

The seventeenth-century surcoat was simply cut, widening from shoulders to hem with plain square fronts and hanging sleeves slit at the shoulder and down the front seam; it varied somewhat in length from knee to mid-calf according to contemporary portraits. It was unfastened and secured at the waist by the girdle, or sword belt. This same style continued until the surcoat died out towards the end of the nineteenth century. The Museum of London possesses the surcoat of the Duke of Clarence (1864–1892). Other names for this garment were "gown" and "kirtle". Like the mantle it was formerly presented by the sovereign from the Wardrobe.

The Hood

According to J. L. Nevinson (*The Robes of the Order of the Garter*) the hood was introduced by Henry VIII although Ashmole cites Wardrobe Accounts to the effect that it was one of the original articles decreed to be worn. It is based on the fifteenth-century chaperon and from the late sixteenth century onwards its appearance has altered little. (The chaperon derived from the earlier hood and consisted of a circular roll that went around the head with a flopping crown and a liripipe either twisted around the head or left hanging down.)

If indeed introduced by Henry VIII its use as a head-covering was soon discontinued and the cap or hat took its place. By the late sixteenth century it was worn over the right shoulder, the liripipe in the form of a flat streamer coming down the front of the body and passing underneath the girdle. In the seventeenth century the padded ring became smaller and the liripipe streamer narrower. This last is shown either passing behind or looped around the girdle or sword belt. It was of crimson velvet lined with white silk, matching the surcoat.

It survives today, much in the same form, worn on the right shoulder.

32. Earl of Nottingham showing early seventeenth century Garter robes. Surcoat with hanging sleeves secured by girdle with hangers and sword.
"Liripipe" of hood in form of broad flat streamer. Hat with small white
plume and jewelled band. 1602. (National Portrait Gallery)

The Cap or Hat

Starting as a fairly low, soft crowned cap of black velvet decorated with white feathers set not to come above the top of the crown, it became by Charles II's time a narrow brimmed hat with a stiff pleated crown, all of black velvet, and a towering plume of white ostrich and black heron's feathers. Charles II's cap, preserved on his effigy in Westminster Abbey, is about six inches high and the plume rises to about twice that height.

Lely's drawings of Knights of the Garter show both the flatter type and the tall variety, looking like an early nineteenth-century top-hat.

By the nineteenth century the crown became lower again, as it is today. The white plumes are restricted to three.

Jewelled bands and brooches were often added to enrich the effect. The feathers seem to have been one of the most costly items in former days: the Earl of Bedford in 1672 paid £20 for black heron's feathers. The ostrich feathers together with the cap, sword and belt, cost £29 7s. 6d. (Scott-Tomson, *Life in a Noble Household*.)

33. Early nineteenth-century Garter dress with surcoat worn open. Large white ribbon bows to secure collar. (Redrawn from Clinch, *English Costume*, 1909)

The Collar and George

The collar is an ancient emblem of the honour and forms part of the
insignia of many orders of knighthood and of civic dignataries and

34. Duke of Leeds in Garter dress. Surcoat worn open, contemporary
periwig. White ribbon bows to secure collar. Shirt sleeves showing below
short sleeves of doublet and surcoat. 1677. (Engraving after Van der Vaart)

other distinguished office holders. That of the garter was added later: it is generally accepted that it was instituted by Henry VII.

The collar is composed of twenty-six enamelled garters each having within it an enamelled rose in red, each garter being linked to its companion by stylised knotted cords of gold which resemble the tasselled cordons of the mantle. The weight of the collar was ordained in the statutes of Henry VIII to be thirty ounces troy of gold, and no more, although Ashmole notes two that were more – one was King Charles I's at thirty-five and a half ounces.

In Henry VIII's decree the roses were double, red and white and white and red in alternate links, but this design does not seem to have survived him, except for a solitary example, a collar made for Queen Victoria with alternate red and white and white and red double roses. This collar, I understand, was also worn by Queen Mary.

Pendant from the collar at the centre front is an enamelled and gold model of St George on horseback, spearing the dragon which is lying underneath the horse's forefeet. Although Ashmole represents St George armoured cap-à-pie as a medieval knight, the majority of representations of the George show more or less a conventional Roman soldier. The George could be, and was often, enriched by jewels at the owner's expense. The collar, however, was never allowed any such adornment.

Henry VIII declared that the collar and George should be worn by every knight of the order "apertly and openly" on the "principall and solempne feastes of the yere", and on other days the "ymage of St George" should be worn on a small gold chain, except in "tyme of warre, sickenes, longe viage", when a silk lace might be substituted for the gold chain. The idea of this was to "have better knowledge of the Knights that shall be of the said order". (Henry VIII Statutes, Act 38. See Ashmole.) This does not indicate that the garter itself was being worn less often as contemporary pictures show both garter and collar together in many instances. These may have been artistic conventions, however, and the actual daily wearing of the garter may have begun to be less scrupulously observed.

The collar is still worn only on "solempne feastes" and special feast days and at opening and proroguing Parliament by the monarch, but normally not after sunset. The collar is secured to the shoulder straps or epaulettes by one and a half inch white satin ribbon bows.

The Lesser George and the Riband

From the last it is but a step to the institution by Henry VIII of the Lesser George to be worn on a chain or riband "loosely before the breast" of every knight of the order. This Lesser George to be an "image of St George . . . the same to be thence forward placed within the enobled Garter". Generally of plain gold, the Lesser George would, by those who could afford it, be embellished with jewels or actually cut out of precious or semi-precious stones. Likewise the garter surrounding the figure was sometimes set with diamonds.

Ashmole states that the Lesser George shows the saint attacking the dragon with a sword, and his plate shows Charles I's Lesser George, worn at the time of his execution, "curiously cut in an Onix, set about with 21 large Table Diamonds, in the fashion of a Garter; on the back side of the George was the picture of his Queen, rarely well limn'd, set in a case of Gold. . . ." A less elaborate example, worn on a jewelled chain, can be seen on the anonymous portrait of Robert Dudley, Earl of Leicester (c 1570) in the National Portrait Gallery. Most Lesser Georges were of the same design as the George, with the saint despatching the dragon with his spear. This is the design used in modern times, in plain gold.

The silk riband mentioned was a popular substitute for the gold neck-chain. There is some evidence that the earliest ribands were black in colour, but "Blue or Sky colour" was laid down by James I in 1622. The riband was worn around the neck, as was the chain, the Lesser George hanging to about the middle of the chest. The width of the ribbon appears to have been quite narrow at first, broadening under the Stuarts. After the Restoration the manner of wearing the riband was altered by Charles II. It is said (Evelyn's *Diary*) that the young Duke of Richmond, Charles' son by the Duchess of Portsmouth, who was invested with the Garter at the age of twelve, put on the riband over the left shoulder and passing under the right arm, where the Lesser George hung. The King is said to have been so taken with this that he ordered it to be the future manner of wearing the riband and Lesser George. On the other hand Ashmole states that the change was made "for the more conveniency of riding and action". The chain seems to have been more or less discarded by this time.

The Hanoverians, in the early eighteenth century, changed the colour of the riband to a dark blue, as they did the mantle and garter itself. Slight variations of blue occurred during the next two centuries, and in 1950 King George VI laid down that in future it should be of the shade of "kingfisher" blue which had been favoured by Queen Victoria.

Dress Worn at Court in 1898 laid down that the riband was to be four inches wide and that "Orders . . . are worn in Plain Clothes only on occasions where the Sovereign or the Royal Family or Foreign Royal Personages are present, or at Official Dinners and Receptions", except that Knights Grand Crosses of the various orders could wear them when being enertained by knights of the same rank, according to "the existing customs". As with other orders the riband and star were only worn with evening dress (or with uniform); in earlier days of the century they were worn with day clothes, as may be seen in various pictures of King George III and others.

Today the riband, when worn with evening dress, passes across the body in front under the coat but not over the shoulder. In fact it is a "sham"; buttoned to the waistcoat at the left armhole and at the right hip, where the Lesser George rests concealing the button. The star is worn with the riband, and the occasions when they are worn are laid down from time to time on much the same lines as the 1898 rules. By modern convention "Decorations" on an invitation card indicates an official entertainment, a convention officially recognised by the Central Chancery of the Orders of Knighthood (e.g. Regulations of 1919).

The Star

When the mantle was worn as a daily outdoor garment the badge of the order on the left breast was thus commonly displayed to the world. But as the mantle passed from being common medieval dress to a ceremonial habit the badge was only seen on rare and solemn days. This worried Charles I who thought the daily display of the badge by the knights should be "a testimony apert to the World, of the honor they hold. . . ." He therefore decreed in 1627 that the knights should wear "upon the left part of their cloaks, coats, and riding cassocks, at all times when they shall not wear their robes, and in all places and Assemblies, an Escotcheon of the Arms of St George, that is to say, a Cross within a Garter. . . ."

Ashmole, after quoting King Charles's Order, goes on to say that soon after "the Glory or Star (as it is usually called) having certain beams of silver that spread in form of a cross, was introduced and added thereunto".

From the beams or rays this version of the badge of the order became known as the star and was worn together with the riband and garter on daily occasions. When trousers replaced breeches and stockings in the early nineteenth century, the wearing of the garter itself became restricted to those times when the form of dress worn was appropriate to it, and the riband and star formed the everyday insignia, or, in some cases, the star alone was worn.

Dress Worn at Court, 1898, says "on ordinary occasions the Riband and Badge, and Star of the several Orders only are worn" at Court with uniform. In plain clothes (evening dress) the same rule is implied. In the 1912 edition, however, for evening dress the occasions listed are noted as either "Ribands, Stars ..." or "Stars, not Riband. ..." A Regulation of the Central Chancery of the Orders of Knighthood issued in 1919 and again in 1932 confirms the wearing of orders with evening dress and prescribes the star only for wear with morning clothes on certain occasions.

The star as originally designed had the clusters of rays at the four cardinal points, longer than the intermediate clusters and the vertical axis was longer than the horizontal. At first it was an embroidered badge, but fairly soon it became made of silver and enamel and in some cases acquired diamonds and rubies to embellish it.

When the Hanoverians changed the blue of the garter and mantle they also altered the shape of the star so that it was squarer in outline. In 1946 King George VI was pleased to order the re-introduction of the original Stuart shape, and that the Georgian stars should be altered eventually as the holders died and the stars were handed back. As stated above, however, the Georgian pattern is still worn by Her Majesty on her mantle in place of the normal badge.

The Sword and Swordbelt

A plain cross-hilted sword in a crimson velvet scabbard was worn on a similar girdle and hangers: in this century a service sword is worn with uniform.

The Underdress

This was originally the daily wear of the knights: even the surcoat and mantle of the order represented medieval fashion. By the Restoration the underdress had changed and had not become stylised like the sur-coat and mantle. In fact, according to King Charles II's Order of May 1661 (Ashmole, Appx. CLXXX), it "followed too much the modern fashion never constant and less comporting with the decency, gravity, and stateliness of the upper Robes of the Order". The order went on to lay down that

> from this time forwards the Companions shall be obliged to a certain and immutable form and fashion, as well for their under-habits as their upper-robes ... that is to say, to the old trunk-hose or round breeches, whereof the Stuff or Material shall be some such Cloth of Silver, as we shall chuse and appoint, wherein as we shall be to them an example, so we do expect they will follow us in using the same and no other.

Mr Nevinson quotes Nicholas (*History of the Orders*, Vol. II), as reporting a Statute of April 1661 to the effect that "the Under-Habit shall consist of a cloth of Silver Doublet or Vest and Trunk Hose". This appears to be the same thing, as the order quoted by Ashmole refers to a review of the statutes carried out in April 1661.

Mr Nevinson carried out a study of the underdress of King Charles II preserved on his effigy in Westminster Abbey (*Connoisseur*, 1936) and describes them as of cloth of silver heavily trimmed with silver-gilt and silver bobbin-lace and silver buttoned. He describes them as "an interesting blend of conscious archaism and contemporary fashion, at a time when little was known of the history of dress".

Although giving the impression of trunk-hose when worn, the hose are in fact a sort of short skirt with no division between the legs and were worn over white silk drawers with white silk stockings sewn on to them. A contemporary pair of breeches for the 4th Duke of Richmond's Garter robes of 1661, however, is divided into two distinct legs. These garments in fact resemble short versions of the contemporary "petticoat breeches" in many ways, including being trimmed with loops of silk and silver ribbons in bunches at the front. They hang upon the hips without support, as distinct from the true trunk-hose which were laced to the doublet with "points".

The doublet is short and skimpy, open in front from the chest downwards and with elbow length sleeves slit down the front seam. This is more or less in the fashion of the 1650s and 60s.

There appear to be no surviving garments for the eighteenth century but pictures show a similar underdress.

In 1805 Lady Louisa Strangeways attended an installation of knights of the Garter and wrote "their dresses were very magnificent. The Knights before they were installed were in white and silver like the old pictures of Henry VIII". (*The Journal of Mary Frampton.*) William Berry (*Encyclopaedia Heraldica*) writing in the period 1828–38 describes the underdress as:

> The stockings and small clothes, which are united like pantaloons, are of pearl-coloured silk: on the outside of the right knee is affixed a knot of open silver lace and ribbons intermixed, in the form of a large rose; and a little below the left knee is placed the garter. . . .
>
> The shoes are of white chamois leather, with red heels [this was a seventeenth-century fashion which soon became restricted to Court wear] with knots and roses like that upon the right knee. The doublet is of cloth of silver adorned before and behind, and down the sleeves, with several guards or rows of open silver lace, each lace having a row of small buttons set down the middle: the cuffs are open and adorned with the same

kind of lace and ribbons, set in small loops; at the bottom of the upper seam of each cuff is fixed a knot of silver ribbons that falls over the gloves, which are of white kid leather laced at the top with silver and adorned at the openings with a knot, like that on the cuff.

The trousers (which are of silver tissue or cloth of silver, the same as the doublet, and adorned with two rows of lace and ribbons intermixed, and set at a small distance that the cloth of silver appears between them) are buckled round the waist, and formed like puffed small clothes, reaching to the middle of the thigh. . . .

Berry's "stockings and small clothes" seem an elaborate version of King Charles II's united drawers and stockings and the "trousers" appear to correspond with the trunk hose.

Surviving examples in this country and on the continent from the nineteenth century agree generally with Berry's description, exhibiting some variations in the arrangement of the lace and other trimmings. The doublets also are longer than in previous centuries: in the case of that of the Duke of Clarence (1864–1892) in the London Museum the immitation petticoat breeches hook and eye on to the doublet for support. By now there is little attempt to make the breeches look like "the old trunk-hose", and in one case at least (King Albert of Saxony, c 1850) doe-skin riding breeches were worn underneath (Nevinson, *Connoisseur*, 1936).

However by now the underdress was not worn on all occasions. Queen Victoria writing in 1844 to the King of the Belgians with reference to the recent visit to England of King Louis Philippe said "the Knights of the Garter did *not* wear the whole costume, but only the mantle".

White stockings, shoes (with red heels) and gloves appear to have been the normal wear with the underdress.

With the use of the underdress being discontinued in recent times the mantle is now worn over morning dress or service uniform or other official costume.

The Officers of the Order

These consist of:

> The Prelate
> The Chancellor
> The Register
> Garter King of Arms
> Gentleman Usher of the Black Rod
> Secretary

Ceremonial Costume

35. Garter robes, and underdress which is now only worn by the four knights carrying the canopy at coronations. (Spectrum Colour Library/A. C. K. Ware, 1953)

36. Procession of Garter Knights at Windsor: low soft crowned hats, tall white plumes. Mantles worn over normal morning dress or uniform. 1977. (Press Association)

37. Officers of the Order of the Garter as dressed before 1673. (Ashmole, *The Institution . . . of the Garter*)

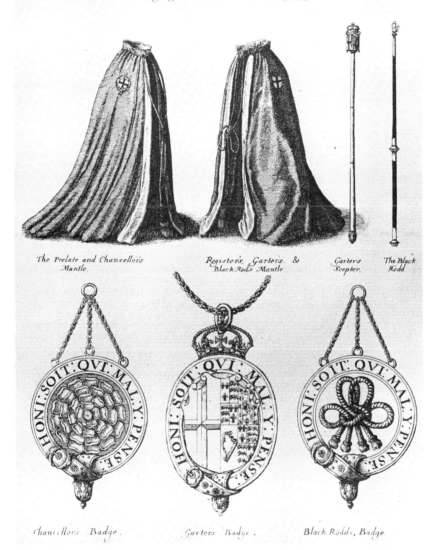

The prefent Habits Enfigns and Badges
belonging to the Offiers of the Order

The Prelate and Chancellors Mantle.

Registers, Garters, & Black Rods Mantle

Garters Scepter,

The Black Rodd

Chancellors Badge,

Garters Badge,

Black Rodds, Badge.

38. Mantles of Officers of the Order of the Garter 1673 pattern and Insignia and Badges. (Ashmole, *The Institution . . . of the Garter*)

The Prelate is always the incumbent Bishop of Winchester and for many years successive Bishops of Salisbury, and later Oxford, held the office of Chancellor. However, in 1937 George VI ruled that the Chancellorship should in future be held by a knight companion of the order.

In Restoration times both these officials wore murrey coloured velvet mantles or robes lined with white sarcenet, blue and gold cordon, but in 1673 Charles II changed both to purple with white taffeta lining. Ashmole notes the fact with the comment, "What inducements the Sovereign had, for changing the colour from Murrey to Purple we have not heard".

As depicted by Ashmole these new mantles were much of a design as those of the knights, except that there is no hood. Also, the garter surrounding St George's arms is on the right side, instead of the left. But, in plain clothes the Prelate should wear a badge or star on the left, as did the Knights. At some later date a neck badge in the form of St George and the dragon surmounted by a bishop's mitre was added. The Chancellor, at least for the time of Charles I, has had a badge of a rose surrounded by the garter, and also carried a purse containing the Seal of the Order suspended from his neck. (See Evelyn, *Diary*, 23 April 1667.) As the Chancellor is now, and in future to be, a knight companion, he wears the normal mantle and hat with his Chancellor's badge, and the Chancellor's mantle will presumably not be seen again.

The Register (ex officio the Dean of Windsor), Garter King of Arms, and Black Rod were, again by Charles II, allotted mantles of scarlet satin lined with white taffeta to replace their older style. When the office of Secretary was created in fairly recent times he was given a similar robe. These four officers have only a St George's shield of arms without the surrounding garter embroidered on the left side.

Black Rod carries it, Garter King of Arms bears a sceptre and all wear neck badges; the Register, two crossed pens, royal cipher and crown: originally this device was on the cover of a book carried by the Register on solemn occasions. "In the morning his Majesty went to Chapell with the Knights of the Garter . . . with the . . . Dean, who had about his neck the booke of the Statutes of the Order". (Evelyn, *Diary*, 23 April 1667.) Garter King of Arms has the royal and St George's arms within a garter surmounted by a crown; Black Rod a garter knot within a garter.

THE POOR KNIGHTS OF WINDSOR, THE ALMS-KNIGHTS, THE
MILITARY KNIGHTS OF WINDSOR

The order of the Poor Knights was originally founded as an alms-house for twenty-six knights "weak in body, indigent and decayed" providing food, shelter and clothes for "such as through adverse fortune were brought to that extremity". According to the statutes quoted by Ashmole their habits were "mantella de rubeo cum uno Scuto Armorum Sancti Georgii carente tantum tamen Garteris" – a red mantle with arms of St George but not surrounded by a garter. It appears that Henry VIII intended, in his will, that the Poor Knights should have annually "a long gown of white cloth". (Ashmole.)

By decree of Queen Elizabeth I they had "besides a goun or surcoat [not mentioned earlier] of Red cloth, and a mantle of Blue or Purple cloth, on the left sleeve whereof is embroidered the Arms of St George in a Plain Scutcheon". Charles I, probably in 1637, reverted to red for the gowns, as it had been before.

Later the numbers sank to thirteen, but rose again to eighteen by the Restoration. The function of these Poor Knights from the beginning was to pray for the souls of the Knights Companions, and for many generations after the Reformation they had to attend chapel twice daily.

From about the fifteenth century the "knights" have not necessarily been such, and in recent centuries the appointments have been made from the ranks of senior army officers.

Oliver Cromwell changed the livery of the Poor Knights to a "sad colour" gown with the Commonwealth arms in place of St George's. At the Restoration the old dress was re-introduced. There is some confusion, I think, in Celia Fiennes description of Windsor in 1698. She refers to the "Poore Knights which go in a peculiar black gown like fryers. . . ." She may have been confusing them with the clergy as she had already mistaken the Minor Canons' quarters for those of the Poor Knights.

The eighteenth century saw the Poor Knights in a sad condition and it was left to King William IV in 1833 to revive them and restore their pride. This monarch changed their name to that of "Military Knights of Windsor" and abolished the old gowns and mantles with their associations of alms and pauperdom. Instead the knights were provided with a contemporary military style uniform of scarlet and blue, which remains much the same today: blue faced scarlet coat with blue trousers with three one and three-quarter inch red stripes; black cocked hat with eight and a half inch red and white swan's plume;

cross hilt sword in black scabbard with white patent shoulder-belt and frog; crimson silk sash; epaulettes with St George's shield and badges of rank; garter buttons; blue cloak, lined scarlet, with cape but no sleeves.

Undress wear consisted of a single breasted dark blue frock coat, gilt buttons, embroidered St George's arms and badges of rank on shoulders, a blue forage cap with a scarlet band and trousers as described above.

THE MOST ANCIENT AND MOST NOBLE ORDER OF THE THISTLE

As with the Garter confusion reigns as to the exact date and circumstances of the origin of the Order of the Thistle. Various dates from 819 to 1535 have been suggested.

Ashmole (1672 edition) states that anciently the knights wore, on the feast of St Andrew, "Parliament Robes, having fixt on their left shoulders an azure Rundle, on which was embroidered St Andrew's cross, environed in Center with Crown composed of Flowers de Lis Or". Badges consisted of a gold collar of thistles interlinked, and a green ribbon from which hung a gold thistle topped with a crown. The motto was: Nemo me impune lacesset. Ashmole also noted a French Order of the Thistle of Bourbon, dedicated to Our Lady, not St Andrew, with a blue mantle but with a green mantlet and hood or bonnet. The collar was of fleurs de lys, with the badge of Our Lady with a green and white enamelled thistle below her feet.

Whenever and wherever the order was first founded, its present form dates from its revival and the publication of statutes by King James II in 1687. This year is the first in which any reference to "Knight of the Order of the Thistle" can be traced, although the statutes are careful to stress that it is a revival of the order originally founded under the protection of Our Blessed Lady and St Andrew. The colours of green and blue, the fleurs de lys, the representation of Our Lady, and the Thistle occur on both sides of the Channel.

King James II's statutes as quoted by Berry in *Encyclopaedia Heraldica*, described the robes of the re-established order as follows:

> That the habit of the Sovereign and Twelve Brethren should be a doublet and trunk hose of cloth of silver, stockings of pearl-coloured silk, white leather shoes, blue and silver garters and shoe strings, the breeches and sleeves of the doublet decently garnished with silver and blue ribbons; a surcoat of purple velvet, lined with white taffeta ... purple [and] gold sword belt ... scabbard of purple velvet.

39. The Earl of Melfort in Robes of the Most Ancient and Most Noble Order of the Thistle. *c* 1687. (Painting by Godfrey Kneller, Scottish National Portrait Gallery)

> That over all should be worn a mantle, or robe, of green velvet, lined with white taffeta, with tassels of gold and green: the whole robe parseminée, or powdered over with thistles of gold.

The badge, St Andrew with his cross before him, was embroidered on the left breast or shoulder.

The hat was to be

> a cap of black velvet ... wide and loose in the crown, having a large plume of white feathers, with a black aigrette, or heron's top, in the middle of it: and the border of the cap to be adorned with jewels. The Sovereign's cap ... two rows of diamonds across the crown thereof.

A gold collar, the links consisting of alternative thistles and sprigs of rue, with a gold badge of St Andrew enamelled or set with diamonds, was worn with the mantle. On other occasions a badge of gold, St Andrew in jewels or enamel on one side and an enamelled thistle on the other, was to be worn from a purple-blue riband.

When James II left hurriedly in 1688 the order seems to have been ignored, but Queen Anne revived it in 1703. She changed the method of wearing the riband to over the left shoulder, as the garter riband, and changed the colour to green (but see Ashmole's statement).

In February 1714 King George I authorised a cardboard and tinsel star for wear on the coat, again as the garter star was worn. A surround of rays was added to the St Andrew badge worn on the collar, and, to quote Ashmole (1715 edition), "now of late they have sewed to their left breast an irradiation (like that of the Knights of the Garter) over a saltire silver, the Irradiation charged with a blue roundel of St Andrew's cross".

It is interesting to note that both James II and Queen Anne wrote in their statutes that the sovereign and successors should "in all time coming, as they might think fit, wear the Badge of the Thistle on the Riband of the Garter". It seems that Queen Anne did on occasions wear a combined St George and St Andrew badge on her Garter riband (de la Bere, *The Queen's Orders of Chivalry*).

It was in these late Stuart days that the powdering of thistles was dropped from the mantle and a hood similar to the garter hood added; in 1703 the mantle is described just as "green velvet" (Statutes, 1703). Some time in the 1860s an enamelled silver star replaced the tinsel one.

Today the insignia of the Thistle consists of a green velvet mantle lined with white taffeta, cordons and tassels of green and gold; on the left breast an irradiated star or badge; a hood of dark blue velvet and white silk ribbon bows on the shoulders to secure the collar; a bonnet

40. Mantle, hat and insignia of the Order of the Thistle worn over normal morning dress, 1953. (Spectrum Colour Library/A. C. K. Ware)

or hat of dark blue velvet, with a gold embroidered badge and a gold cord; a gold collar enamelled in proper colours of alternating thistles and sprigs of rue, with the badge of a figure of St Andrew with his cross surrounded by golden rays suspended from it.

The star of St Andrew's cross is in white enamel or silver irradiated with intermediate rays, in the centre a thistle in proper colours on a gold field surrounded by a green circle with the motto in gold. A dark green riband is to be worn over the left shoulder, with a plain gold badge, when the collar is not worn. Officers of the order today at court wear either service uniform, or third class household uniform, if civilians.

THE MOST HONOURABLE ORDER OF THE BATH

This order, in its present form, was instituted by King George I in 1725, and at that time was intended to be a military order for the reward of outstanding services to the state by officers of the navy and army. The principal figure behind the idea was the First Minister, Sir Robert Walpole, prompted, it has been said, by John Anstis, the then Garter King of Arms.

But long before this, the notion of a bath or bathing was associated with the more ceremonious creation of a knight, as opposed to the simpler method of dubbing by the sword. The various ceremonies entailed in this elaborate ritual in the Middle Ages included a vigil before the altar and a bath symbolic of spiritual purification. In this country the custom seems to go back to Norman times. Later this form of ceremonial creation became restricted to coronations or to mark other great state occasions.

Froissart describes such a creation of new knights by King Henry IV in 1399 referring to him as "the duke" in accordance with the then prevailing idea that the title "king" should not be bestowed until after the coronation ceremony.

> On Saturday before the coronation, the new King went from West-minster to the Tower of London, attended by great numbers, and those Squires who were to be Knighted watched their arms that night; they amounted to forty-six; each squire had his chamber and bath. The next day after Mass the duke created them Knights, and presented them with long green coats with straight sleeves lined with miniver, after the manner of the prelates. These Knights had on their left shoulder a double cord of white silk, with white tufts hanging down.

The "double cord of white silk" indicated to some degree a novice knight; they would be removed by his lady when he had carried out a

41. Knight of the Bath in long blue gown; short sword at girdle; knotted "lace" on left shoulder; small plumed hat. *c* 1475. (After Writles Garter Book, MS. belonging to the Duke of Buccleuch)

suitable feat of arms. Later the cords were plaited or braided rather than removed when the knight had proved himself.

The last creation of such knights by the bath was at the coronation of King Charles II, of sixty-eight young men at Westminster. On 19 April 1661, Evelyn records that he "saw the bathing and rest of the Ceremonies of the Knights of the Bath, preparatory to the Coronation; it was in the Painted Chamber Westminster". (In a splendid throwaway line he added "I might have received this honour, but declined it".) On the twenty-third he attended the coronation in the Abbey and among the "magnificent traine on horseback, as rich as embroidery, velvet, cloth of gold and silver and jewels could make them" he picked out the "Knights of the Bath, sixty-eight, in crimson robes exceeding rich and the noblest show of the whole cavalcade, his Majestie excepted".

James Heath in his *A Chronicle of the Late Intestine War* gives a very full account of this, the last of the old order. After prayers and a supper provided by the king, they were taken to "Other near rooms, where their Bathing Vessels and Baths ... were prepared; There, after they had Bathed more or less as each of them found convenient, they remained all Night". In the morning they dressed in long russet gowns with wide sleeves and a hood with an ash-coloured and russet silk girdle with a white napkin or handkerchief hanging from it. Thus attired they attended morning service in the Henry VII Chapel and there also took the Oath of Knighthood.

> This done they returned ... to the Painted Chamber, and put on the Habit of the Order, which was a Mantle, and Surcoat of red Taffeta lined and adged with white Sarcenet, and thereto fastened two long strings of white silk, with buttons and tassels of red silk and gold; and a pair of white Gloves tyed to them, a white Hat and white Feathers: in this Garb ... girded with a sword, the Pummel and Cross-Hilt whereof were guilt, the Scabbard of white Leather, and belt of the same, with guilt spurs carried by their Pages, they marched ... to Whitehall. Here, in the Banqueting House the King delivered the accolade with the Sword of State. Before this, the Knights' own swords had been given up to the Lord Chamberlain, who, when the Knighting was done, handed the Knight's sword to the King who put it "that it might hang on his left side; and then the said scabbard *with the Order hanging at it*. [my italics]

What exactly was "the Order hanging at it"? It has been suggested that a badge of three crowns was granted to Knights of the Bath in 1605 – presumably for those created at the coronation of James I in 1604. Later, Charles I is said to have ordered the badge to have been worn around the neck on a red ribbon (de la Bere, *The Queen's Orders of Chivalry*). Was this what the king handed over with the sword and scabbard? Another puzzle is the pair of gloves tied to the cordons of the mantle and no mention of the white lace or cord on the left shoulder.

Lord Herbert of Cherbury was created a Knight of the Bath in 1604 and in his diary (quoted in Strong, *The Elizabethan Image*) records the ceremony and says:

> the second day to wear robes of crimson taffety ... and the third day to wear a gown of purple silk, upon the left sleeve thereof is fastened certain strings weaved of white silk and gold tied in a knot ... which all the Knights are obliged to wear until they have done something famous in arms, or until some lady of honour take it off and fasten it on her sleeve. ...

William Pope, first Earl of Downe, another knight of 1604, was painted in his crimson mantle with a pair of gloves tied in the cordons which are attached to the neck of the mantle to fasten it. Lord Herbert's account introduces a "purple gown", of which we have not heard before and do not hear of again.

Turning to the "revival" of the Bath by George I in May 1725 we find that in fact John Anstis, as the technical expert involved, created a

42. Surcoat of the Order of the Bath. Worn by General Sir William Clinton, C.B.E. at the coronation of George IV, 1821. (National Army Museum)

new order in the statutes in which features of the old Bath ceremonies were combined with some derived from the Garter ceremonies.

In 1730 John Pine produced an illuminated work, *Procession and Ceremonies*, recording the installation of the first knights in the Henry VII Chapel, Westminster Abbey, and showing the robes and insignia both of the knights, and of their attendant esquires, three of whom accompanied each knight for the installation ceremonies. The robes consisted of a crimson surcoat, lined with white and with a white lined crimson mantle to match with silk cordon with gold and crimson tassels. The surcoat and mantle were of silk – variously described as

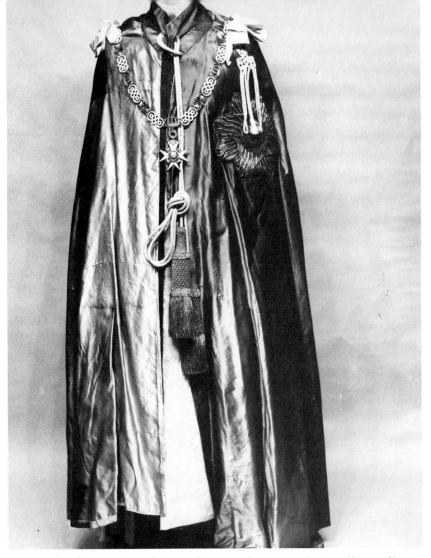

43. Mantle of the Order of the Bath. Worn by General Sir William Clinton, C.B.E. at the coronation of George IV, 1821. Collar from another source. (National Army Museum)

taffeta or satin. The sovereign's mantle was trained and required to be supported by a page. On the left breast or shoulder was embroidered an eight pointed star carrying a red circle on which were three imperial crowns in gold surrounded by the motto "Tria juncta in uno" – the device and motto as used in Carolinian times. The suggestion is that originally the motto alluded to the three kingdoms of England, Scotland and France; later the allusion was to England, Scotland and Ireland. A further suggestion is that it is of religious origin in honour of the Holy Trinity.

The collar was of 30 ounces Troy, gold (as was that of the Garter) compound of "several imperial crowns of gold, tied or linked with Gold Knots enamelled White, representing the White Laces mentioned in the Ancient Ceremonials. . . ." (Addition of 1 June 1725 to Statutes of May 1725.) In November a second design was approved to replace the first. This had nine crowns and eight devices made up of a sceptre with roses and thistles issuing from it all enamelled in proper colours and crowns and sceptres linked by seventeen gold knots enamelled white as before. Later, after the Act of Union in 1800, the shamrock of Ireland was added to the sceptre, and the collar remains much the same today. Attached to the collar was the badge, a gold oval inscribed with the motto and surrounding a sceptre, three crowns, and a rose and thistle. Minor variations in design occurred during the eighteenth and nineteenth centuries. This remains the style of the badge of the civil division of the order today. (Berry, *Encyclopaedia Heraldica*.)

The 1725 statutes decreed an underdress of white doublet, not unlike the contemporary waistcoat, white breeches, stockings and white boots "edged and heeled crimson", white sword-belt and scabbard and a plain cross-hilt sword and gold spurs. The hat was of white silk, high crowned, and decorated with a towering plume of white ostrich feathers.

The esquires at the installation wore red doublets, breeches and stockings and shoes and a white silk surcoat lined with crimson. On the left of the surcoat was a blue shield with three embroidered crowns. There was also a hood. There was sold at Christie's in 1971 a complete esquire's dress – doublet, breeches, surcoat, garters, belt and hat of black silk – reputed to have been worn at an installation in 1786.

The officers of the order wore white mantles, lined with crimson and with a blue shield as above (but on the right shoulder), and fastened with cordons, like a knight. The Dean of the order (the one in 1725 was a bishop) wore the mantle of a knight. All the officers were supplied with appropriate badges for the neck. The King of Arms had a two-foot silver mace with the arms of the order and the sovereign, with a crown above, and the Usher a gilt mounted red rod.

The 1725 ceremonies, like those of 1661, and presumably earlier creations of Knights of the Bath, were attended by the sovereign's Master Cook, complete with chopping-knife and block. At the conclusion of the installation the Master Cook reminded the knights as they passed by of the oath they had taken and if they failed to keep it, it was his duty to hack off their spurs.

The star of the order as worn on the mantle was also sewn on the coats of the knights. The star was not provided until about 1800, being

44. Sir William Hamilton wearing Bath Robes and underdress of 1725 pattern. 1775. (Painting by David Allan, National Portrait Gallery)

up to then bought by individuals; it was silver and gold thread and silk embroidery on a cardboard backing and fairly soon wore out. Some privately made metal stars were also in wear. It was not until the mid-nineteenth century that silver stars were officially bestowed. The Queen, who is Sovereign of the order, wears on her mantle a star, originally made for Queen Victoria, of silver, gold and enamel.

The mantles were supplied by the Lord Chamberlain's Office: the rest of the outfit the knights bought themselves. As with the Garter, the ostrich feathers were a very heavy item: in the early 1800s they could cost over £20. The installation of new knights in 1812 was the last one attended by esquires: thereafter they and their surcoats disappeared from the scene.

In 1815, at the end of the Napoleonic wars, the order was enlarged and altered and new statutes written. The requirements for vigil and bathing, long in desuetude, were abolished, membership of the order

45. Detail of mantle of the Order of the Bath, left shoulder and side. Stand collar showing slit for cordon to pass through, white silk ribbon bow to secure collar, white silk plaited cord and Star of post-1815 design for military division. (National Army Museum)

was divided into three classes, a new departure in English chivalry. Also provision was made for civil as well as military members of the highest class. There were now Knights Grand Cross (G.C.B.), Knights Commanders (K.C.B.) and Companions (C.B.). New insignia were designed, and the old designs were kept for the civil division. The military division had a laurel wreath and the extra motto "Ich Dien" added to the badges and stars. Only members of the highest grade, the Knights Grand Cross, were entitled to the mantle, hat and collar. At the same time the attachment of the gloves to the mantle by the cordins or laces was discontinued.

In 1821 came the coronation of the Prince Regent as George IV and as has been previously noted it was dressed in a theatrical manner. The G.C.B.s, and for this occasion K.C.B.s, were granted a short mantle, worn from the left shoulder, whilst for underdress both grades had doublets and trunk-hose, a red sash and red heeled boots with crimson tops, the lot topped by a ruff around the neck and a black velvet hat to replace the former white one. This was the last time that the full dress was worn. Subsequent occasions up to about 1861 when the order assembled, G.C.B.s alone wore the mantle and collar with court dress or uniform. After the Prince Consort's death (he was Great Master of the Order) the order was only infrequently convened and the mantles rarely, if ever, seen until the present century. Then they appeared at Edward VII's coronation and in 1913 at the first of the revived installation ceremonies.

In 1847 the order was again enlarged and the civil division extended to K.C.B.s and C.B.s

Today services of the Order of the Bath and installations of Knights Grand Cross take place in Westminster Abbey once in every four years. G.C.B.s and the officers of the order wear their appropriate crimson or white mantles, the knights with their collars. To quote *Dress Worn at Court* (1912):

> Knights Grand Cross of the Most Honourable Order of the Bath wear mantles of crimson satin, lined with white taffeta, and tied with a cordon of white silk, with two tassels of crimson silk and gold attached thereto; and on the left side of the mantle, below a white silk lace, is embroidered a representation of the Star [Military] . . . of rays of silver, charged with a Maltese Cross Or, in the centre whereof, on a ground argent, are three Imperial Crowns . . . within a circle gules inscribed . . . "Tria Juncta in Uno" in letters of gold . . . encompassed by two branches of laurel . . . issuant from an escrol Azure . . . inscribed "Ich Dien" . . . and the Star . . . of Civil Knights . . . of rays of silver . . . charged with three Imperial Crowns . . . within a circle gules whereon is inscribed 'Tria Juncta in Uno" in letters of gold.

46. Mantle of the Order of the Bath (Knight Grand Cross, Military Division) worn with George IV coronation "Elizabethan" underdress, but shoes instead of boots. 1953. (Spectrum Colour Library/A. C. K. Ware)

The black velvet hats have not been worn for forty years or more, except now by our present sovereign. Neither do the officers of the order wear hats: previously they had crimson ones similar to the knights' black velvet, but without plumes. The officers are entitled to wear service or household uniforms.

47. Latest type of hat of the Order of the Bath, black velvet *c* 1821. Not now worn, (National Army Museum)

It has been recorded that the gloves were originally suspended from the white lace on the left shoulder (see Riske, *History of the Order of the Bath and its Insignia*). There seems to have been some confusion in the past between the "lace" and the cordons. Further confusion has also been caused by mistaking the white silk ribbon bows used to secure the collars of various orders on the shoulders with the "silk lace" of the Bath shoulder knot.

Ashmole's 1715 edition speaking of the Bath knights states "they never used only a silk lace", which seems to indicate that no badge was then worn on the mantle. However, the original 1672 edition only says, "Knights of the Bath made by the present Sovereign [Charles II] . . . were created . . . and appointed to Knights Batchellor . . . they Watched and Bathed, they took an Oath, they were girded with a Sword and Belt, and lastly Dubbed by the King with the Sword of State".

The badge of the order is either worn on the collar (for G.C.B.s) or on a crimson ribbon round the neck. The badge can also be worn on the riband, which is crimson and goes over the right shoulder.

The Museum of London has a specimen of a Bath mantle of bright crimson satin; the star is embroidered in silver with a white braided and knotted "lace" on the left shoulder above the star, and white ribbon bows on each shoulder to secure the collar.

48. Members of the Most Honourable Order of the Bath assembled in Westminster Abbey for the Order's Service and Installation. Mostly Military Division Knights. Mantles worn over normal day dress. 1968. (Press Association)

The 1913 revival of the installation ceremony "which had been omitted for so many years" (King George V Order for 22 July 1913) caused *The Times* to comment upon the sad state into which ceremonial dress seemed to have fallen, despite two coronations since the beginning of the century: "The Officers of Arms will doubtless see to it that the Mantles themselves are worn in the correct way, as on recent occasions distinguished men have shown a deplorable inability to dress themselves properly."

THE MOST DISTINGUISHED ORDER OF ST MICHAEL AND ST GEORGE

This order was originally founded in 1818 to reward the loyalty of the inhabitants of Malta and of the Ionian Islands during the Napoleonic wars: Malta had come under the Crown in 1814, and shortly after that the Ionian Islands became a British protectorate. The order, like the Bath, consisted of various classes; Knights Grand Cross, Knights Commanders, and Companions (or Cavalieri), of which only the first have the right to wear the mantle, hat and collar of the order.

The size of the order was increased in 1832 and again in 1850. In 1864 the Ionian Islands were ceded to Greece, and four years later the order was opened to all British subjects serving or domiciled overseas. More increases were made during the nineteenth and early twentieth centuries, including the award of the order to the services during the First World War. When the Order of the British Empire was instituted

49. Star, collar and badge of the Most Distinguished Order of St Michael and St George, shown against the mantle with cordons and tassels. 1950–60. (Spectrum Colour Library/A. C. K. Ware)

50. Order of St Michael and St George, King of Arms, Crimson satin lined with Saxon-blue mantle with officer's badge on the right breast. Silver gilt crown and gilt mounted ebony rod. Worn with special uniform. 1950–60. (Spectrum Colour Library/A. C. K. Ware)

in 1917, the Order of St Michael and St George became once more restricted to honouring those who rendered valuable overseas service in the Empire, Commonwealth or in relation to Foreign Affairs.

The mantle was of saxon-blue satin, lined with scarlet silk. The term "saxon" blue which is used today is the colour also known as "saxe" blue; a medium tint with a rather cold greyish hue. There are two cordons of blue and scarlet silk and gold, with heavy tassels.

On the left of the mantle is the embroidered star, seven rays of silver, from between each of which comes a smaller gold ray; in the centre is St George's cross in red, with superimposed a blue circle with the motto "Auspicium Melioris Aevi" and a figure of the Archangel Michael with a flaming sword, trampling down Satan. The hat, described as a "chapeau", which was blue satin, lined with scarlet and with black and white ostrich feathers has not been worn for about thirty years. Originally the collar was of gold; now it is of silver-gilt. It is made up of crowned lions, Maltese crosses and the letters S.M. and S.G. In the centre front are two winged lions holding a book and a sling of arrows. The Maltese crosses are enamelled white.

The badge is a white enamelled seven-armed cross showing fourteen points. On the front is the design of St Michael as on the star; on the back is St George and the dragon. When the collar is not worn the badge is suspended on a four inch riband of saxon blue with a central scarlet stripe. The riband goes over the right shoulder. The star, to be worn on the left breast, is as embroidered on the mantle.

Knights Commander and Companions have no mantle, hat, collar or riband. The stars and badges are of a smaller size and Companions receive only a badge. In both cases the badges are worn round the neck on a narrow ribbon of the order. The officers of the order are entitled to wear a court dress similar to household uniform, but with scarlet velvet collar and cuffs, and laurel leaf embroidery.

THE ROYAL VICTORIAN ORDER

The Royal Victorian Order was founded by Queen Victoria in 1896 as "a reward for personal services to the Queen and her successors". At its institution there was a strict understanding that the whole cost of the order should be borne by the sovereign, without any government expense. The order is today considered a most desirable honour, and it is also bestowed as an honorary award upon distinguished foreigners. One of the acts of King Edward VIII during his brief reign was to open the order to ladies.

There are five classes, Knights Grand Cross, Knights Commander, Commanders and Fourth and Fifth Class Members. In addition three degrees of medal are awarded to people who have rendered very long service to the Royal Household. The medals are also occasionally awarded to foreigners, and to distinguish these King George VI, in 1951, ordered that the honorary awards to foreigners should be marked by a central white stripe in the red and white edged dark blue ribbon.

Knights Grand Cross wear a dark blue satin mantle, edged with two inches of red satin (half an inch at the collar) and lined with white silk. Dark blue silk and gold cordons and tassels. A red satin hood edged with blue is worn on the right shoulder: this now appears in the form of a circular flounce with an attached hanging strip (a vestigial liripipe). A specimen in the Museum of London has in addition a white ribbon knot and the right side of the mantle has a slit arranged for the arm. On the left of the mantle is embroidered a large star of the order, a silver star of eight points, with a representation of the badge in the centre.

51. The Royal Victorian Order. Star, collar and badge shown against mantle. 1953. (Spectrum Colour Library/A. C. K. Ware)

The gold collar is elaborate, of octagonal plaques enamelled blue and bearing a gold rose jewelled with a carbuncle. The plaques are linked by frames repeating in white enamelled gold cut-out letters the phrases "Victoria Britt. Reg. Def. Fid. Ind. Imp." Centre front is a larger plaque, enamelled red, white and blue and with an effigy of Queen Victoria in gold. The badge hangs from this central plaque, and is a white enamelled Maltese cross, in the centre a crimson oval with V.R.I. in gold, surrounded by a blue enamelled riband inscribed "Victoria", which is the motto of the order.

When not worn on the collar the badge is suspended on a riband passing across the right shoulder. The riband is dark blue, with narrow red-white-red stripes at each side. For men it is three and three-quarter inches wide and for ladies two and a quarter inches. The star which is worn on the left breast is an eight pointed star of clipped silver with the badge in the centre, the Maltese cross in frosted silver, not white enamel.

Knights Commanders and the inferior classes wear variations of the star or badge of smaller sizes. Ladies who are Dames Commander wear the badge on a bow on the left shoulder.

THE MOST EXCELLENT ORDER OF THE BRITISH EMPIRE

The Order of the British Empire, the youngest and largest of the orders of chivalry, has been described as "the order of chivalry of the British democracy. Valuable and useful service is the only test of admission, and in the opinion of many it is the most important order of the British Commonwealth". (de la Bere, *The Queen's Orders of Chivalry*.) The order was founded by King George V in 1917 and was originally to award non-combatant war service. The following year it was extended to include military awards. Its great innovation was that from the beginning it was to include women. There were five classes and a medal.

The original riband of the order was purple, and in 1918 a central scarlet stripe was added to that of the military division. The badge carried a representation of Britannia. In 1937 the riband was replaced by one of rose pink with grey edges, the military division being distinguished by the addition of a grey stripe in the centre also. The badge was also changed in design to show King George V, founder of the order, and Queen Mary, in place of Britannia. Officers of the order were granted third class civil uniform.

From December 1957 silver oak leaves have been added to the appropriate ribands in the case of awards made specifically for acts of gallantry. The mantle of the order, restricted to Knights and Dames Grand Cross, is rose pink satin with a grey silk lining. Cordons of grey

52. The Most Excellent Order of the British Empire. Star, collar and badge. 1953. (Spectrum Colour Library/A. C. K. Ware)

silk with tassels of pink and silver. The star is embroidered on the left side.

The collar, restricted like the mantle, is of silver-gilt with alternating roundels showing the royal arms and the imperial cypher, six of each, joined by links in the form of ropes with the imperial crown, two tridents and two "sea lions" – beasts like mermaids, fish from the waist down. The badge suspended from the collar is a cross patonce in grey enamel with a crown at the top and today the centre bears the portraits of King George V and Queen Mary in gold surrounded by a crimson circle with the motto "For God and the Empire". The riband, to which the badge is attached when the collar is not worn, passes from the right shoulder to the left side. It is four inches wide for men and two and a quarter inches for ladies. The latter, if G.B.E. of the military division, do not have the central grey stripe, as do the men. Queen Mary, when Grand Master of the Order, was anxious that all ladies should wear a similar riband to the new civil riband which she had adopted in 1937.

The star is of clipped silver with eight points, rayed, with a gold medallion at the centre showing King George V and Queen Mary, in profile, as on the badge.

Knights and Dames Commanders wear badge and star, smaller than those of G.B.E., and the inferior classes only the badge.

THE OBSOLESCENT ORDERS

THE MOST ILLUSTRIOUS ORDER OF ST PATRICK

Under the date 5 February 1783 Fordyce's *Chronology* records "His Majesty created a new order of Knight-hood for Ireland, called Knights of the illustrious Order of St Patrick". The order was given precedence after the Garter and Thistle, but before the Bath, and was intended as an equivalent of the first two for awarding to the Irish peerage. It consisted of the sovereign and fifteen knights, the Lord Lieutenant of Ireland being Grand Master. In 1833 the number of knights was increased to twenty-two. The motto was "Quis Separabit". From 1924 the order began to decline and by the 1960s only two knights survived – the Dukes of Gloucester and Windsor.

The mantle was sky-blue, satin or silk of Irish manufacture and with a white silk lining. There was a matching hood on the right shoulder, and cordons of blue and gold with similar tassels. On the left was embroidered the star of eight rayed points, in the centre a red St Patrick's cross, with a green clover leaf on its face, each lobe of the trefoil bearing an imperial crown and surrounded with a blue enamel circle bearing the motto and the date MDCCLXXXIII. The gold collar was of alternating Irish harps and enamelled roses, linked with knots in the form of the cordon and tassels. From the centre the badge was suspended from a harp surmounted by a crown. The badge is oval, and like the centre of the star has St Patrick's cross, trefoil and crowns, motto and date.

There have been minor variations in the badge and star. For instance in the early nineteenth century the star, in the centre, had around the blue circle containing the motto and date an outer border of trefoils. The badge was similarly bordered: in 1912 the star had "a representation of the badge of the Order, but without the wreath of trefoils". The silver star is as described above.

A smaller badge was worn on a light blue riband across the right shoulder, resting on the left hip, when the collar was not worn. Up to 1916 the silver star was not provided at investitures and had to be purchased privately. As with the Orders of the Thistle and the Bath, Officers of St Patrick were to wear service or third class household uniform.

THE MOST EXALTED ORDER OF THE STAR OF INDIA

The order was instituted in 1861 and the insignia are said to have been designed by the Prince Consort but the *Illustrated London News* states they were "designed and made by Messrs. Garrard, of the Hay-

53. The Most Exalted Order of the Star of India. Star, collar and badge shown against mantle with cordons. 1950–60. (Spectrum Colour Library/ A. C. K. Ware)

market" (17 August 1861). No appointments have been made to the order since 1947. It was intended as an award to ruling Princes of India and to distinguished British administrators and soldiers who devoted their services to that country. The order has two peculiarities: first, the highest of the three classes of the order is Knight Grand Commander and not Knight Grand Cross; this is to avoid embarrassing non-christians who are members. Second, the insignia are more costly than any other, and are liberally decorated with diamonds, and the design of the star is unique.

Knights Grand Commander have light blue satin mantles with white silk linings, with cordons of white silk with blue and silver tassels. On the left is embroidered the star, enriched with diamonds. The collar is enamelled gold of roses, lotus flowers and palm branches tied with ribbon, all in proper colours. From an imperial crown in the centre hangs a badge: an oval medallion of an onyx cameo profile of Queen Victoria, surrounded by a light blue enamelled border with the motto "Heaven's Light Our Guide" in gold letters, the whole surmounted by a five pointed star.

The riband is light blue with white borders, four inches wide and on it is worn a secondary badge, known as the "investment" badge, similar to that described above but heavily encrusted with diamonds and with the motto also in diamonds.

The star is of gold wavy rays, like flames, in the centre a blue enamel ribbon with the motto surrounding a five pointed star, like that surmounting the badge. The star and motto are all in diamonds. To quote the *Illustrated London News*, "A considerable degree of costliness has been, with an appropriateness to Eastern ideas, attached to this decoration, while there is an artistic embellishment about it which tones down the general effect, and renders it at once rich and graceful".

THE MOST EMINENT ORDER OF THE INDIAN EMPIRE

Instituted originally in 1878, on New Year's Day, to commemorate Queen Victoria's newly acquired title of "Empress of India", this was not an order of knighthood, as it was composed of Companions only, known as C.I.E.s. On 20 August 1886, as part of the Golden Jubilee celebrations, the order was extended and up-graded. It was further extended in 1897 but has not been awarded since 1947. It finally consisted of Knights Grand Commanders, Knights Commanders and Companions.

Knights Grand Commanders wore a mantle of purple satin lined

54. The Most Eminent Order of the Indian Empire. Star, collar and badge shown against mantle with cordons. 1953. (Spectrum Colour Library/A. C. K. Ware)

with white silk, with white silk cordons ending in purple and gold tassels: the star was embroidered on the left side.

The collar is of gold, of lotus flowers and peacocks in their pride, connected by plain chain links. In the centre front is the imperial crown with an elephant on each side. From the crown depends the badge, a gold and enamel rose, in the centre a profile of Queen Victoria within a circle bearing the motto "Imperatricis auspiciis". The earliest type of badge also bore the word "India" on each petal of the rose. The badge is surmounted by another imperial crown. The star is ten pointed, alternately gold and silver, the centre being a portrait of Queen Victoria surrounded by the circle and motto, but with an imperial crown at the top resting on the circle. The riband is dark blue and worn from the right shoulder to the left hip where the badge is attached when the collar is not worn. Knights Commanders have no mantle and the star is all silver, and smaller in size. Companions wear the badge only.

THE ORDER OF THE CROWN OF INDIA

On New Year's Day 1878 the Queen also instituted an order for Indian and distinguished British ladies – the Order of the Crown of India. The order bestowed no titles, precedence or initials upon the ladies who were awarded it. The last appointments were the Queen and Princess Margaret in 1947. The only insignia was a badge, an oval surmounted by the imperial crown and bearing within the cypher VRI, the whole enriched with diamonds, pearls and turquoises. The badge is worn on the left shoulder, on a ribbon bow of light blue watered silk edged with white.

CHAPTER III

Women's Court Dress

From early times it has been the custom to wear one's best clothes at important social and official functions, especially those associated with the monarch. So the court became the natural show place for the most costly and elegant of clothes for both men and women; for those whose lives as courtiers were spent within the royal household, and for those whose attendance at court was occasional.

Celebrations such as New Year's Day and the birthdays of the various members of the royal family called for even grander clothes to be worn by courtiers and by their majesties. Articles of clothing, personal jewelry and the like were favourite and welcome gifts to royalty on birthdays and other occasions: among other New Year gifts to Queen Elizabeth I in 1564 were "a cawle" (a netted, often lined, cap of gold work) and "three forehead cloths" (triangular pieces of material worn over the head and caul, point behind, and tied under the chin) "of cambryk netted with gold". In the same year the Earl of Oxford brought the Queen perfumed gloves from Italy "trimmed only with foure tuftes of roses in culler'd silk". In a way these were rather backhanded presents as royalty was expected to reciprocate in kind or cash to the giver: in 1544 Princess Mary gave thirty shillings to "a gentleman of my Lord Admiral bringing a coffer with X payr of Spanyneshe Gloves from a Duches in Spayne".

The dress at court of both sexes was in the ruling fashion of everyday clothes, although grander. It was not until the late eighteenth century that court dress began to exhibit a degree of "fossilisation" which marked it off from contemporary fashion. This tendency for court dress to be in the style of former times is more noticeable in men's

PLATE I

(a) French style Court Dress with wide side hoop. Described as a winter gown of blue satin trimmed with bands and tails of sable secured by white ribbon bows. There is also lace at the neck, stomacher, cuffs and on the overskirt and petticoat. The hair and headdress are more exaggerated than the English fashion at this time. *c.* 1750 (Plate by Voysard after Le Clerc).

(b) Court Dress of green silk, round décolleté with modesty-piece, low waist, irregular low skirt yoke and hem line, beaded bodice and beadwork over-skirt. The train apppears to be too long for the Regulations, although the picture appeared "officially" 1929. (Reville design for *Dress and Insignia Worn at Court*, 1929. Copyright of The Lord Chamberlain.)

court clothes: the women's, although succumbing to a degree, managed to keep up for the most part with the essential fashionable line of the day, the accessories providing the main distinction. Despite this, one of the causes of the divergence of styles was the fact that women's court dresses retained the exaggerated side-hoops of the 1740s until the nineteenth century when the combination of a high waist line and George IV finally abolished the archaic style in 1820.

In addition to such celebrations as royal birthdays, attendance upon the royal family for political, administrative and social reasons took place regularly. From early times the king would receive friends and officials in his bed or dressing-rooms during the prolonged formalities of the daily toilet, and his queen would receive similarly in the "withdrawing room" later in the day. From these practices grew the eventual rituals of the "levee" and the "drawing room", held at prescribed and regular intervals. Formal receptions and balls were other features of court life which required attendance in court dress. Eventually the levee became the occasion for the presentation of men to the monarch, with the drawing room for the similar presentation of the ladies, particularly when they were "coming out". From this grew the ritual of debutantes.

Mrs Armytage (*Old Court Customs and Modern Court Rule*) stated that "it is difficult to trace out or fix the exact date when court receptions assumed the rules which at present regulate these ceremonies", and again, "there are no existing records of any Court regulations being issued as to dress till of late years". This last statement is not strictly accurate, since during the eighteenth and early nineteenth centuries various edicts as to dress were promulgated, although it was not until 1898 that the first edition of what in the next century was to become the courtiers' bible of dress was produced. This was a nineteen page pamphlet, anonymously produced, titled *Dress Worn by Gentlemen at Her Majesty's Court*.

THE SEVENTEENTH CENTURY

The return of the king in 1660 saw, among other things, a reaction in women's clothes against the plain costume of the Civil War and Commonwealth years. Colours became more brilliant, trimming more lavish. The bodice of the fashionable dresses was long and heavily boned in a corset-like manner. As the century progressed the bodices became longer and even more like a corset. The neckline was low, exposing the shoulders and upper half of the breasts: a variety of "berthas" and scarves served at least partially to conceal the nudity. After 1680 the neckline was higher.

Skirts were pleated into the waist and hung in natural folds to the ground. The front was usually open to expose an underskirt or petticoat. Trained skirts had come in about 1650 and by 1680 the overskirt was very long. In the last twenty years of the century the outline became taller and narrower, the skirt fitting closer, the overskirt hitched up at the hips and the train narrower: a "bustle" was sometimes added and the trained overskirt bunched up at the back.

The underskirt or petticoat was usually richly trimmed with lace, fringes, or embroidery. In August 1660 Mrs Pepys paid £5 for cloth and "rich lace" for a petticoat, "but she doing it very innocently", her husband "could not be angry". Except that it was a "light colour" and the lace all silver we know no more. The next year Mrs Pepys had a "green petticoate of floured sattin, with fine white and black gimp lace ... which is very pretty". The cost is not mentioned. In 1662 Pepys records that the maids-of-honour in attendance on Queen Catherine of Braganza in December were all dressed in velvet gowns. In the summer of 1664 they wore silver-lace gowns, apparently a revival, for Pepys adds "I did not think would have been brought up again".

Queen Catherine, who was Portuguese, arrived in England in 1662, accompanied by her own ladies who were, like the queen, dressed "in their monstrous fardingals", as Evelyn describes them. This is echoed by Pepys and other observers – "their farthingales a strange dress ... I find in them nothing that is pleasing". This outmoded costume of the Portuguese Court, a survival of fifty years and more, foreshadowed the equally outmoded side hoops worn with English court dress a century or so later.

One of the new queen's early remarks was of the time spent in dressing by the English ladies: "The Queen is much concerned that the English ladies spend so much time in dressing themselves. She fears they bestow but little on God Almighty and on housewifery", Lord Cornberry wrote to Lady Worcester on 10 June 1662. However, the influence of Charles and the atmosphere of the court and town generally seems to have had no mean effect on Catherine, so much so that her original stuffy attitudes and unfashionable dress were alike discarded, and a few years after the remarks quoted above she was competing with the most advanced of the English fashionables: she "exposed her breast and shoulders without even ... the slightest gauze; and the tucker instead of standing up on her bosom, is with licentious boldness turned down and lies upon her stays". (Jesse, *Memoirs of the Court ... of the Stuarts*). Also, if we are to believe Pepys (20 October 1666) "the

Queen hath a great mind to alter her fashion, and to have the feet seen: which she loves mightily". But the fashion, judging by contemporary pictures, does not appear to have been altered: a minimal amount of foot is seen occasionally, although one print of the King and Queen shows the front of the dress an inch or so off the ground and most of one foot exposed. She appears to be pregnant, however, and this might account for the elevation of the front skirt.

The Queen's birthday was on 15 November and in 1666 Pepys and his wife were privileged spectators in a

> loft, where with much trouble I could see very well . . . and it was indeed a glorious sight to see Mrs Stewart in black and white lace, and her head and shoulders dressed with diamonds, and the like many great ladies more, only the Queen more . . . the business of the dancing of itself was not extraordinary pleasing. But the clothes and sight of the persons were indeed very pleasing, and worth my coming, being never likely to see more gallantry [finery] while I live. . . .

But Evelyn, writing nearly twenty years later of the Queen's birthday in 1684, thought "the Court had not been seene so brave and rich in apparell since his Majesty's Restauration".

A popular version of the fashionable gown was the mantua; a dress with an unboned, loose bodice and trained overskirt divided in front to show the usual decorative underskirt. It was often fastened at the waist by a sash or belt. Originally it was worn as an informal housedress or negligee, often being referred to as a "night-gown". It worked its way up the social scale and became acceptable wear for social and formal occasions by the 1680s. Originally made of Mantuan silk – hence the name – it also appeared in brocades and other rich silks. The Queen did not always approve of wearing mantuas formally and in 1683 apparently disagreed with the Duchess of York who, according to a letter of John Verney, when at Newmarket gave "the country ladies leave to come to her in mantos".

A feature of the century was the widespread habit of women to go bareheaded, outdoors as well as within. However, headwear was worn and during the later part of the century two styles were popular for indoor use: the "cornet", a coif like cap, and, from about 1690, the "fontange", a stiffened linen and lace structure supported on wire and worn forward, with an attached cap sitting behind on the back of the head. The fontange stood high up over the hair, which often had artificial curls piled up in front of it. With both types long lace or linen streamers, or lappets, were worn falling down to or below the shoulders. Such lappets remained a feature of court headdress down to modern times.

The hair from 1660 was generally set in curls – corkscrew side curls, from 1660 to 1670 held out from the face by wire, were being replaced from the 1680s by curls closer to and on top of the head, with long ringlets hanging behind. False hair and wigs were much used. Mrs Pepys in 1662 had made "a pair of peruques of hair in the fashion now in for ladies to wear; which are pretty, and are of my wife's own hair, or else I should not endure them". The full periwig, however, was mostly confined to wear when riding. Dye and hair powder was also in use; Sir John Cooke sent some of the latter to a friend from France, noting that it was "of the best Montpellier affords . . . there is powder cheaper, but not so proper for the hair". (Verney, *Memoirs*, quoted in Gunn, *The Artificial Face*.)

Face powder, rouge and patches were all in use. The patches, of various shapes, were of black silk or velvet stuck on the cheeks, either to cover blemishes or emphasise some feature. Pepys had divided views: "To the King's house [theatre] and . . . met with Knipp [Mrs Knipp, an actress], and she took us up into the tireing-room . . . where Nell [Gwynn] was dressing herself . . . But Lord! to see how they were both painted would make a man mad, and did make me loath them. . . ." (*Diary*, 5 October, 1667). Later in the month he sees a Mrs Pierce "still very pretty, but paints red on her face, which makes me hate her". (26 October.) His attitude to patches was quite different: in 1660 he writes of Princess Henrietta and of his wife, "but my wife standing near her with two or three black patches on, and well dressed, did seem to me much handsomer than she". We presume that Mrs Pepys's patches were the result of innocent vanity and not used to cover "pimples about her mouth" which Pepys gives as the reason for Lady Newcastle's "many black patches" recorded years later. (*Diary*, 22 November 1660 and 26 April 1667).

Shoes from 1660 were narrow fronted, square or slightly concave, generally with a high heel and fastened by straps tied or buckled over a tongue. With "full dress" embroidered silk or other material was *de rigueur*. Silk stockings in bright colours supported by tied or buckled garters. Again with full dress elbow length gloves of fine leather and silk were correct.

A display at neckline and sleeve of the lace and frills of the chemise was a feature of this period and the sleeve was sometimes slit in front to allow the chemise sleeve to be seen. Purely decorative aprons, plain white, or of transparent fabric with lace, embroidery or cutwork decoration were fashionable and were probably worn at court.

55. Mary II, Queen of England,
wearing fontange headdress of lace
with long matching lappets.
Elaborate bodice with stiffened
stomacher, long gloves, and fan. The
lappets were retained as part of court
dress for more than three centuries.
1688. (Mezzotint by John Smith after
Van der Vaart. Crown copyright,
Victoria and Albert Museum)

What perhaps started as a court fashion was the wearing of a distinctive riding habit, modelled on masculine lines: "I find the Ladies of
Honour dressed in their riding garbs, with coats and doublets with
deep skirts, just for all the world like mine . . . with perriwigs and with
hats; so that, only for a long petticoat dragging under their men's
coats, nobody could take them for women in any point whatever;
which was an odd sight, and a sight did not please me", wrote Pepys in
June 1666. And in September of the same year Evelyn noted, "The
Queene was now in her cavalier riding habite, hat and feather, and
horseman's coate, going out to take the aire".

Fashion in the Restoration period was largely under French influence and was also a reaction against the past sad days of Parliament
and Puritanism. An extravagance of costume was observable in both
sexes, and the restored court plunged into a sea of lace and ribbons
and silk and fine linen. Gold and silver and jewels were worn by men
and women alike. On 4 February 1666 Evelyn described the jewels of

the audience at a court masque; "the excessive gallantry of the ladies was infinite, those especially on ... Castlemaine [Lady Castlemaine, one of Charles II's favourites] esteem'd at £40,000 and more, far out-shining the Queen"; and again, on the Queen's birthday in 1674, "the Court exceeding splendid in clothes and jewells, to the height of excess". It is Evelyn also who records for us a "French pedling woman, one Mad. de Boord, who us'd to bring peticoates and fanns, and baubles out of France to the Ladys. ...."

James II's brief and unedifying reign made little impression on fashion. On the King's birthday on 14 October 1686 Evelyn records of the ball at night, "the Ladys no less splendid at Court ... but small appearance of qualitie".

The reign of William and Mary turned the court into a very dull place. It was said of William that he was the plainest man, and of no fashion at all, and his queen wrote that the court was a noisy world full of vanity and that she hated the court ladies who crowded round her. It has been noticed above how the fashion became more elongated and upright – rigid and more covered up during the last years of the century.

THE EIGHTEENTH CENTURY

During this period female dress underwent several major changes and by the end of the century court dress had established itself as a style apart; just as from the end of the seventeenth century the court itself became but the centre of a formalised and restricted circle, itself a style apart from the rest of the nation's life. Since the death of Charles II the court had ceased to be the centre not only of pleasure but of patronage, politics, literature, art and of all the other activities of a lively and progressive nation. The decline of the court was com-pounded by the burning down in 1698 of Whitehall Palace itself, leaving in London only the little palace of St James as the focal point of what court life remained.

Queen Anne, who succeeded William III in 1702, was a confirmed invalid who kept court unwillingly, although she apparently held "drawing rooms" two or three times a week, at St James's or at Wind-sor. Swift in his *Journal to Stella* comments upon their dullness. Nevertheless the Queen was most particular as to her own dress and was not slow in reproving anyone she considered improperly dressed in her presence.

The fashion was that which had emerged at the end of the last cen-tury, a stiffly bodiced slim line, the height accentuated by the tall fontange on the head. This had reached its highest by 1700 and thereafter got lower, subsiding into a mere frill by 1710. By the same year the waist line rose and the bodice was less boned, or quite boneless. As the century progressed the corset proper as an undergarment developed.

In the eighteenth century the gown and petticoat together formed a complete dress: in most cases the gown was bodice and overskirt joined together, the bodice open or closed in front, the skirt open showing the petticoat or underskirt (the "open" robe in modern terms). Sometimes the gown was complete in itself with the overskirt closed and no separate petticoat (the "closed" robe in modern terms). A third variety was a separate bodice and petticoat (skirt), the bodice usually in the form of a jacket falling outside the petticoat. Closed bodices were generally buttoned down the front to the waists. The open bodice was closed in front by a "fill-in" or false front with edge-to-edge fastening down the centre front; generally made of the same material as the gown. Or the open bodice was closed in front by a "stomacher" – a triangular, stiffened and decorated panel, pinned or laced in place. The front edges of the open bodice were finished off with flat revers, known as robings, ending at waist level until about 1750, when they continued down the open petticoat in some cases.

Within these divisions there were a variety of styles, some named, some not. Of the named types the mantua, or manteau, continued to be worn during the first half of the century and was seen at court: Mrs Delany records Lady Hertford in 1729 wearing "a blue manteau, embroidered with gold and a white satin petticoat".

The custom of wearing especially grand clothes at court on royal birthdays, New Year, and also on accession and coronation anniversaries was by now well established, despite the decline in the general importance of court life, and the expense of new clothes became a burden upon the less wealthy courtiers and court officials. The custom was appreciated by the London tradesmen, and the mercers, weavers and silkmen petitioned Queen Anne to hold court balls "on her birthnight and other public occasions which are certainly the greatest support to our and almost all other trades" (Cowper MSS, quoted by J. M. Beattie, *The English Court in the Reign of George I*).

By 1710 the fashion had moved to wider skirts which needed additional support in the form of hoops, giving either a dome-shaped outline, or a dome flattened front and back (the oval or fan hoop), or an extreme exaggeration of width over the hips (the oblong or side hoop). The first form persisted up to the 1780s, the latter two disappearing between 1740, when the skirt was at its largest, and 1760, except that, as noted above, the side hoop was retained for court wear.

The petticoat, from about 1710 to 1750, was often flounced in court dresses, and so were the sleeves from the mid 1730s. Trains generally were unfashionable from 1710 to 1760, but were retained for court wear: some were detachable from the waist.

In early 1738 Mrs Delany "after much persuasion . . . consented to go with Lady Dysart to the Prince's birthday, humbly drest in my pink damask, white and gold handkerchief [a square worn around the neck and tucked into or secured at the front of the neckline], plain green ribbon [probably a bow tying the ends of the handkerchief together in front] and Lady Sunderland's buckles for my stays". Either Mrs Delany wore a back-lacing corset which acted as a stomacher (which we know she did at times) or she applies this word to the stomacher itself. She goes on to say

> I never saw so much finery without any mixture of trumpery in my life . . . Lady Huntingdon's as the most extraordinary I must describe first. Her petticoat [she probably wore an open robe] was black velvet embroidered with chenille, the pattern a large stone vase filled with ramping flowers . . . gold shells and foliage embossed and most heavily rich; the gown was white satin embroidered also with chenille . . . it was a most laboured piece of finery, the pattern much properer for a stucco staircase than the apparel of a lady – a mere shadow that tottered under every step she took under the load.

The courts of both George I and his son George II were said to be both dull and low in tone. "Drawing rooms", or receptions, were held once or twice a week. A redeeming feature of the time was Caroline, George II's queen, and when in 1736 she "desired people not to make fine clothes" for her birthday, but to "reserve them for the Prince's wedding" it was said that her drawing room was unusually crowded, perhaps an indication of the effect that the costly new clothes customary at these celebrations had on people and purses. (Egmont MSS, quoted in Beattie, *The English Court*.) Later in the reign this is shown in a letter of Lady Suffolk's: "my zeal about my new gown came partly from its being the only one I shall have for the winter". (*Letters*, 1758.)

Court gowns of all kinds of silk and velvet (which was largely confined to court wear) were often of multi-coloured or design-laden pattern, whereas up to the middle of the century plain one colour materials were usual for everyday wear. Apart from black and white, reds, blues, green, yellow, pinks and purple were favourite colours. Elaborate trimmings with diamonds and other jewels, gold and silver embroidery, and rich fur were all to be seen.

56. Court dress of type known as a "mantua" worn over exceedingly wide
side or oblong hoop. Red silk heavily embroidered with silver. 1740–45.
(Crown copyright, Victoria and Albert Museum)

In the 1750s the decolletage was both wide and low, "naked-
shoulder'd and open-breasted" as the *Gentleman's Magazine* put it, and
overskirts and petticoats became very short. "While I am conniving at
low stays and short petticoats I will permit no lady whatsoever to make
both ends meet", wrote Edward Moore in *The World*, in 1756. By the
1760s both skirts and necklines had become once again more modest
in their proportions; but low necklines seem to have persisted for court
wear; in 1762 Horace Walpole wrote "there is a Court-dress to be instituted . . . stiff-bodied gowns and bare shoulders".

In 1765 Charlotte, Queen of George III, asked all the ladies attending court to wear only Spitalfield's silk, as she did, to encourage the
English silk trade. Most of the ladies complied with the Queen's
request, but few persisted in using imported silk. The following year,
on 7 June 1766, the *Ipswich Journal* reported, "The rich dresses in which
the Nobility appeared yesterday at Court and which were fabricated at
Spital-fields evidently showed that no Nation on Earth can vie with
them".

Two familiar styles of the eighteenth century dress were the sack, and its variation, the sack-back; and the polonese. The distinguishing feature of the sack family was the multiple pleats falling from the centre back neckline, where they were stitched down for some inches, thence flowing freely to be lost in the folds of the back of the gown. The polonese had the overskirt of the gown drawn up into three puffed-out bunches at the back; this was achieved by cords or ribbons pulling up and securing the folds; the petticoat was thus exposed all round and was generally shortened to above-ankle length. The sack and sack-back flourished from 1720 to 1780 in general wear, but some time longer at court. The polonese was very fashionable for about fifteen years from 1770.

In July 1786 Fanny Burney, Assistant Keeper of the Wardrobe to Queen Charlotte, wrote ". . . at St James I can never appear, even though I have nothing to do with the drawing-room, except in a sacque; 'tis the ettiquette of my place".

The Museum of London has a sack-back robe with matching underskirt and stomacher which dates from the time Fanny Burney was writing. It is lavishly trimmed and of high quality silk and silk lined throughout. The cut is for wide side hoops and with a train, and thus it is most probably a court dress. In 1788 Queen Charlotte and her daughters "in sacque dresses" received a deputation at Kew (Mrs Papendiek, *The Journals*).

Eleven years earlier, in 1777, Mary Frampton records the dress of the Queen and Princesses for the Prince of Wales's birthday in August. "We all retired to dress, all in New Clothes in hon^r of the day – Her Majesty and the Princesses wore blue and silver polonaises" (*At Court and At Home, 1756–1816*). Some of the princesses were only children of seven and eight, and Mary Frampton noted that, surprisingly, they looked "well in such a costume".

For some time it had been customary for newly-wed brides to wear white at court, possibly adapting their wedding-dresses, as was done in the nineteenth century. By the 1770s this custom was lapsing: in 1774 Mrs Delany wrote "the fashion of brides being presented in white is out, and so, tho' she has a pretty white and silver she is to be presented in pink with Brussel's lace. The trimming cost 70 pound". Seven years later Lady Althorpe, a bride of a fortnight, was at a drawing room in "silver tunic trimmed with gold, many jewels . . ." (*Autobiography and Correspondence*). This seems to approach white again very nearly.

In 1774 Mrs Papendiek recorded that "it was permitted for Spectators to be present on all public days at St James's. . . . For those who

57. French court dress of the style worn both sides of the Channel: wide hoops, train, ruffles at sleeves, décolletée, and the fashionable plumes. By this time hoops had become quite small for everyday fashion, and in many cases were omitted altogether. 1777. (Engraving by Martini after Moreau le Jeune. Crown copyright, Victoria and Albert Museum)

were in course of time to be presented, this permission was a great advantage for it gave them an insight into Court ceremonies, and . . . the peculiar dress essential for all those who attended them at that date – the large hoop, long lappets, heavy plumes etc.". Later she wrote "the headdress was a cap with Court lappets . . . the . . . Princesses . . . had not yet been introduced at Court, they wore no lappets".

58. Side hoops for court wear: short under petticoats showing below stocking tops falling down over garters; or legs of drawers. If the latter this was a French fashion and such garments were not worn this side of the Channel until the early nineteenth century. 1785. (From a French satirical engraving)

In addition to the above, trains and ruffles were essential: "the Queen then leaves the dressing-room, her train being carried by the bedchamber-woman" (Fanny Burney, 1786). "The Queen's train about 3 yds. in length . . . those of the Court attendance were 2 yds. long and could be looped up elegantly" (Mrs Papendiek, 1780s). The ruffles, double or treble, were worn on the sleeves of the gown.

Fanny Burney describes herself as being dressed "all at Kew except tippet and long ruffles which she carries in paper to save from dirty roads". This was in the summer of 1786 at a time when the Royal Family was living at Kew Palace and would go to London for the day to hold court at St James. Later, in 1799, the *Ipswich Journal* reported a court ball remarking that "some ladies appeared, contrary to Court etiquette, without ruffles, to display their embroidered sleeves".

Fanny's tippet was one of the various neck coverings common throughout the century, another of which was the handkerchief, a square folded diagonally and worn with the points at the back and ends tucked in the bosom, or secured by ribbon or brooch. Also worn were: a double or treble cape-like "ruff" set on a neck band, tied in front and falling down to the shoulder; the tucker, frilled or lace edging round the bodice neck line, leaving the bosom bare (this was "dress" wear only); or the modesty-piece, a small strip of lace or linen on the upper border of the corset, rising above the neckline to cover "the pit of the bosom".

The tippet itself was a narrow white shoulder cape, like a fichu, with short falling ends in front, closed by a pin or clasp. They could be worn high or low: "a tucker edged with diamonds ... and no more of a tippet than serves to make her fair bosom conspicuous rather than hide it". (Mrs Delany 1773/4).

Mrs Papendiek mentions "heavy plumes" as essential at court: this is in the year 1774, and is an early, perhaps the earliest, note of this type of head adornment as a requisite at court, and we find them hereafter becoming increasingly popular, not only for court but for other "dress" occasions, despite the alleged disapproval of Queen Charlotte: "the Queen disliked the nodding of the funeral plumes". (*London Magazine*, 1775, quoted in Cunnington, *Handbook of English Costume in the Eighteenth Century*). The fashion for plumes was not confined to this country: we also find the wearing of feathers on the Continent at this time. The 1770s was a period of extreme hair fashions, the coiffure reaching an excessive height and exuberance.

Georgiana, Duchess of Devonshire, is popularly supposed to have introduced the feather headdress, which was generally of ostrich plumes, of any colour. In March 1775 Mrs Delany wrote: "The three most elevated plumes of feathers are the Duchess of Devonshire, Lady Mary Somerset and Lady Harriet Stanhope, but some say Mrs Hubert's [or Hobart] exceeds them all". And the next year, "the ladies head dresses grow daily and seem like the Tower of Babel to mean to reach the skies!"

59. Hair style, with front hair dressed high over a pad or frame, side curls, back hair plaited and turned up into a "chignon": decoration of feathers, ribbon and flowers. French *c* 1777–80. (From a contemporary fashion drawing)

In 1786, for the King's birthday celebrations, the Princess Royal wore a "head ornament with white feathers and one black, on which were placed a number of diamonds"; and on the same occasion we read for what seems to be the first time, of the arrangement which became the only acceptable court style, that is, the Prince of Wales feathers. "Miss Vernon . . . the headdress displayed the Prince's plume, three red feathers so disposed as to require nothing more than Ich Dien, to make it completely the royal crest" (both quotations from the *Ipswich Journal*, 18 February 1786). For many years after this, however, other arrangements and number of feathers were permitted.

The 1780s saw breadth rather than length as desirable for a hair style, and in the 1790s hair became plain and simple, sometimes cut quite short, and by the end of the century it was worn upswept, with small curls and "Grecian" effects. Again the *Ipswich Journal* told its eager Suffolk readers in 1798 that at court "white ostrich feathers are much in use and worn in an upright position". The year before, 1797, the same paper reported of the Queen's birthday "velvet caps ornamented with gold were the most prevalent, with a profusion of white ostrich feathers".

60. Court dress with high waistline, train and hoop now restricted to court wear. Elaborate hair style with extremely tall ostrich feather plume, jewelled ornaments and lappets. English, 1798. (From fashion plate in Heideloff, *Gallery of Fashion*, 1798)

61. Ordinary day dresses of
the classical style. High
waists, simple flowing skirts.
Note popularity of tall
feathers for everyday wear.
English, 1795. (From fashion
plate in Heideloff, *Gallery of
Fashion*, 1798)

Wigs were sometimes substituted for the extravagant concoctions of
hair in the 1770s and 1780s. White powder was also worn for dress and
court wear until the 1790s. In 1786 Fanny Burney describes the
Queen's dressing: "we help her off with her gown and on with her
powdering things, and then the hairdresser is admitted. . . . . She never
forgets to send one away while she is powdering, with a consideration
not to spoil my clothes". By 1795 powder was out. "The ladies have left
off wearing powder", recorded *The Times* in April 1795 (quoted in Cunnington, *Handbook of English Costume in the Eighteenth Century*).

From the 1780s gowns had been getting simpler, waists were beginning to rise, the skirts lost their hoops and were long and trained and
fell in natural folds with only the false rump (the "bustle" of the
nineteenth century), a crescent moon padded with cord and tied round
the waist to rest at the back, and perhaps a stiffened under-petticoat
beneath. "Hoops were no longer worn, but a horsehair petticoat,
quilted in fine glazed stuff . . . having no whalebone, and a pad was
added at the bottom of the waist behind", recorded Mrs Papendiek in
1786.

In about 1794 the Classical Style emerged; high waisted, straight,
close-skirted, made in light weight muslins, linens or silks. But summer
or winter alike from the mid-1790s white or coloured muslin was by
far the commonest fabric used.

The last two decades of the eighteenth century was the time when court dress became to an extent static for some forty years, retaining from this period the hoop, which, as waists rose, rose with them, the headdress and the train. This last could be an embarrassment when dancing and in 1785 at a court ball the dance dresses had "a small slope 4 in. to 6 in. long instead of a train so as not to interfere with the dancing". (Mrs Papendiek.)

Mrs Papendiek, who in 1786 told us that hoops were "out", describes, two years later, an afternoon reception by Queen Charlotte and notes that "two ladies of the bedchamber, two maids of honor . . . [the Princesses] two ladies, all in Court hoops" were in attendance.

In the 1790s a single skirt (i.e. no overskirt) and a separate bodice and train was usual. The bodice was fitted, close fastened in front or at the back with buttons or a lace. The train was attached at the waist. Bodice and train generally matched and were of different colour and fabric from the skirt or petticoat.

Decoration for dresses featured embroidery, metal thread embroidery, lace, fringe, tassels, fur, jewels, foil, artificial flowers and leaves and feathers, all of which are mentioned between 1770 and the end of the century.

Colours in plain, floral or striped fabrics, ranged from white to black through buff, blue, cherry, green, lemon, orange, pink, purple, puce, scarlet and silver, and in one recorded case "coloured and spotted like a leopard's skin" (*Ipswich Journal*, 18 February 1786) were seen during the same period. In 1783 "Emperor's Eye" or "Knife Steel", presumably a grey-blue, was the "in" colour, and the Seige of Gibraltar which ended in 1783 was commemorated by two popular colours, "Smoke" and "Elliott's Red Hot Bullets". (General Elliott was Governor of the Rock and the red hot bullets were in fact cannon-balls fired by an ingenious gunner to set fire to the floating wooden gun-platforms the Spaniards were using.)

The *Gentleman's Magazine* for January 1779 recounted that "laylock sattin trimmed with fur, beads and wreaths of flowers" was the popular thing at the Queen's birthday ball. Fabrics mentioned for court dresses range from aerophane (a fine silk crepe, c 1790) to velvet, via gauze, including gold and silver gauze, lutestring (a brilliant taffeta), muslin, satin, silk, tabby (watered taffeta), tiffany (another silk gauze), and tissue (gold, silver or silk gauze).

There was one court fashion that was peculiar to the year 1789 – in March that year the court returned to Windsor with King George III recovered after a year's illness and loss of reason. Entertainments were held to celebrate the King's recovering and Mary Frampton wrote that:

> the dresses were the Windsor uniform [as far as I know this is the only reference to such a dress except for day clothes of ladies of the Royal Family] the old ladies wearing a long purple train, the young ladies without any. The gown was of white tiffany, with a garter blue body; the sleeves were white, and ornamented, like the coat [i.e. petticoat, or skirt] with three rows of fringe corresponding with that of the bottom of the gown. All the ladies wore bandeaux round the front of their headdress with the words "God Save the King". . . .

Later, at the service of thanksgiving held at St Paul's:

> the Queen, Princesses and Ladies wore open gowns of purple silk, edged and finished off with gold fringe; . . . petticoats of Indian muslin over white satin with deep fringes of gold at the bottom . . . white satin bandeau, on which the motto [God Save the King] was embroidered in gold letters.

On the King's birthday, at the drawing room, "in many instances the motto was studded in diamonds on a purple ground, and the effect was most brilliant. This was the last occasion upon which it was expected to be worn". The wearing of a bandeau with the loyal motto was not confined to court ladies in London or Windsor. When the Royal Family went to Weymouth in the July of 1789 for the sea-bathing, Fanny Burney was delighted to see that:

> the bathing machines make it their motto . . . the royal dippers wear it in bandeaux on their bonnets to go into the sea, and have it again in large letters round their waists to encourage the waves. Flannel dresses tucked up, and no shoes or stockings, with bandeaux and girdles, have a most singular appearance: when first I surveyed these loyal nymphs, it was with some difficulty I kept my features in order. . . . . Think last of the surprise of his Majesty when the first time of his bathing, he had no sooner popped his royal head under water than a band of music, concealed in a neighbouring machine, struck up "God Save Great George Our King".

Decorative aprons were a feature of the century and were probably worn, at times, to court. White silk stockings, perhaps with gold or coloured silk embroidered clocks, secured by garters of silk tied above or below the knee, or by 1779, spring garters, with fine spiral springs built in, were worn with pointed toed high heeled shoes of satin, velvet or silk. Low heels or wedges, or flat shoes, were introduced in the 1790s. These were of thin leather, cut low and often known as "slippers". Also in this decade were flat heeled sandals, tied over the foot and around the ankle with criss-cross ribbons.

Long gloves, sometimes embroidered, of white kid, and fans, were worn or carried. Rouge and white paint were used, but declined in favour in the 1780s, although false eyebrows remained fashionable, sometimes made of mouse-skin. Patches were given up about 1790. The fashions of 1780s onwards, with the bouffant neck-scarf or neckerchief, known as the "buffon", puffed out over the breasts in the decolletage, made it necessary for some ladies to supplement their charms by "false bosoms" and "spring bodices".

Spectacles were forbidden at court sometime towards the end of the century, a ban which remained until Queen Victoria's day.

Finally, by this time court dress for the ladies had settled down to a pattern which in its details of train and feathers, headdress and lappets, gloves and decolletage, survived until the ending of courts and presentations in the twentieth century.

As we have seen, ladies of the court in the eighteenth century needed many clothes; as Fanny Burney said "the Court-days, which require a particular dress" and "I find that on the King's Birthday, and on the Queen's, both real and nominal, two new attires, one half, the other full dressed, are expected from all attendants that come into the Royal presence" (4 June 1787). Bedchamber women were made an allowance for clothes, but other appointments, and those ladies visiting or attending court with no official position, could find the strain considerable unless some dodges could be found to lessen the expense. To quote Mrs Papendiek in 1785, "the price of lace was very high . . . such things as lace were handed down . . . a silk gown would go on for years, a little furbished up with new trimmings . . . and a young woman . . . might with no discredit to herself, appear time after time in the same attire". That same year she herself appeared on the King's Birthday at "a brilliant Court . . . my puce satin for this fourth year I had trimmed with a row of flat steel [embroidery] down each front. . . ." Nevertheless, five years later she remarked, somewhat scathingly I think, on the attire of two ladies at a presentation drawing room on the King's birthday: "Mrs and Miss Stowe passed; the mother in some second-hand vamped up dress: the daughter in white silk, with aerophane petticoat and trimmings . . . her mother's pearls and lappets".

One can feel the relief with which Fanny Burney, after her retirement from the Queen's service due to ill-health, records the King's Birthday in 1792: "how different was my attire from any other such occasion the five preceeding years! It was a mere . . . undress without feathers, flowers, hoop or furbelows" (*Diary*, 4 June 1792).

But let the last word on the century come from Mrs Delany: "bestow as little time on dress as possible, but let it always be neat and suitable to your circumstances (or position), and never extravagantly in the fashion, which is very vulgar and shows levity of mind" (letter to Miss Sparrow, 1780).

THE NINETEENTH CENTURY

The changes in form and fashion of women's dress in the last century ranged from the simple, close classical line of the opening years through an ever increasing expansion of skirts until the middle of the century and later, and thence via the bustles of the 1870s and 1880s, to the gores and flare of the last decade, with its passing backward glances at earlier times. The court dress, once it had freed itself of the obsolete hoop, followed the fashionable line, always, of course, with the addition of the train and the accompaniment of veil, lappets and plumes.

If for no other reason the court lady of 1820 had to be thankful to the new King, George IV, for the abolition of the, by now ridiculous, hoop; but before it finally went it was to draw expressions of ridicule and discomfort. Susan Sibbald in her *Memoirs*, writing of about the year 1800, records: "it was very awkward getting in or out of a carriage", despite the technology which enabled the hoops to be folded when worn. Louis Simond, an American of French origin, watched the ladies going to Court in sedan chairs in 1810: "to enable them to sit in these chairs, their immense hoops are folded like wings, pointing forward on each side" (*An American in Regency England*). And as late as 1817 new and "improved" hoops were being produced. *La Belle Assemblée* for June 1817 drew "the attention of the nobility and gentry ... to the newly invented Court hoop, which enables a lady to sit comfortably in a sedan, or other carriage, while the hoop is worn, with the same ease as any other garment; and by this unique and unrivalled novelty the splendor and dignity of Court costume is not only preserved, but considerably heightened". The magazine went on to say that at the shop selling the new hoops could "be found every article of costume to suit not only the female moving in the gay scenes of fashionable splendor, but the more retired fair one of wealth and title, who emerges but seldom from her own protected circle to grace the public rooms or the brilliant drawing-room". The death notice for the hoop was the Lord Chamberlain's "Direction" of 15 June 1820 (Public Record Office LC 6.1) for the coming royal birthday drawing room. "His Majesty is graciously pleased to dispence with Ladies wearing Hoops, they will be expected on the ensuing and future Drawing Rooms to appear in Court Robes and Lappets. . . ."

During the century the regulations relating to court wear were published periodically by the Lord Chamberlain, interspersed with special notices relating to court mourning, but they do not appear in the first (1898) edition of *Dress Worn at Court*, and we have to wait until this century before ladies are included. The rules for feathers were elastic at first: five seems to have been the commonest number; in 1805, "I was dressed in white crape train and petticoat, with silver embroidery on the sleeves and round my waist, and on my head a very pretty bandeau of diamonds and five white feathers" (*Correspondence of Sarah Spencer, Lady Littleton*). Mrs Stevenson, wife of the American Ambassador records the price of five "Court feathers" as 65 dollars in 1836, and the next year, "five feathers one guinea a piece" (Boykin, *Victoria, Albert and Mrs Stevenson*). Later the five feathers were split into twos and threes – two for single girls and three for married women: ". . . a triumphant wreath on the top of my head and two little coaxing feathers behind my left ear" ("Going to Court", *London Society Magazine*, 1863).

And in about 1882, *Manners and Tone of Good Society* by "A Member of the Aristocracy" laid down that "It is compulsory for both married and unmarried ladies to wear plumes. The married lady's Court plume consists of *three* white feathers, and the unmarried lady's of *two* white feathers. . . ."

At first the colour of the plume, as in the eighteenth century, was a matter of taste, but though most colours were employed, white feathers were always the most popular. In 1817 Mr Rush, the United States Minister noted at one of Queen Charlotte's drawing rooms at Buckingham Palace, "No lady was without her plume, the whole was a waving field of feathers; some were blue, some tinged with red; here you saw violet and yellow, there shades of green, but most were like tufts of snow. . . ." Again, the *Court Magazine* of June 1834, describing the latest court fashions refers to "the hair is ornamented with a superb plume of white ostrich feathers. . . ." It was customary for the monarch to kiss on the cheek the ladies who were presented: a pleasant custom abandoned by William IV and never revived. His reason for giving up was that he got their feathers in his mouth when so doing. (Turner, *The Court of St James*.)

Lace lappets or tulle veils and jewels in some form of headdress were also necessary. In due course the feathers became attached to wire or other types of hair-grip. As with the feathers, the lappets and veil came to distinguish the married from the single. Again quoting *Manners and Tone of Good Society*, in the 1880s ". . . a lady must either wear lace lappets or a tulle veil. As a rule the former are worn by married ladies,

62. "The newly invented Court hoop", worn under a dress which shows the fashionable high waist, shorter skirt and small puffed sleeves. There is an elaborately trimmed petticoat with a simpler, lighter, overdress caught up high. Headdress of five ostrich feathers, ribbon, jewels and lappets. English, 1817. (Fashion plate, *La Belle Assemblée*, June 1817. Robert Harding Associates)

and the latter by unmarried ladies; but this also is a matter of individual taste".

The fashionable colour for the classical style dresses of the early nineteenth century was white, and so it is not surprising that white reasserts itself for court wear. Lady Lyttleton was in white and silver in 1805, and in 1813 Mrs Calvert was in "a white satin petticoat with a patent net drapery – gold Brussels and fringe – gown; and train of green velvet ornamented with gold; headdress of seven white ostrich feathers and diamonds". Coloured trains were often worn with the white dresses.

In the Museum of London there is a dress of 1816 belonging to the ill-fated Princess Charlotte; it is of white silk machine-made knitted net embroidered with silk and silvered glass beads, fashionably cut with a train. This was a court dress of the Princess's, as was an earlier example, recorded by Cornelia Knight (*Autobiography*) in 1812, "white and silver, and she wore feathers for the first time".

Colour, however, was not excluded, and in that same year, 1812, Miss Knight's own dress at a drawing room was described in the February *Mirror of Fashion* as "of orange-coloured satin, with draperies of silver gauze, tastefully separated with net, silver rolio forming a lacing between each, through which the colour of the satin was dis- covered: the whole trimmed with handsome silver cords and tassels: robe [overdress] black velvet".

Poor Princess Charlotte died in childbed in 1817, the year after her marriage, aged twenty-one, and the Court went into mourning: "Ladies to wear black bombazine, plain muslin or long lawn crape hoods, shamoy shoes and gloves and crape fans"; later modified to "black silk or velvet, coloured ribbons, fans and tippets, or plain white or white and gold or white and silver stuffs with black ribbons" (Lord Chamberlain's Regulations, November 1817). On 26 February the following year, 1818, Queen Charlotte held her first drawing room after the Princess's death. Among those present were Mr Rush, the American Minister, and his wife. After getting into St James's Palace they could hardly stir for the crowd, and three-quarters of an hour were spent getting upstairs – the throng often jammed motionless, but let Mr Rush tell his own story:

> The whole group stood motionless. The hoop dresses of the ladies sparkling with lama, their plumes, their lappets, the fanciful attitudes which the hoops occasioned, some getting out of position, as when in Addison's time they were adjusted to shoot a door, the various costumes of the gentlemen, as they stood pinioning their elbows, or holding their swords, the common hilarity from the common dilemma; the bland recognition passing between those above and below, made up altogether an exhibition so picturesque that a painter might give it as illustrative so far of the Court of that era.

Upon gaining the ante-room Mr Rush continues with the description of the plumes quoted earlier:

> Then the diamonds encircling them caught the sun through the windows, and threw their dazzling beams around. Then the hoops! I cannot describe these. They should be seen. To see one is nothing, but to see a

thousand and their thousand wearers! I afterwards sat in the Ambassador's box at a coronation. That sight faded before this. Each lady seemed to rise out of a little gilded barricade, or one of silvery texture. This topped by a plume, and "the face divine interposing", gave to the whole an effect so unique, so fraught with feminine grace and grandeur, that it seemed as if a curtain had risen to show a pageant in another sphere. It was brilliant and joyous. Those to whom it was not new stood to gaze as I did – Canning for one. His fine eye took it all in. You saw admiration in the great statesmen, Lord Liverpool, Huskisson, the Lord Chancellor, everybody! Now I saw radiating on all sides British Beauty, and I had the inward assurance that my countrywomen were its inheritresses. *Matre pulchra filia pulchrior.* So appeared to me the drawing room of Queen Charlotte: the whole was harmony, though parts of the ladies' dresses may have been incongruous. Like old English buildings and Shakespeare, it carried the feelings with it. It triumphed over criticism. ("Memoirs", quoted in *The Gentleman's Magazine*, 1872.)

By 1824 the waist line had come down to more-or-less natural level, and shoulders and skirt hems were expanding throughout the decade and the skirt itself shortened to the ankle. The evening dress skirt was shorter than the day skirt, and the bodice was always decolletée; this last feature persisted throughout the century.

63. Court dress with white petticoat embroidered with large design. Dark blue overdress with yellow appliqué, lace bertha, undersleeves and lappets. Ostrich plumes in headdress. 1833. (After *Court Magazine*, April 1833)

The 1830s continued to see the skirt expand, and for the first five or six years the sleeves expanded also, but from about 1836 the sleeves shrank and the shoulders drooped and the waist-line began again to fall, and show a tendency to become pointed. Bustles, worn in the 1820s, became a necessity in the 1830s to help support, with the petticoats, the ever-widening skirts. Corsets were increasingly in demand as the waist became more pointed.

A Court dress of 1834 is illustrated and described in the *Court Magazine* of June that year:

> Under dress of white gaze Chine with a rich border of gold lama. Robe of Gros Pompadour, vermilion ground, and rich antique pattern of gold. The corsage cut low, square, and pointed at the bottom, is trimmed on each side of the front with a blue satin border, richly embroidered with white; it is edged with gold and laced with gold cord. Fancy jewelry girdle, from which is suspended a cordon of coloured gems, terminated by a lozenge and tassels of fancy jewelry. The back of the corsage is trimmed with blond lace, a là Medicis, but not very deep. Mantelet of tulle illusion lightly embroidered in gold. Under sleeves of white gros d'orient; the upper ones of tulle illusion are à la Mameluke embroidered to correspond with the mantelet. The skirt just meets at the point [of the waist], opens down the front en tablier, and is trimmed round with a border corresponding with that on the corsage. The hair is ornamented with a superb plume of white ostrich feathers, blond lace lappets, and a ferroniere and combs of gold and coloured gems. Necklace and earrings en suite.

Medicis were standing collars at the back sloping down to meet the neckline at the sides. A mantelet was a half-shawl, rounded at the neck. Mameluke sleeves were one of the very full sleeves of the day. The "tulle illusion" appears to be similar to tulle Arachne, a very fine clear silk bobbin net, which according to Cunnington (*Dictionary of English Costume*) was embroidered with gold and silk threads. Tulle was a favourite component of court dresses and in 1826, on account of the reduction in duty and consequent large imports of tulle from France, ladies were requested to use only English tulle for court wear in order to give employment to English workers.

Sallie Coles Stevenson, wife of the American Ambassador Andrew Stevenson, who represented his country at the Court of St James from June 1836 until October 1841, was a vivacious, popular and observant lady who kept up a lively and fascinating correspondence with her family and friends across the Atlantic. In various of her letters she describes occasions of state and visits paid to the court. She also gave details of her dress at these times. In April 1837 she went to a drawing room held by William IV, one of the last functions of that reign:

I have procured my dress from Paris, a white satin embroidered before
and around the tail – the train of maroon velvet, very rich and beautiful,
the whole to be trimed [sic] with blond, and a little blond ruff a la Queen
Elizabeth to cover the neck behind [like the collar a la Medicis,
above?] – five feathers one guinea a piece and the head dressed with bows
of velvet and pearl etc.

Two days later she dresses for the drawing room: "I went first with
the barber – such cutting of hair (I was astonished to see how well it
looked) then came the mantua-maker to dress me with my maid Dunn
as an assistant, and Jenny the housemaid and Mary Ann the cook, to
look on, or rather to peep at me, for they are too respectful to come in
without permission." Then to court, "at the door our trains were taken
from us [they were carried over the arm] and spread out by a person
stationed there for the purpose." After all was over she wrote: "You
know how much dress becomes me, and rouge I can tell you makes me
look ten years younger."

The rouge, evidently new to her, at first presented a problem: "I was
somewhat puzzled to know how to put it on, whether it was to be wet
or dry or how." The rouge had been procured from Paris by a friend, a
fellow American, Lady Wellesley and was "a pot of the best". Rouge
was, as Mrs Stevenson put it, "a part of the Court dress as much as the
train".

64. Court dress of white gauze Chine
petticoat and vermilion and gold
overdress. Lappets and plumes. 1834.
(After *Court Magazine*, June 1834)

Drawing rooms were often held on Sundays, after church, and the practice grew up of ladies attending the court in the hats or bonnets they had worn at church. However, on 27 May 1834, the *London Gazette* printed a notice that "for the future ladies attending their Majesties Drawing Rooms must appear with feathers and lappets, in conformity with established order".

During the 1840s and 1850s the skirt expanded even more, necessitating, in the late 1850s, the re-introduction of a mechanical support; the cage crinoline. Court dresses were now as wide as the old hooped ones, if not so ridiculous in appearance. Also by this time the plume of feathers was worn lower down on the back of the head. The train, now a separate article, was attached at the waist.

The anonymous author of *The Habits of Good Society*, 1859, wrote of court dress:

> This costume consists, first, of an entire dress, generally made of some plain but costly silk.
> The dress, therefore, forms one component part; next comes the petticoat, usually of some lighter material; and lastly, the train.
> The dress is made, even for elderly ladies, low; and the boddice is trimmed in accordance with the petticoat and the train.
> The petticoat is now usually formed of rich Brussels lace, or of Honiton lace, or tulle; and often looped up with flowers.
> The train is of the richest material of the whole dress. Formerly it was often of satin; now it is of moiré or glacé silk, though satin is again beginning to be worn.
> It fastens half round the waist, and is about seven yards in length, and wide in proportion. It is trimmed all round with lace, in festoons, or on the edge, with bunches of flowers at intervals, and is lined usually with white silk.
> The petticoat is ornamented with the same lace as the train, sometimes in flounces, sometimes in puffings or bouffons of tulle, sometimes *en tablier*, that is, down either side.
> The boddice and sleeves are all made in strict uniformity with the train and petticoat.
> The head-dress consists of feathers, and comprises a lappet of lace, hanging from either side of the head down nearly to the tip of the boddice. Diamonds or pearls, or any other jewellery sufficiently handsome, may be worn in the hair, but the two former are most frequently adopted. The same ornaments should be worn on the boddice around the neck and arms.
> The shoes should be of white satin, and trimmed according to fashion. The fan should be strictly a dress fan; those spangled are the most suitable for a costume which requires everything to be as consistent as possible with the occasion.

In 1861, Grant & Gask of Oxford Street advertised "Superb Court Trains (some of which are worked in pure gold)" and others silk robes at greatly reduced prices "due to Court mourning" and "no orders from America" (*Illustrated London News*).

Make-up, although still used, was by now not admitted too openly. It had to be discreet and private, and young ladies were discouraged, on moral as well as hygienic grounds, from its use. Ladies of an older school, however, retained the freer habits of an earlier age and in 1863 we read of "an old lady next to us, and her rouge and pearl powder gazed candidly from under her mouse-skin eyebrows" (*London Society*, April 1863) on the way to court. The mouse-skin, as we have seen, was an eighteenth century beauty aid that apparently survived on some faces well into the nineteenth.

In *Life among the Troubridges* (Hope-Nicolson), we read, in the 1860s of two court dresses, one white satin with the eyes of peacock feathers and gold beads edging the train, and the other of white silk with a red velvet train.

After the Prince Consort's death in 1861 Queen Victoria withdrew into virtual isolation, and thereafter many drawing rooms were held on her behalf by one of her daughters, and later, by the Princess of Wales. For instance, Princess Helena held a Drawing Room at St James's Palace on the Queen's behalf on 18 May 1865. The Princess wore a rich white silk dress and train decorated with tulle and with wreaths of, presumably, artificial, narcissi; with an emerald and diamond diadem, plumes and veil. This was one of the last drawing rooms held at St James's, as in that year the function was transferred to Buckingham Palace.

65. Court dress of fashionable cut over large cage crinoline. Overskirt caught up in front. Train from shoulders. Headdress with feathers worn low down at back. 1863. (After *London Society*, 1863)

By the end of the 1860s the skirt, which throughout the decade, supported by its cage, had shown a tendency to move backwards, had become more or less straight in the front with the back absorbing the bulk of the garment to produce in the 1870s an epoch of bustles which survived, except for a few years between 1878 and 1882, until 1890.

One of the Troubridge family presented in 1876 had a dress of cream silk and net in the fashionable style with a long-waisted bodice and a cream grosgrain and net train, with a tulle veil. Veils, formerly preferred by unmarried girls were now beginning to be preferred to lappets by most ladies.

In 1878 the Lord Chamberlain issued further instructions, with especial reference to the plumes:

> ... Ladies who attend Her Majesty's drawing-rooms must appear in full Court dress with trains and plumes according to regulations, that is, so that the feathers can be clearly seen on approaching the Queen and with white veils or lappets. Coloured feathers are contrary to regulations, but in deep mourning black feathers may be worn.

A couple of years earlier the Queen had had occasion to complain of the number of ladies who had appeared without any plume at all, let alone the accompanying veil or lappets.

There is ample evidence that the honour of presentation at drawing rooms was, certainly in mid and late nineteenth century days, both a test of character and endurance. The Queen held her drawing rooms at varying times in the afternoon, but in July 1837 it was announced that "the State apartments will not be open for the reception of company coming to Court until half-past one o'clock". Later this rule was

66. Arrival at the Palace, problems of the cage crinoline. 1863. (After *London Society*, 1863)

67. St James's Palace: debutante approaching the throne room. Others waiting in "The Pen", a corridor-like waiting room. 1863. (*London Society*, 1863)

changed to that commanding all attending, whatever time the drawing room was held, to be at Buckingham Palace not later than one o'clock. No food or refreshments of any kind were provided from first to last. The crush was so great, both at St James's and later at Buckingham Palace, where the accommodation was bigger, that it was a struggle for debutantes to retain their places in the ante-rooms and to make their way to the presence. In April 1863 *London Society* describes the company, "pushing as only fine ladies can push, frowning and dragging as only the British dowagers can ..." and in the 1880s it was reported that dresses were torn and debutantes weeping before the ordeal was over. In 1891 *Punch* (28 March) repeats the criticism, "We were driven from one bitterly cold room to another ... one had many fellow sufferers and these poor creatures pushed against us and fought with us."

The court dresses of the 1870s and 1880s were the fashionable bustled evening dress with the addition of the court train. These could be separate, but the Museum of London has a specimen of about 1880 of white damask and satin with a built-in train. The train tended to get longer in the 1880s, some, according to *The Queen* in 1886 were twelve to fifteen feet in length. According to Mrs Armytage (*Old Court Customs and Modern Court Rule*), "the Court train is carried on the left arm until the door leading across the picture gallery is reached, when it is spread out by the pages-in-waiting, and the progress ... into the Queen's presence is very slow, and regulated by the wearer of the preceding train, treading on which must be carefully avoided". After passing the presence, "one of the attendant pages gathers up the train and throws it over the lady's arms (which should be extended to receive it) almost as soon as the Queen is passed". The lady then retreated backwards for several paces.

Manners and Tone of Good Society in 1882 reiterates that low cut evening dresses are to be worn, with short sleeves and trains not less than three yards long: these can be fastened either at the shoulder or from the waist. White was imperative for wear by unmarried ladies and also the fashion for married ones "unless their age renders their doing so unsuitable". The dresses of debutantes and of married ladies could be trimmed with either white or coloured flowers according to individual taste. The wearing of a dress that was not decolleté, could only be by special permission of the Lord Chamberlain upon production of a doctor's certificate stating that a low cut bodice was precluded for reasons of health. Fans were traditionally carried, but in the 1860s, at least, small posies were also seen. By the 1890s quite large bouquets were popular and supplanted the fan in most cases.

A number of gorgeous court trains survive from the 1890s; the dresses presumably having been subsequently worn for evening dress, and in some cases converted to wedding dresses. The Museum of London has a very magnificent specimen of pale yellow velvet, turned over and lined with gold tissue, with embroidered border of irises and leaves in their proper colours, with gold net applique, and gold and silver cord and diamante trimming. Also in their collection is a complete dress of 1898. It is of cream satin with a short train; the front of the dress is decorated with small pearls, rhinestone, beads and mauve chenille. The train and sleeves are also edged with ruched tulle.

Mr Peter Watson, of Saffron Walden, has in his collection a court train 11 feet 6 inches long, of net appliqued with lace and silk motifs, lined with frills of chiffon and edged with sequins and beads.

Necklines in the 1890s were square, or round or cut in a wide deep

68. Presentation to Her Majesty. Tight fitting bodices, tunic overskirts, bustles and trains from waist, feathers worn low. *c* 1875. (From *Sidelights on English Society*, 1881, after an earlier *Illustrated London News*)

V; bodices reflected the fashionable small waist, often pointed at the front. Shoulder straps, coming in in the later 1880s were popular for the first two or three years of the decade, after which short puffed sleeves came in and became ever bulkier until about 1897. The bodice was lavishly trimmed, the skirts less so, though often with trimming down the side seams; some with flounces at the bottom. Dresses were single, without the overskirt of earlier days in most cases. Writing in the 1890s Mrs Douglas (*The Gentlewoman's Book of Dress*) advised that "At the Drawing Room you cannot be too resplendant. The richer your brocade, the more fitting the occasion. Yet let your richness be in taste, and have your design as good as your material". Long white gloves, bouquets as mentioned before, three feathers on top of the head, and veils, together with the train, completed the picture.

69. Court or presentation dress with
large puff sleeves, low square cut
bodice, all in contemporary fashion
for evening dress; train from
shoulders; headdress with veil and
three feathers, 1895. (After Clephane,
Our Mothers. Possibly from *The
Graphic*)

Queen Victoria's court was formal in the extreme and her insistence
on the minutiae of etiquette was inflexible; so was her attitude to the
correct dress of both sexes. Such also had been the nature of her uncle
George IV – it has been said that anyone present at court in his day
might be ordered to leave – and it was inherited by her son and grand-
son, Edward VII and George V, at whose courts, despite the increasing
informality of twentieth-century life, the rules, modified sometimes as
necessary, were expected to be obeyed.

It was Queen Victoria who abolished the ancient custom of court
balls as part of the monarch's birthday celebrations. Also we find the
Queen giving, not receiving, New Year's gifts, among other things
cloaks, calico and flannel to the poor of Windsor (*Illustrated London
News*, 6 January 1849).

Throughout the reign, *Punch* had kept its eye on court proceedings
and court reporters, and at times waxed sarcastic. The "Almanack"
for 1857 reported: "Ignorance of the Higher Classes. How few of those

ladies of rank who attend Her Majesty's Drawing Rooms know how to clean their own white ostrich feathers". On 21 February 1891 *Punch* quoted *The Times* Court Circular of the 11th: "The following Ladies and Gentlemen had the honour of . . . being received by Her Majesty in the Drawing Room. Well Sir, and where are they usually received? In the kitchen? The report does not mention if it was the front or back Drawing Room".

THE TWENTIETH CENTURY

The new century coincided with a new reign when King Edward VII succeeded to the throne in 1901. He was very much a stickler for correct behaviour and dress, at court and elsewhere: he demanded that ladies dining at Windsor should always wear tiaras, and there is a story that he struck off the court list the name of an unfortunate lady who tripped over her train one day. Among the changes made by the new king was the substitution of evening courts, held at nine o'clock, for the afternoon drawing rooms. It is conceivable that the wearing of full evening dress for an evening event was regarded as an improvement upon the previous custom of dressing up in mid-morning for a drawing room.

The little pamphlet, *Dress worn at Court* of 1898 was expanded into a solid volume during the new reign and covered a greatly extended range of courtiers, officials and their dress. Ladies now had a page. The 1908 edition, *Dress Worn at His Majesty's Court*, "issued with the authority of the Lord Chamberlain" and edited by Herbert Trendell, M.V.O., his Chief Clerk, says of "Ladies attending Their Majesties' Courts" that they

> will appear in Full Dress, with trains and plumes. For Half Mourning black and white, white, mauve or grey should be worn. Feathers should be worn so that they can be clearly seen on approaching the Presence, with white veils or lappets. Coloured feathers are inadmissable, but in deep mourning black feathers may be worn. White gloves only are to be worn except in case of mourning when black or grey gloves are admissable.
>
> High Court Dress. The King has been pleased to permit that a High Court Dress, according to the following description, may be worn in future at Their Majesties' Courts, and on other State occasions, by ladies, to whom from illness, infirmity or advancing age, the present Low Court Dress is inappropriate viz., Bodices in front, cut square or heart shape, which may be filled in with white only, either transparent or lined, at the back high or cut down three-quarter height. Sleeves to elbow, either

thick or transparent. Trains, gloves, and feathers as usual. It is necessary Ladies who wish to appear in "High Court Dress" to obtain permission through the Lord Chamberlain, unless they have already received it.

Quite a number of pre-1914 court dresses survive, both in museums and in private hands. In Worcester County Museum there is a cream corded silk specimen of about 1904 which is said to have been altered from a wedding dress. This sequence is unusual: it is much more common to find the presentation dress altered for bridal wear or for ordinary evening dress. This last was very common, as, with the train detached, the gown was merely the fashionable evening wear of the year.

The Museum of London has a 1908 specimen of white satin, two piece, embroidered in a floral design in white and silver, chiffon sleeves, the skirt slightly trained, and with a splendid green velvet court train, nine feet and one inch long, lined with white satin and decorated with silver braid and tassels: this hooks onto the dress at the shoulders. There is also a headdress of three white ostrich feathers and a net veil mounted on a hair clip.

Dress Worn at His Majesty's Court was republished in 1912 with certain differences. For the first time appears the direction that three feathers are to be worn "mounted as a Prince of Wales's plume". The centre feather was to be a little higher than the others and the whole worn slightly on the left-hand side of the head. Coloured feathers and black for mourning are also forbidden. A tulle veil, not longer than forty-five inches is to be attached to the base of the feathers, and lace lappets may be worn. The dress is also regulated; the skirt to extend not less than fifteen inches on the ground at the back, and the court train to be three yards, from the shoulders, not more than fifty-four inches on the ground, and the same width at its end. Directions as to court half-mourning, gloves, and high court dress are as before.

King George V had succeeded his father in 1910 and the coronation courts of 1911 saw some splendid examples of court dress. In 1908 a change in the fashionable line had occurred: the full, flared, gored skirt which had reigned for some ten years gave way to a straight, narrow skirt which in its extreme form from 1909 to 1914 was the "hobble". At the same time there was a tendency for dresses to become simpler, the bodice and skirts increasingly being united to make a one-piece dress. The evening dress often had a tunic or overdress and the waistline was rising.

I am told by a lady who was presented in 1914 at the last pre-war court, that many debutantes, herself included, carried fans instead of the then more usual bouquet. This was because at the previous court a

70. Edwardian presentation gown of cream satin, low round neckline; bodice swathed in ruched and frilled chiffon. Trained skirt, with court train twenty feet long attached to shoulders. Matching silk taffeta gored and trained petticoat. Dress decorated with wreaths of artificial flowers and leaves, and embroidered net overskirt. 1908. (Courtesy of Holly Trees Museum, Colchester)

71. Debutante's gown. Fashion
drawing from an advertisement. Such
drawings of original designs were
made to customers' requirements by
the leading court dressmakers. 1912.
(After *Dress Worn at Court*:
advertisement by Debenham and
Freebody)

suffragette had secreted a petition amongst her flowers and handed it
to their majesties as she was presented by her mamma. My friend and
her fellow debutantes were carefully scrutinised before admission to
the presence.

From 1914 to 1918 no courts were held and for the first few years
after the war garden parties took their place. For these, afternoon
dresses and hats were worn. When courts were resumed in 1920 they
were attended by ladies in ordinary evening dress, minus feathers,

72. Mrs Grant in her presentation gown of white slipper satin, trimmed with white sequins, tunic overdress style with high swathed waist and square cut low neckline. Very voluminous train of silk and net. Headdress of veil and three "Prince of Wales" feathers. Long white gloves, bracelet and fan. Mrs Grant attended the last drawing room before the First World War. 1914. (Courtesy of Mrs Grant, Cheltenham)

trains and veils. However this was short lived: all were back in the next couple of years, but with colour of dresses optional and the train shortened to two yards.

The post-war dresses were altogether less elaborate in construction than the pre-war models, and skirts were generally getting shorter during the mid-1920s. Veils were still to be a maximum of forty-five inches, and the Prince of Wales plume was now to be composed of three "small" white feathers. Black feathers were again permitted in case of deep mourning. Although gloves must be worn, like the dresses they could now be of any colour. Lappets, bouquets or fans were all optional.

The evening dresses of the 1920s became both light-hearted and exiguous, with falling waist lines and rising skirts: with over-drapery, uneven hems and deep decolletage, back and front. Sleeveless, or with tiny shoulder straps, the dresses were of lame, georgette, satin, lace, crepe-de-chine, and often with heavy bead embroidery, sequins, or pearls, as decoration. These dresses, especially during the years 1926–28 when skirts were at their shortest, often looked mismatched with the long court train and veil. As Lady Angela Forbes wrote (*How to Dress for all Ages and Occasions*, 1926) "A too short frock with a train will make the most graceful girl look gawky, and present an incongruous and unbalanced appearance. . . ." Lady Angela stated a preference for a white dress for debutantes, although, as she said, they "have dipped into the realm of colour". She also remarked that once-upon-a-time beaded and embroidered dresses were the perquisite of the married woman, but no longer so in 1926; although the "debutante does not as a rule wear the rich gold and silver lamés, but this is more on account of the price . . . than the conventional idea of what a girl may or may not wear!" In 1929 it was stated that details of dress would be issued with the summons cards.

Longer skirts returned with the 1930s and as the decade advanced they became fuller and the dresses altogether more formal again.

The 1937 edition of *Dress and Insignia worn at His Majesty's Court*, edited by G. A. Titman, is the latest, and in fact, is still operative, so that if, as I at least hope, our present or some future monarch re-institutes courts and other formal functions, the rules as to dress will present no problems. "Low evening dresses with Court trains suspended from the shoulders" are enjoined. The train must still be two yards long, and is not to exceed eighteen inches on the ground. Feathers, veils, gloves and colours were as previously detailed. There is added "Sketches of typical Court Dress are on view at the Lord Chamberlain's Office, St James's Palace".

73. Court gown by Reville Ltd. "of pale pink satin beauté embroidered in diamanté, crystals and microscopical bugles, the smooth princess line being broken below the hips by a shaped band of the embroidery. Satin train matches gown". Headdress of "Juliet" cap type with veil and Prince of Wales plumes. Very large ostrich feather fan. 1934. (*Country Life*, 19 May 1934)

74. Group of debutantes about to be presented at the last presentation party. 1958. Afternoon dresses, long gloves and hats. (Press Association)

During the late nineteenth and twentieth centuries the ladies attending court, as debutantes or otherwise, obtained their court dresses from the great court dressmakers, such as Reville, Lucile and Poiret, from lesser known dressmakers, or from the better stores such as Liberty, Marshall & Snelgrove and Harrods. One writer who attended the coronation of 1937 – the last at which court dress was obligatory for those in the Abbey who had no official or lordly apparel – described the headdress of veil and feathers saying that it was most becoming and that even plain women looked elegant in it.

In the 1930s the problem of attaching a quite heavy train to an exiguous neckline was solved by a number of ingenious ideas, such as, attaching it cunningly to a corselet, which with its suspenders anchored to the stockings, distributed the weight between them and shoulder-hooks at the top.

In 1936 King Edward VIII, during his brief reign, substituted garden parties in lieu of courts. With the outbreak of the Second World

War in 1939 courts and all other such functions again went into abeyance. When they were re-started in the late 1940s they reverted to daytime and ladies attending wore afternoon dresses and hats. Even this was not to survive very long, and the last debutante presentations at court were in the summer of 1958. Since then the only functions of any similarity are the Queen's garden parties at Buckingham Palace, where once again, afternoon dress is worn.

CHAPTER IV

Men's Court Dress

Correct court wear for men for the last century and a half has been of two kinds: an official uniform based on early nineteenth-century models for the Royal Household, Privy Councillors and senior civil servants, and the court suit, which derived from late eighteenth-century fashion for those gentlemen attending court who were entitled to neither a civil uniform nor a uniform of the services. The court suit will first be described and traced from the Restoration period until today, as it is, in one form or another worn, as we have seen, by such officials as the Speaker of the House of Commons, the Serjeants-at-Arms, and also by certain civic and legal dignitaries, even in these egalitarian days. Like the women's court dress it evolved from the normal styles of contemporary clothing, whereas the court uniform was deliberately designed and introduced in the reign of George IV.

THE SEVENTEENTH CENTURY

At the time of the Restoration the normal wear was a doublet and breeches, some closed at the knee, others open like shorts. Shirts were often exposed at the waist and in front by leaving the lower doublet buttons undone and pouching the shirt over the breeches. Ribbon was lavishly used for trimming. At the neck a falling band, in the form of a deep turn-down collar on a high neckband, bordered in fashionable circles with wide lace, was worn. Some were square cut and bib-like in front. A plainer style, square fronted spreading under the chin without lace, was affected by Puritans and soldiers.

75. King Charles II and Catherine of Braganza. The King wears a short doublet showing shirt at waist, with sleeves slit to expose shirt sleeves; petticoat breeches decorated with ribbon fancies at waist and knee; cloak with Garter star, and badge round neck; lace edged cuffs and falling band; stockings and boots with lace trimmed "canons". Wide-brimmed tall-crowned hat with plumes. 1662. (After James Heath, *A Chronicle of the late Intestine War*, 1676)

In 1660 a variety of open breeches with exaggeratedly wide legs, known as petticoat breeches, pantaloons or Rhinegraves, was introduced, mainly as a court fashion. (It is to be noted that "pantaloons", in the nineteenth century was a name applied to very close-fitting trousers.) Pepys recorded on 6 April 1661, "Met with Mr Townsend, who told of his mistake the other day, to put both his legs through one of his knees of his breeches, and went so all day". And in *Tyranus, or the Mode*, published in the same year, John Evelyn describes them as "a kind of hermaphrodite and of neither sex".

With the return of the King and the court, French influence, already at work for some years this side of the Channel, became even more marked and the fashionable man's clothes exhibited an extravagance of cut and decoration that called forth disapproving criticism from the more sober minded. To quote *Tyranus* again, "It was a fine silken thing which I spied walking th'other day through Westminster Hall, that had as much ribbon about him as would have plundered six shops and set up twenty country pedlars; all his body was drest like a May-pole, or a Tom o' Bedlams Cap".

A pair of petticoat breeches in the Victoria and Albert Museum, from the Verney family, are trimmed with "at least two hundred and fifty yards of ribbon in bunches" (from Mr J. Nevinson). In 1671 the Earl of Bedford paid £87 18s 6d for silver lace for trimmings. It is interesting to note that five years earlier he had paid sixteen shillings to have a suit made up. (Scott-Tomson, *Life in a Noble Household*).

Five years later occurred an event that not only introduced a new form of dress to court, but radically altered the whole style of men's clothes and laid the foundations for the fashion of the next three centuries, in fact until today. Pepys records on 8 October 1666, that "The King hath yesterday, in Council, declared his resolution of setting a fashion for clothes, which he will never alter. It will be a vest, I know not well how: but it is to teach the nobility thrift, and will do good". On the 13 October Pepys was at Whitehall and met the Duke of York, just returned from hunting. "So I stood and saw him dress himself, and try on his vest which is the King's new fashion, and he will be in it for good and all on Monday next, and the whole Court . . . ." And two days later. "This day the King begins to put on his vest, and I did see several persons of the House of Lords and Commons too, great courtiers, who are in it; being a long cassocke close to the body, of black cloth, and pinked with white silk under it, and a coat over it, and the legs ruffled with black riband like a pigeon's leg: and, upon the whole, I wish the King may keep it, for it is a very fine and handsome garment". On the 17th of the month "The Court is all full of vests, only my Lord St Albans not pinked, but plain black; and they say the King says the pinking upon whites makes them look too much like magpies, and, therefore, hath bespoke one of plain velvet".

Another contemporary observer, T. Rugge, in his *Diary*, describes the new suit as

> a close coat of cloth, pinkt with a white taffety under the cutts. This in length reached the calf of the leg, and upon that a sercoat cutt at the breast, which being loose and shorter than the vest six inches. The breeches the Spanish cut [with a high waistline, ending below the knee, either open-ended or closed by ribbon ties or garters] and buskins [boots] some of cloth, some of leather, but of the same colour as the vest or garment . . . ."

On 1 November Pepys's tailor "bring my vest home, and coat to wear with it, and belt and silver-hilted sword . . . and I like myself mightily in it, and so do my wife". For the Queen's birthday ball on the 15th Pepys and his wife saw the King "and all the dancers" in vests of silk and silver cloth.

76. Petticoat breeches and short doublet both lavishly trimmed with fancies; sleeves with multiple slits (paned) showing lining. From Verney Family. 1662–65. (Crown copyright, Victoria and Albert Museum)

Evelyn also records the change: on 18 October 1666 "To Court. It being the first time his Majesty put himself solemnly into the Eastern fashion of vest . . . after the Persian mode . . . ." The Persian idea seems to be Evelyn's own and should not be taken too seriously. He mentions the "stately and easy Vest . . ." in *Tyranus* and in his diary for 18 October he recalls this and concludes, "I do not impute to this discourse the change . . . but it was an identity that I could not but take notice of". Evelyn also says that "divers courtiers and gentlemen" bet with the King that he would not keep to his resolution never to abandon the new style, bets which they won, I hope, for on 22 November in 1666 Pepys was told that "the King of France hath, in defiance to the King of England, caused all his footmen to be put into vests . . . which, if true, is the greatest indignity ever done by one Prince to another"; and in a few years the vest and tunic were replaced by the coat and waistcoat. "Vest", however, still remains as the tailor's name for a waistcoat.

The coat and waistcoat which followed, from about 1668, were of the same length and until 1680 were loosely cut and reached to the knee. By the 1690s the coat was well fitted with a defined waist, fuller skirts and in length just below the knee; the waistcoat was shorter, and came above the knee. Coat and waistcoat both had outside pockets, set low, but rising towards the waist by the end of the century. The waistcoat was sleeved and could be worn without the coat. Sometimes, to save money, the back was made of inferior material (as it is today) and was known as "cheats".

77. Loose and unwaisted coat and waistcoat. 1670–80. (From etching by S. Le Clerc)

Coat and waistcoat had buttons from neck to hem, but these were rarely fastened all the way. Sometimes no waistcoat was worn. Coat sleeves were elbow length at first, with deep turn-back cuffs; getting longer towards the end of the century, though still with large cuffs. The open buttons and short sleeves ensured a good display of shirt and of its cuffs or ruffles at the wrist. From about 1665 the bands worn at the neck were being replaced by the cravat or neckcloth, a scarf of fine linen or muslin with, in many cases, lace ends: this was loosely knotted, or tied in a bow with short ends, under the chin.

In the 1670s closed breeches with a full seat and wide legs gathered into a band to fasten below or above the knee were popular. Some had a flounce at the knee, turned-up like a cuff and stitched in place. Pockets with vertical slits in the front of the legs, and fob pockets in the waist-band were incorporated. Another type of closed breeches was closer fitting, with a full seat, gathered on to a waist-band and the legs fastened below the knee with strap and buckle ties, or buttons.

Stockings appropriated to themselves the name "hose" from about 1660, knitted silk or wool being the most popular. Some tailored cloth stockings persisted for rough wear. They were held up by garters. With petticoat breeches long-legged stirrup-footed hose were drawn up and fastened underneath the breeches by ribbon ties passed through eyelet holes. Over them were worn footed stockings with wide spreading tops which turned down into deep frills which were known as canons or post-canons. These canons were only worn with open breeches.

Boot hose, to wear under riding boots to protect the finer stockings had, also, decorative turn-down tops, often made of lace. Fairly high heeled shoes with tapering square toes, fastened mostly by ribbons tied in a bow, from 1660, sometimes by a buckle, were popular; the latter became universal after 1680. Colour was usually black and for court wear the heel and edges of the soles were coloured red.

Although periwigs or perukes were known in England from the sixteenth century they became a fashion feature, rather than a cosmetic aid. After the Restoration the King and court could be seen in the very large type of periwig that was brought from France. The fashion for loosely hanging shoulder-length hair was common in this country and for the first few years after 1660 the periwig was regarded somewhat askance: however, the more elaborately natural styles of long hair did not, perhaps, differ in appearance very much from the wigs, which in a few years were accepted generally as well as at court. Pepys bought one, after some heart-searching, in October 1663: in 1665 he "suffered his own hayre to grow long, in order to wearing it" but by May of that year he found "the convenience of perriwigs is so great, that I have cut off all short again, and will keep to perriwigs." The "convenience" was, no doubt, easier control of dirt and lice.

The large French wig was by the end of the century known as the full-bottomed wig: from 1660 to 1675 it was a mass of irregular curls around the face and down to the shoulders, then for another fifteen years or so of evenly arranged tight curls and then, till about 1710, made high above the forehead with a centre parting and dressed in a "horn" at each side, the side curls over the shoulders, loose, and generally falling lower on one side than on the other.

Periwigs could be expensive: the best were of human hair – Pepys had one made of his own – but substitutes such as horse hair and goats hair were made up into inferior models. Pepys paid £3 for one of his, and for that of his own hair "21s 6d more than the worth of my own hair," which is not specified. This was in 1663. In the same year John Masters of Kent paid £5 for a "perrewig" (John Master's Expense Book published in *Archaeologia Cantiana*) and the Earl of Bedford in 1672 paid sums ranging from £6 to £20 for wigs, and ten shillings to have one cleaned (Scott-Tomson, *Life in a Noble Household*).

John Aubrey in his *Brief Lives* says that "peruques not commonly worne till 1660. There was one Gregorie in the Strand that was the first famous periwig-maker; and they were then called Gregorians (mentioned in Cotgrave's Dictionaire in verbo perruque)".

The full-bottomed wig continued for court wear until the middle of the eighteenth century, although from about 1730 it was discarded in favour of shorter models by fashionable men. Numerous models were designed, each with its distinctive name; and both wigs and the natural hair when worn, were commonly powdered.

Hats in the early 1660's were the tall-crowned broad, flat brimmed type, but they were changing about 1665 to a flatter-crowned model, again with a wide brim. Plumes and ribbon trimmings until the 1680s, then being replaced by a small ostrich feather fringe along the brim, or by a braid edging (from about 1675). The lower-crowned hat had the brim cocked in a variety of styles, and this had by 1690 evolved into the type with three equally spaced cocks, giving a triangular plan worn with one of the points to the front.

THE EIGHTEENTH CENTURY

In the eighteenth century the coat became better fitting and in the first decade the skirts began to flare from the waist, rather as the women's skirt expanded. There was a back vent and pleated side vents: these latter sometimes stiffened with wire to give support to the flare. In 1711

78. Court suit of red/brown silk and metal strip woven in diagonal leaf pattern: matching coat, waistcoat and breeches. Coat and waistcoat trimmed silver lace. 1720–40. (Courtesy of Museum of Costume and Textiles, Nottingham)

the *Spectator* (No. 146) notes "wire to increase and sustain the bunch of fold that hangs down on each side".

The coat and waistcoat were generally only fastened at the waist to display the frill-fronted shirt. With heavily embroidered coats, hooks and eyes, instead of buttons, gave an edge-to-edge closure: these may have been the "little silver hasps" in lieu of buttons mentioned by Addison and Steele in the same year (*Spectator* No. 175). The waistcoat, or vest, was cut similarly to the coat, but now ended above the knees. It was sleeved until the 1750s.

Both coat and waistcoat became shorter from about 1740 and the fronts of the skirts began to curve backward from the waistline, thus exposing more of the breeches. This backward movement of the skirt fronts carried on steadily throughout the century.

Knee breeches were generally worn, until about 1750 with the stockings pulled up over them, but from about 1735 the knee-band of the breeches began to be fastened over the stockings below the knee, a method which superseded the earlier fashion by the middle of the century. The knee-band was fastened with buckles, which began to be made to match the shoe buckles. By the 1780s breeches were tight fitting and long in the leg and high waisted.

The custom of extra good clothes with additional decoration for court balls and drawing rooms, and birthdays continued, and during the reigns of George I and George II much expense was incurred by courtiers and high officials of the Royal Household in providing themselves with suitably splendid garments. In 1715 one of the Prince of Wales's household spent over £30 on new clothes for the King's birthday. For court wear gold and silver stuffs, brocade, velvet and cloth were the materials for coats which often matched the breeches. Cloth coats were always embroidered. Court waistcoats were generally of different colour or material; gold or silver brocade, damask, silk or satin, heavily embroidered or laced in silver or gold. From the 1730s, at least, cloth for court wear was popular. "The Noblemen and Gentlemen wore [at Court] chiefly velvet or dark cloth coats ... and breeches of the same ... their waistcoats were either gold stuffe or rich flowered silk." (*Weekly Register*). But the next year, for the Prince of Wales's wedding suits were "in gold brocades of £300 to £500 a suit ... others in cloths flowered or sprigged with gold ... the waistcoats were universally brocades." (*Reads Weekly Journal*). Both quotations are from Cunnington, *Handbook of English Costume in the Eighteenth Century*.

In 1722 a Mrs Osborn had written of court dress "and most people very fine, but I believe the gentlemen will wear petty-cotes very soon, for many of their coats were like our mantuas. Lord Essex had a silver tissue coat, and pink colour lutestring wascote, and several had pink colour and pale blue padesway coats, which looked prodigiously effeminate" (quoted in Beattie, *English Court Life in the Reign of George 1*). Padesway, or Paduasoy, from "pou de soie" was a strong silk grosgrain. Lutestring at this time was a fine taffeta.

There is a fawn figured silk suit in the Museum of London showing the characteristic cut and flare of the early eighteenth-century coat, and the Nottingham Museum of Costume and Textiles has a similar suit of gold striped brownish crimson silk brocade, quite lavishly decorated with silver lace, which was probably originally worn at a royal birthday during the years 1720–40. Mrs Delany in 1738 writing of the Prince of Wales's birthday said there was "much finery, chiefly brown, with gold or silver embroidery and rich waistcoats". These fine clothes sooner or later became soiled and a number of cleaners' shops was opened in London, at least as early as the first half of the eighteenth century. In 1742 *The Daily Advertiser* carried an announcement that "Jane Franklin, Maiden Lane, cleans silver and gold laced cloath, buttons and buttonholes".

When, in 1755, Lord Essex became a Lord of the Bedchamber to George II, his father-in-law, Sir Charles Hanbury-Williams wrote him a long letter of advice, urging him to attend

> "Levées very frequently when you are out of waiting, and by being extremely punctual and exact in your attendance when you are in waiting. Be sure always to be at your post five or ten minutes before the time appointed.
>
> The King loves to see people well dress'd; therefore when you go to Court, and particularly when you are in waiting, be sure to put on fine clothes." (Ilchester and Langford-Brooke, *The Life of Sir Charles Hanbury-Williams.*)

By the 1760s the coat had shortened to above the knee and the waist and flared skirt almost disappeared, the garment being close fitting with the fronts curving back more markedly, especially after 1770. By the 1790s very little of the front skirts remained, they were almost reduced to tails at the back. Stiffening to the skirts of the coat was discarded and from the 1780s padding was being placed in the fronts over the chest. The front curve, from the 1770s, often began at mid-chest, giving, with the padding, a "pigeon-chested" appearance. If coats were buttoned, it was at waist or chest only; sometimes only the top button being used.

In the last quarter of the century the "frock" of the type known as the "French frock" was allowed at court. The frock, distinguished by

79. Diagram showing typical suit
c 1780. This is the style which set the
pattern for future court wear. (Based
on a suit in the Museum of London)

its turn-down collar, or "cape", from the coat, which was at first collarless, but from about 1765 acquired a small stand collar, had been adopted for informal and "undress" wear about 1730. Based on the workman's protective overgarment of the same name, it gradually replaced the coat on formal occasions, and became more fitted. The French frock was, when worn as full-dress, fully trimmed, with buttoned cuffs and gold embroidered button-holes. When worn in place of the coat it was often referred to as a "frock-coat", and it is advertised as such in 1787 but must not be confused with the frock-coat of the nineteenth century.

"What is generally called a French Frock is the court dress," wrote the *Gentleman's and London Magazine* in 1777, which in the same year commented also on the shortening waistcoat: "the waistcoat worn a few years ago would now make two; the length is now so shallow" (quoted in Cunnington, *Handbook of English Costume in the Eighteenth Cen-*

tury). The waistcoat had now taken on a modern look; it had shorter skirts, the fronts parting at an angle from the lowest button, just below the waist. This angle became wider during the 1780s, and in the last decade of the century a square-cut front was the rule, generally buttoned from the 1770s. By the end of the century the short waistcoat, square-cut across the high-waisted, long breeches, and the open, tailed coat, gave a masculine line of apparent slender height, complementing the high-waisted close classical styles of the women.

Court wear, like the women's, froze a few years before this ultimate line was achieved, and by the end of the century was already somewhat out of date in appearance, although the prevailing fashion for plainer, cloth, dress coats was followed and the peacock element in court dress was being reduced to the still elaborately embroidered waistcoats worn with it.

The wars on the Continent were also having an effect on what was worn. For Her Majesty's birthday on 19 January 1795, the *Salisbury Journal* reported that " the gentlemen were chiefly in military uniform and the ladies in velvet; the former certainly pourtrayed the state of the country . . ." The Journal added that for this occasion the King wore a prune-coloured broad cloth coat with an embroidered white satin waistcoat.

But in the 1770s and 1780s gorgeous coats were very much to the fore: Lord Villiers in 1773, according to Mrs Delany, appeared "in the morning at Court in a pale purple velvet coat, turned up with lemon colour, and embroidered all over with Ss of pearl as big as pease, and in all the spaces little medallions in beaten gold, real solid, in various figures of cupids and the like. (as Smith would say) at best it was only a fool's coat."

In 1782 the Prince of Wales favoured dauphin-bluish tint velvet embroidered with pearls and foil (Mrs Armytage). A coat, believed to be for court wear, of about 1770 in the Museum of London is of purple and shot green silk velvet, embroidered at the collar, front edges, skirt vent and pleats, cuffs and pocket flaps.

For the King's birthday in 1791 the Prince of Wales wore a

bottle-green and claret-coloured striped silk coat and breeches, and silver tissue waistcoat, very richly embroidered in silver and stones, and coloured silks in curious devices and bouquets of flowers.

The coat and waistcoat embroidered down the seams and spangled all over the body. The coat cuffs the same as the waistcoat. Diamond buttons to the coat, waistcoat and breeches, which with his diamond epaulette and sword made the whole dress form a most magnificent appearance.

(*St James's Chronicle* June 1791.)

This must have been a sight and Mr Pitt, six years later, must have cut a sad figure, despite his "new dress of brown cloth, the pockets and skirts of which were covered with gold embroidery" worn for the Queen's birthday in 1797 (*Ipswich Journal* 21 January 1797). In this year it was noted that steel buttons were the leading fashion of the day, and these eventually found their way on to certain types of court coats.

Queen Anne insisted on the full-buttoned wig in her presence, and according to Jonathan Swift, Prince Eugene was told that "it was not proper to go to Court without a long wig." As the Prince apparently only had a tye-wig (short, with bunched curls tied in a small queue at the nape of the neck) with him one wonders how he overcame the problem.

Wigs declined in size and by the middle of the century the bag-wig, short with a pig-tail or queue, was most popular. The queue was enclosed by a black silk bag held by a draw-string and a stiff ribbon bow at the back; a variation after the middle of the century was a rosette in place of the bow. When wigs finally disappeared at the end of the century, the bag, in the form of a silk patch covered with an elaborate ribbon bow, all black, was transferred to the back of the coat collar where it still survives (a less elaborate version is part of the uniform of the Royal Welch Fusiliers).

Red heels to shoes went out of fashion by about 1720, though favoured by some of the beaux until 1750 and for court wear until about 1760, when there too they were unfashionable for about ten years, until reintroduced by Charles James Fox in the early 1770s. At the King's birthday in 1771, the *Ipswich Journal* of 8 June reported: "it is not a little remarkable that Mr Charles Fox had red heels to his shoes, though that fashion has been exploded above half a century".

Buckles were commonly used to fasten the shoes until about 1793, when shoe-strings, appearing from the mid-1780s, replaced them generally. This caused consternation among the buckle makers, who in 1791 sent a deputation from Birmingham, Walsall and Wolverhampton to the Prince of Wales "with a petition setting forth the distressed situation ... from the fashion ... of wearing shoe-strings instead of buckles. His Royal Highness graciously promised ... his example and influence". But, to no great avail, although buckles were retained in some orders of court dress until today.

By the last decade of the century both coat and frock had become narrow in the back, the front line curving well away from the lower chest and the skirts almost disappearing in the front, becoming coat-tails at the back. If fastened at all, they were buttoned at the waist or slightly higher. Waistcoats were square cut and breeches long and close

80. French costume showing eighteenth century cut, possibly a court suit; chapeau bras carried under arm. 1810–11. ("Habit habille" after fashion plate from *Costume Parisien*, 1810–11)

fitting. Like the shoes, the knee-bands of the breeches lost their buckles in favour of ties: again, however, buckles remained.

The court suit however retained somewhat fuller skirts and a cut reminiscent of the 1770s and 1780s. It was of dark cloth or velvet, embroidered in silk or metal, a fashion disappearing from everyday clothes. The waistcoat was silk, white the usual colour and apparently retaining the diverging angled fronts and not adopting the square-cut waist. A black velvet suit of coat and breeches, the coat lined with cream silk and undecorated except for its buttons, which are covered with gold and silver thread, is in the Museum of London. This is believed to be a court suit of 1785–95, although I should have expected more decoration: a black cloth court suit of about 1800 in the same museum has the coat embroidered in silks with a floral design and also a trimming to the front edges of narrow point net.

The three-cornered hat of the eighteenth century was modified in the 1760s and 1770s for dress wear into the opera-hat or chapeau bras.

Both these were, if there was any difference, variations whereby the hat was made flat, to be carried under the arm only, and not for wear. The wig and the heat it engendered in the head was mostly responsible for this fashion.

THE NINETEENTH CENTURY

The black cloth court suit in the Museum of London mentioned briefly at the end of the previous section introduces the new century. Appropriately for the dawn of a century of progress, the narrow point net with which the fronts are adorned is machine made.

During the opening years of the new century trousers or pantaloons became increasingly popular and were fashionable day wear by about 1807. Pantaloons, or "tights", were close fitting and worn either with boots, or extending over the foot and strapped under the shoe. Breeches remained correct wear for evening and ceremonial or court wear; they were part of evening dress until the 1820s or 1830s, and of ceremonial court wear until today.

During the first decade the court suit was of the same style of coat, with the fronts curved away, single breasted, in cloth or velvet. Common colours were black, brown, dark green, purple or blue. Breeches matched or could be of silk of a similar colour. The coat, and sometimes the breeches, were embroidered. The waistcoat was most generally of white satin, embroidered or not. A wig-bag on the back of the coat neck. White silk stockings, black buckled shoes, and a sword. The chapeau-bras was carried under the arm.

Nottingham Museum possesses a court suit of dark brown cloth dated from 1815–20. The coat is lined with pink silk and the buttons are cut steel; the matching cloth breeches also have cut steel buttons; the white silk waistcoat has a stand collar, embroidered with a floral design. The accompanying hat is the chapeau bras, by now a flat crescentric shape; it was occasionally worn, but generally just carried folded under the arm. It is the type known as a "bicorne" – a later, not contemporary, name – and if worn was orientated fore and aft.

Wigs, except for some elderly people, and the learned professions, had gone out with the eighteenth century; as had hair-powder. But there were exceptions: Richard Brinsley Sheridan, in his fifties at Brighton appeared at the Pavilion before the Prince of Wales in 1805 "powdered as white as snow, as smartly dressed as even he could be from top to toe . . ." (Creevey, *The Creevey Papers*). Among the elderly unfashionables Creevey mentions Lord Thurlow, one time Lord Chancellor, also at Brighton, who "always dressed in a full suit of

81. Court suit in dark brown cloth. 1815–20. (Courtesy of Museum of Costume and Textiles, Nottingham)

cloaths of the old fashion, great cuffs and massy buttons, great wig, long ruffles etc". In fact, this was the style into which court dress proper had by now fossilised.

In the second decade of the century the crescent-shaped chapeau-bras was becoming known simply as the cocked-hat, as the tall hat took over as the general headwear for men. Another, shorter lived, name was "opera hat", a name later transferred to the spring-actuated collapsible top-hat invented by one Mr Gibus.

Brown continued in favour as a colour for court coats; a fashion lucky for Lord Petersham, who, according to Princess Lieven in 1821, was "handsome, but the maddest of all the mad English. For instance, a few years ago he was in love with a certain Mrs Brown, and his passion declared itself in the following way. He purchased a brown carriage, brown livery, brown hat, brown spurs, brown harness, and finally, being obliged to have an embroidered coat for Court wear, he had it in brown, embroidered with dead leaves. You see the kind of man he is." (Letter to Prince Metternich, *Private Letters of Princess Lieven.*)

In April 1822 the Lord Chamberlain laid down that for men appearing at a drawing room "full Court dress, sword and bag" must be worn by all those not in uniform.

The court suit of the 1830s and 1840s is of the same pattern as previously but is sometimes decorated with embroidery and sometimes not. A drawing by Richard Doyle, Senior, of 1831 shows a plain coat with only buttons on the cuffs and pocket flaps as decoration. The *Gentleman's Magazine of Fashion*, ten years later describes

> Court dress: A blue coat cut à la Francaise, stand collar, single-breasted, slopes away to tails (no cut in). Pocket flaps embroidered in gold, also collar and cuffs. White satin waistcoat, gold buttons, corners sloped off. Breeches white cassimers. Band at knee embroidered in gold and fastened with gold buttons. Shirt frill of lace and lace ruffles.

Also in the same year (April 1841) "Military style evening dress coat [this may mean a tail coat] stand collar [the "military style"]; collar, flaps and cuffs embroidered in gold. White satin waistcoat, white cassimer trousers gold lace down outer seams. Shirt frill and ruffles. Cocked hat." No colour is given for the coat, but, again, in December 1841 the magazine describes a black dress coat, "unembroidered, with a stand collar (à la militaire) worn with white cashmere trousers is mentioned. The trousers are hollowed to fit the boot".

Trousers were becoming acceptable wear for some formal occasions during the 1830s: as early as 1831 pantaloons were worn with court uniform for levees. Presumably the white trousers mentioned above were levee wear only.

The Museum of London has two suits of about 1840–45. One in dark blue cloth, the other is black cloth: both have matching breeches and embroidered white silk waistcoats. One has cut steel buttons on coat and breeches: in the other the buttons are missing.

In 1849 *Court Etiquette* by "A Man of the World", stated that "those who are without a distinguishing dress must procure the claret-coloured coat, sword, knee-breeches and buckles, lace shirt-frill, ruffles, long white silk stockings, shoes, shoe-buckles, and other elements of a Court suit from their respective tailors." The anonymous author also adds the information that those gentlemen "more economical than fastidious . . . may actually succeed in hiring many of these articles", although he gives no hints as to where they may be hired from.

82. Court suit. 1831. (From drawing
by R. Doyle Senior)

Claret-colour and mulberry seem to be very popular in the 1830s
and 1840s. How they differed and what colours they actually were in
the earlier nineteenth century is not easy to say. The Oxford Dictionary
gives mulberry-coloured as an adjective dating from 1837 and defines
it as "dark purple". "Claret" seems to have settled down by the
nineteenth century as the accepted generic name for the red Bordeaux
wines and claret-coloured is the colour of claret. However the dictionary also gives "maroon", from 1791 as "brownish-crimson, or
claret colour", whilst D. R. Hay in his *Nomenclature of Colours* published
in 1845 calls "the lightest of the shades of red purple" a "deep
marrone", apparently a variant of maroon. Hay's colour as illustrated
in his book is, in fact, a pretty dark purple.
Cloth seems the most general material for these court suits, but
velvet was also used. Christies, during recent years, have had through

their hands a number of blue velvet Court suits of the nineteenth century.

A suit illustrated in *Punch* in August 1842 (The Presentation of the Chinese Ambassador) shows the back view, with buttons at the back waist and at the bottom of the tails, an elongated wig-bag, coming well down the back, worn with ruffles and white stockings and sword. The cocked hat is now much less deep than the previous chapeau-bras.

83. Court suit back view, wig bag at neck of coat, ruffles at cuffs, cocked hat. 1842. (After drawing in *Punch*)

A dark purple (claret, mulberry or maroon) suit with cut steel buttons in the Museum of London has a "wing" cuff: that is the top of the cuff extends backward from the sleeve for an inch or two, sloping down to the normal width, close to the sleeve, at the wrist. The suit has white silk waistcoat with woven floral stripes. The date is about 1850. A suit of a similar date in private hands is "dark mulberry" with a plain cuff, cut steel buttons and a matching waistcoat.

The *Tailor and Cutter* in 1869 confirmed that dark cloth trousers with a gold lace stripe were worn for levees, and cloth breeches for drawing rooms, and a levee suit in the Museum of London, of about 1870, has dark green trousers with a narrow gold lace stripe. The coat is of the single-breasted "swallow-tail" variety with a narrow gold lace on the collar, cuffs and pocket flaps. This was the "new" court dress introduced apparently from the 1840s on. The new style was described as a dark cloth single-breasted dress coat with a stand collar, white collarless waistcoat, matching trousers with a gold lace stripe for levees, matching breeches with white silk stockings for drawing rooms, and a white neckcloth.

This same pattern was described by Mrs Armytage in 1883 as "dark

84. Rather romanticised illustration of velvet court suit with embroidered white silk waistcoat. 1863.
"I feast my eyes on velvet sheen
    The buttons glitter on my breast,
No faithful subject of the Queen
    Will go to levée better dressed."
(After *London Society*, 1863)

coloured cloth dress coat, to be worn unbuttoned, single-breasted, stand collar, pointed pocket flaps, gold embroidery on collar, cuffs and pocket flaps. White waistcoat, trousers or breeches of same colour as coat with one row of gold lace, sword and white neckcloth". Alternatively, says Mrs Armytage, this style may also be made in velvet. She also states that "the most minute details are printed by the Lord Chamberlain's Office". The swallow-tail or tail coat, the dress coat with a square, horizontal cut-away at the front and two tails representing the back skirt, was by the 1860s confined to evening dress and was universally black. There was a turn over collar and lapels. The new court coat therefore differed from this standard only in respect of its collar and colour.

85. Velvet court dress at a presentation. 1874. (After *Illustrated London News*, 22 March 1874)

Despite the "minute details" from the Lord Chamberlain it was not until 1898 that *Dress Worn by Gentlemen at Her Majesty's Court* appeared in pamphlet form: when it did, it detailed court dress, much as Mrs Armytage's description, for "All Gentlemen who have no special Uniform". The gold embroidery on collar, cuffs and pocket flaps was specified as "similar to 5th class of Civil Uniform". Buttons are specified as convex gilt with mounted crown (i.e. in relief). Mrs Armytage is somewhat ambiguous but makes clear that it is the trousers that have the gold lace stripe. White breeches are to be worn, stockings may be of black or white silk, shoes are to have gilt buckles. In addition, the hat is to be a beaver or silk cocked hat, with black silk cockade, gold lace, loop and button. The sword, "the same as that worn with Civil Uniform" is suspended by a silk shoulder belt, worn underneath the waistcoat. The neck cloth is to be white.

The velvet version of the new court dress, as described in this 1898 edition, has the coat cut as described above, but without the gold embroidery. Buttons could be gilt, steel or "plain". The waistcoat is either of black velvet, or is a normal white one; the trousers are velvet; the hat is as above, but with gilt or steel loop and button, no lace. The sword is of gilt or steel with a silk shoulder belt. The neckcloth is white. When breeches were worn they were to be black velvet with black silk hose; shoes have gilt or steel buckles.

The velvet suit is all black: the cloth version is described as of dark colour "of similar colours to present Court Dress", but no clue is given as to what these colours are. Old court dress, described as "Now Obsolete" is merely given as "cloth or velvet coat"; no colours are stated, except black for mourning. With this old dress the white silk waistcoat is to be embroidered, the breeches are to match the coat and are worn with white silk stockings. In addition buckled shoes, court stock [not described], sling sword, cocked hat, frill, ruffles and wig-bag are prescribed.

Some of the shoe buckles at this time were apparently very insecure and it was said that the Palace was littered with stray buckles after a drawing room or ball. (Ponsonby-Fane, *Connoisseur* Vol. 11.)

86. New style velvet court dress, 1894. (After Holding, *Uniforms of the British Army, Navy and Court*, 1894)

Queen Victoria was in general most strict as to the dress worn at court and on other occasions; however she did sometimes relax in favour of, at least, elderly gentlemen. Baron Stockmar, for instance, got away with trousers instead of breeches at court, and later the older men were allowed a pattern of breeches which came down to the feet and buttoned at the ankle, obviating the need for silk stockings, which they were supposed to imitate; however, it appears that they merely imitated peg-top trousers (Frederick Ponsonby, quoted in Hibbert, *The Court at Windsor*).

The Commissioners of the Great Exhibition apparently were ill at ease even in the normal court suits. *The Times*, on 2 May 1851, commented on their appearance at the previous day's opening ceremony, "They are nearly all in Court dresses [sic] and in some instances the experienced eye can detect the awkwardness of manner which such unwanted habiliments superinduce". Awkwardness of manner was avoided by the American ambassador, James Buchanan, who appeared before the Queen wearing black coat, white waistcoat, and pantaloons; although Andrew Stevenson had, on his appointment to St James's in 1836 gone to an audience with William IV "buttoned up to the throat, . . . cocked hat, very rich and handsome sword . . . gold lace enough about him to adorn a dozen well-dressed footmen". (Boykin, *Victoria, Albert and Mrs Stevenson*.)

THE TWENTIETH CENTURY

Although much in social and official life was relaxed with the advent of King Edward VII, satorial correctness was always expected and, despite his innovations in dress, no degree of slackness was countenanced in the wearing of either uniforms or plain clothes: "Woe betide the courtier or lord who deviated by the position of even the obscurist star from what was correct". (Roger Fulford in Nowell-Smith, *Edwardian England*.)

Dress worn at Court appeared in enlarged and illustrated editions during King Edward's reign: in 1908 both old and new style velvet court dress was described. The new style was described as a single-breasted black silk-velvet coat, worn open but with six buttons. It had a stand collar, gauntlet cuffs and four buttons at the back, two at the centre waist and two at the bottom of the tails. The lining was black silk except to the tail, where it was white. The buttons were of cut steel. It was worn with a white satin or black silk waistcoat and black velvet breeches, with three steel buttons and steel buckles at the knees. The stockings were black silk, the shoes black patent leather with steel buckles. The hat is merely designated black silk or beaver; the sword is to have a steel hilt and black scabbard, the belt is worn under the waist-coat. White gloves and a white bow tie are worn. For levees, velvet trousers could be worn with patent leather military boots – presumably Wellingtons.

The old style is in velvet, the coat "cut-back frock style", single-breasted with seven buttons and button holes but the coat was actually fastened edge-to-edge on the chest by a hook and eye. There were six buttons at the back; two extra half way down the tails. There is a black silk flash or wig-bag and lace frill and ruffles were prescribed. All other items were as for the new style (including the waistcoat which was no longer, therefore, to be embroidered).

87. Old style velvet court
suit. 1908. (After *Dress
Worn at Court*, 1908)

88. New style velvet court
suit. 1908. (After *Dress
Worn at Court*, 1908)

In addition cloth court dress "for Courts and Evening Parties" is detailed. This is described as single-breasted, worn open but with six gilt buttons and dummy button-holes. A stand collar, gauntlet cuffs and two buttons at back centre waist and two at the bottom of the tails were detailed. It was to be of dark cloth: "mulberry, claret or green, not black or blue", with gold embroidery on collar, cuffs and pocket flaps as for 5th class civil uniform. Breeches were to match, with gilt buckles. The waistcoat could be white corded silk or marcella with four small gilt buttons. Stockings, tie, gloves, shoes and hat were as for the new style, but gilt buckles on shoes and a gold loop on the hat were added. The sword was "Court Dress with gilt hilt. Black scabbard gilt mounted. Gold knot". At levees trousers, instead of breeches, to match the coat were worn with patent leather military boots.

Two years after King George V's accession, in 1912, a new edition of Dress worn at Court was published. This was substantially the same as that of 1908. For the new style the only differences are that pocket flaps with three points are to be on the waist seam, the coat is lined with white silk, and the tails with black, and most important, "The Regulation allowing trousers to be worn with this style of Court Dress has been cancelled". Of the other items, the hat is to have a steel loop as a black silk cockade or rosette, and the sword belt is described as "black silk waist belt worn under the waistcoat, with blue velvet frog". The old style is similar to that in the previous edition, but the pointed pocket flaps, with three buttons, one under each point in this case, are again mentioned. The waistcoat also has pointed pocket flaps and three buttons under each, and is to have skirted fronts. All the other items are the same, except the sword which is of the sling type, with slings instead of a frog on the black silk waistbelt.

Cloth court dress is still embroidered on collar, cuffs and pocket flaps as for the 5th class civil uniform. The buttons are described as gilt, convex, mounted with the imperial crown. Matching cloth trousers with a row of five eighths of an inch wide gold lace are prescribed for levees. "A black or very dark Inverness cape, or a long full dark overcoat" could be worn with the velvet or cloth dress.

These three types of court suit were all pictured and described in the *Tailor and Cutter Year Book of Fashions* for 1913. The *Army & Navy Stores Catalogue* for 1912 advertises "Silk velvet Court coat £10 10s 0d" and "Embroidered Court coat [cloth], mounted buttons" at the same price. Velvet breeches were £4 4s 0d, cloth breeches £2 5s 0d and the gold laced trousers £3 15s 0d.

The First World War caused courts and similar functions to be suspended until the early 1920s. In February 1924 the *Tailor & Cutter* published a sketch of an "unofficial" style of dress which they said was introduced during the war and was now to be extended to ministers in place of their elaborate uniforms. It is described as "Black dress coat, silk facings; vest white marcella or same material as coat; black cloth

89. Old style velvet court suit. 1938. (Courtesy of Museum of Costume and Textiles, Nottingham)

90. Back view of 89 showing buttons on tails and wig bag. (Courtesy of Museum of Costume and Textiles, Nottingham)

91. Alternative dress. 1924. (After
Tailor and Cutter, February 1924)

knee-breeches, with three buttons, black strap fastening with black buckle; black silk stockings plain black court shoes with bows and white gloves". The picture shows an ordinary dress shirt, collar and white bow tie and an opera hat is carried. This "unofficial" dress sounds remarkably like the "frock dress", which originated some time in the nineteenth century. Winterhalter's picture of Queen Victoria and the Prince Consort with their children, painted in 1846, shows the Prince sitting wearing what may be court dress, but which, again, looks like frock dress.

Mrs Armytage in 1883 describes frock dress as a dress coat and waistcoat, breeches or pantaloons, worn with a "white cravat" at dinners and evening parties when uniform is not worn. *Dress Worn at Court*, 1898 gives a similar description, adding that the dress coat is lappelled, and that orders, decorations and medals are worn. According to Mrs Armytage this costume is to be worn at dinners and evening parties where uniform is not worn.

The 1908 edition of *Dress Worn at Court* gives an extended description, mentioning silk facings to the coat, black or white waistcoat, black cloth or stockinette breeches (pantaloons are not mentioned and obviously not now allowed), with three black buttons and buckle at the

92. King Edward VII in frock dress with Garter insignia and wearing caped cloak; carrying "Gibus" opera hat. 1890s. (From a painting by A. Stuart-Wortly)

knee. Plain court shoes with bows ("no buckles") are specified and the
cravat is replaced by a white tie. In addition there is a folding cocked
hat in corded silk with a black loop and rosette and white gloves. It is
worn, as before, for "Dinners, Balls and Receptions".

The 1912 version is the same, except the hat is now an opera hat,
which is shown in the portrait of Edward VII by Archibald Stuart-
Wortly painted about 1897, that is, eleven years before *Dress Worn at
Court* was saying a cocked hat, and fifteen years before the opera hat is
authorised in the 1912 edition. Kind Edward is also wearing the insignia of the Garter (as is Prince Albert in the 1846 picture).

This informal court wear is, I think, undoubtedly the "unofficial"
style shown by the *Tailor & Cutter* in 1924, and the authorisation for
ministers to wear it as an alternative to civil uniform on state occasion
was an example of King George V's thoughtfulness and consideration
for the members of the first Labour Government, elected in January of
that year. He met the members of the Cabinet of that government first
in February, the same month that this authorisation was given. It was
also a sign of the new government's respect and liking for the King that
so many of them in fact wore the full uniform, even if, like many a
courtier before and since, they had recourse to hiring their finery.

A re-issue of *Dress Worn at Court* in 1929 shows no significant change
in any of the orders of dress, but in 1937, the last edition had minor
variations. For new style velvet court dress the correct white satin waistcoat is emphasised by the instruction "NOT white corded silk or
marcella", and a black velvet version is introduced also. The cocked
hat is described as "beaver", silk being omitted; and an additional
item describes the shirt to be "as worn with evening dress, stiff front
and cuffs". The prohibition of trousers with this style is repeated.
There is no change in old style velvet, but the cloth coat is now to be
decorated by gold embroidery "similar to the edge of a Privy Councillor's uniform coat", a change which had also been made in this
edition.

There were slight variations in the velvet and cloth court suits in the
case of the judiciary and legal profession. It is not within the scope of
this book to deal with legal dress in general, but the Lord Chancellor
in his other capacity is included, and he wears a black velvet or blue
cloth court suit of the old style, according to the occasion (see Chapter
I). This style of old velvet dress is worn also by the Speaker of the Commons and by judges, King's or Queen's Council and barristers at
Court. In addition the judges and King's or Queen's Council wear
black silk gowns. For levees a similarly cut black cloth ("legal cloth
court dress") suit is worn. This legal cloth dress is also worn by the

93. Her Majesty the Queen leaving 10 Downing Street. Sir Winston Churchill, K.G. in frock or alternative dress with Garter insignia. 1955. (Press Association)

Serjeants-at-Arms at courts or in the Houses of Parliament.

In 1929 and 1937 *Alternative Court Dress* gives details of the version of 1924 and it is identical with the 1912 "frock dress", except that a stiff evening dress shirt and a winged collar are added to the list and the opera hat is omitted. In connection with this last is a note "In the case of alternative dress as headgear does not form part of it, no particular kind of hat is prescribed therefore". This alternative dress may be worn "in lieu of either Civil Uniform or Court Dress . . . by gentlemen other than Members of Their Majesties' Households and of the Diplomatic and Consular Services on all occasions when Uniform and Court dress is prescribed".

In 1939 the Army & Navy Stores, lists in their catalogue "Court Dress, any style to order, in velvet, or new pattern black cloth (alternative) Evening Dress". They do not now commit themselves to a price, but will "submit estimates on application".

The rules of the 1937 edition of *Dress Worn at Court* still hold, but the occasions when garments of high ceremony are worn are few. For the ladies the court dress with its train and accessories of feathers and veil has been swept out of modern life, at least for the present; but the court dress of the men still persists, even if no courts are held. Officials of the Houses of Parliament, Lord Mayors, judges and barristers, among others, keep alive the old tradition in their daily, or almost daily wear.

CHAPTER V

Court Uniforms

Court uniforms, as opposed to court dress, are worn by a wide range of office-holders, including the Civil Service, Privy Counsellors and Household Officials, among others. One uniform, the Windsor Uniform, is also worn by the monarch and members of the royal family. The origins of such uniforms were Continental, particularly coming from the Germanic states during the eighteenth century, although there is possibly an early nineteenth-century French influence.

According to the *Memoires* of Stanislas Poniatowski, Augustus III, Count of Saxony and King of Poland, in 1751, had a "court uniform, yellow, blue and silver", and the Swedish court uniform came about in 1778. In 1779 both Frederick the Great of Prussia and our own King George III were wearing a personal uniform and in both cases it was blue with red facings. George III, like other members of his family, loved uniforms and all the minutiae of military dress: he was especially fond of that of the Horse Guards Blue, and often wore their blue and red uniform, even going so far as to raise "a special Windsor troop and make himself a captain". (Hibbert, *The Court at Windsor*.) Also at this time a blue livery was "worn at Wilton by the servants of Esther, Lady Pembroke, a woman he deeply admired – with scarlet and gold accessories". (Joseph Taylor *Relics of Royalty*, 1820 quoted in Hibbert, *The Court at Windsor*.) So apart from his second-cousin, Frederick, he had local and familiar precedents for the colours of his new court uniform.

Mrs Delany (*Autobiography and Correspondence*) accompanied the Royal Family to Bulstrode on a visit to the Duke of Portland in August 1778 when the King was "in a blue and gold uniform, and so were all his attendants in uniform". This, and the occasions when the picture of "The Trusty Servant" at Winchester College, was repainted in honour of a visit of the King and Queen, and also in 1778, when the trusty servant was given a coat of blue and red laced with gold, seem to be the earliest records of the Windsor uniform, although the name was not applied until 1781, when the August number of the *Gentleman's Magazine* refers to it thus. (Morshead, *Connoisseur*, 1935.) Gainsborough painted the King wearing it in 1782 and many subsequent portraits of the King and his family show it.

94. King George III wearing Windsor uniform with top hat and cockade. (After portrait by P. E. Stroehling)

Originally there was a gold-laced full dress, and an undress without lace. The full dress does not seem to have survived very long, and the undress version, without the gold lace, is the one that survives until today. The cut of the coat varied according to fashion and both day and evening versions probably existed, as it was worn for hunting and also late into the evening.

At the time that King George III was creating the Windsor uniform he was also settling into Windsor Castle as his principal home: Windsor, of all places, was that which he loved best, and obviously the two events went together, as the application of the name to the dress implies. However, in the earlier years its wear was not confined to Windsor, and certainly during the King's illness in 1788, when he was temporarily removed to Kew Palace, and in 1789 after his recovery, it is noted at both Kew and in town. Fanny Burney at Kew on 29 November 1788 "perceived a Windsor uniform", and Mrs Papendiek wrote of the Thanksgiving Service at St Paul's on 23 April 1789: "The King was in the full dress Windsor uniform, blue with red collar and cuffs, gold lace buttholes etc.", and at a concert in Westminster Abbey that same year, "the King, his sons and attendants were in the Windsor uniform . . . ." At this time its use was not confined to court occasions or in the King's presence, for, Mrs Papendiek noted it at balls given by the French and Spanish Ambassadors in 1789, when "the gentlemen wore the full dress Windsor uniform". The Prince of Wales wore it in Yorkshire at least once that same year. (H.M.C.R. Carlisle MS. 670.) Indeed, it seemed to serve as a generally useful court dress worn as an alternative to the usual court suit to a variety of functions as well as being the costume particular to the Royal Family and the immediate entourage.

King George IV kept up its use at Windsor, and probably at Brighton, but his successor, William IV, discontinued it. Queen Victoria revived it and when reviewing her troops in 1839 wore, according to Lady Lyttelton (*Correspondence of Sarah Spencer, Lady Lyttelton*), "a smart chacot [shako], with plenty of gold about it, and the Windsor Uniform riding habit and the beautiful blue ribbon and (I believe) the Star of the Garter over all". This statement is confirmed by the Queen's diary.

The uniform was worn with trousers or knee breeches: Prince Albert is wearing it with knee breeches, in Winterhalter's painting of the visit of Louis Philippe in 1844. The Queen, writing to her daughter Vicky, Princess Royal and Crown Princess of Germany in 1858, about the confirmation of the Prince of Wales said that "he wore his Windsor uniform" (the ceremony took place at Windsor).

It is probable that it was only during Queen Victoria's reign that a "sealed" pattern for the uniform was produced, and the orders of dress settled down to trousers for day and breeches for evening wear, with the same coat, a cut-away dress "tails". Later, evening dress trousers were substituted for the breeches: in 1883 Mrs Armytage records Windsor uniform as a "blue dress coat, scarlet cuffs and collar, gilt Garter buttons, morning or evening trousers, etc." *Dress Worn at Court*, 1898, has much the same description: "The Windsor Uniform, worn only at Windsor Castle by the Royal Family and certain Officers of the Household etc., consists of a Blue Dress Coat lappelled, Scarlet Cuffs and Collar, Gilt Buttons, of Garter Star within Garter surmounted with Crown, with Morning or Evening Trousers, and Waistcoat. Orders, Decorations and Medals are worn." The uniform was now definitely limited to a specific place and to specific persons. For day wear dark trousers were usual, and a top hat was worn.

King Edward VII confined the use of the Windsor uniform to evening wear only and the 1908 edition of *Dress Worn at Court* states that it is worn only at Windsor Castle by the Royal Family and certain Household Officers. It is described as a dark blue cloth evening dress coat, with four buttons on each side, two at the back waist and two on the bottom of the tails. The collar and cuffs are scarlet, and have three buttons on each cuff. All buttons are gilt with a mounted garter star within garter surmounted by the imperial crown. The waistcoat is a single-breasted white marcella, roll collar and three small buttons as above. A matching black waistcoat is worn when the court is in mourning, together with a black crape band on the left arm of the coat. The trousers are black. Breeches are re-introduced and are of black cloth or stockinet, with black buttons and buckles. Plain black court shoes with bows are worn with breeches but with trousers, black boots could be worn. A white tie and gloves are required, and presumably, a white starched shirt. No hat is mentioned.

The Windsor uniform was worn with knee-breeches in the evening in King George V's reign, and it is occasionally used by the Duke of Edinburgh and the Royal Family and Household today, particularly during Ascot week, a practice probably originating this century.

There have been few changes since 1908. In 1912 the white waistcoat was to have "no long pointed fronts" and in 1937 the buttons on the coat are reduced to three each side. "Evening dress material" is specified for trousers, and gloves are omitted.

The Windsor uniform was painted on "The Trusty Servant" at Winchester for a Royal visit but perhaps an even stranger exhibition of loyalty occurred in Manchester in the late eighteenth or early nineteenth century when the angel roof of the Cathedral was painted to show the supporting angelic choir in the same uniform. The source of this information is an appendix to *A Memoir of the Rev. Cecil Daniel Wray, M.A.*, published in Winchester in 1867. The present Cathedral archivist has been unable to trace any other reference or possible date, and today the angels are unpainted. "The Trusty Servant" has breeches and waistcoat of scarlet, and there is a tradition that such was the original uniform, but I know of no other instance of it being so, or being specifically mentioned in writing.

Despite the fact that William IV did not seem to care for the Windsor uniform, and did not make use of it as a household dress during his reign, he is to be credited with granting its use to the officers of the Royal Hospital Chelsea. As it is a civilian uniform, badges of rank were not worn with it, and when a military tunic, still in Windsor colours, replaced the original dress, badges were still omitted, and are to this day.

A variation of the uniform, known as the Windsor Livery, was worn by a select number of public servants, of which the gate-keeper of the old British Museum was one, and the staff of the Royal Academy, probably others.

The Windsor uniform was a dress for the private use of the Royal Family and such others as the monarch decreed, worn specifically at Windsor, despite some aberrations in the late eighteenth century: there was no civil uniform for state occasions for most of the state officers and officials in their governmental or other capacities. It is said that King George IV introduced the civil uniform, as still worn, for the Royal Household, ministers of state and superior civil servants based on the Windsor model modified by the dress of the French Marshals. (Morshead, *Connoisseur*, 1935.)

This was at the end of 1820, and it is surely no coincidence that the Bourbons re-introduced in 1820 a court uniform following the lines of that created by Napoleon in 1804 or 1805. On this dress the gold lacing was strictly laid down as to quantity and position according to the rank or station of the official wearing it. Its inception in this country is attributed to George IV in a memorandum of Sir Henry Ponsonby's, made in 1880, embodying the recollection of Lord Ailesbury, a courtier under both William IV and Victoria. Sir Owen Morshead saw this memorandum in the Lord Chamberlain's Office at St James's Palace, but it is no longer there and is presumably somewhere in the Public Record Office.

The Public Record Office does have among the Lord Chamberlain's documents an Order of 23 April 1822 for men attending drawing rooms stating court dress was essential "except those in uniform" though this may, of course, refer to military as well as civil.

An example of the French "grande tenue" of a senior minister of the Empire is shown by the Gros portrait in the Louvre of Comte Daru wearing a magnificent laced full skirted coat, white breeches, cloak, sash and plumed hat. Pictures by Goya of late eighteenth- and early nineteenth-century Spanish noblemen indicate that set designs and patterns of gold lace were incorporated in Spanish court dress also at this time.

George IV, when Prince of Wales, had made a previous attempt to introduce some kind of uniform for his household. Writing in 1783, Mrs Papendiek notes, "The Prince's people were to have a uniform. Although extremely costly and elegant yet a uniform it was: another innovation upon attendants as gentlemen"; apparently the idea was regarded as echoing the livery of menial servants. This proposed uniform of the Prince's may have been a sign of his antipathy to his father in the setting up, as it were, of rival colours.

In 1820 the fashionable coat was the cutaway swallow-tail, generally double-breasted, with fairly short and broad tails and usually with a square cut-in at normal waist level. This tail coat, known at the time as a morning coat, was in fact now the only "dress" coat for evening wear. Both day and evening versions could have a velvet collar: gilt buttons were sometimes used.

As we have mentioned before, George IV's coronation was marked by, among other things, Elizabethan, and even more outré, dress for those taking part in the ceremonies. Like most of the monarchs of his House and their successors, George IV had a deep interest in uniforms, and clothes generally. After his splendidly dressed coronation it is not surprising that the new King should wish for an equally splendid costume for his Household, ministers and officials to wear when attending him on state occasions. Whether the French influenced the British pattern as is suggested, is perhaps uncertain, but George IV was certainly an admirer of the French taste in the arts, an admiration no doubt encouraged by his Whig friends. The court uniform appears in the first third of the nineteenth century in a form remarkably like that which survives into our own times. There was a blue tail coat known as a "Coatee", suitably faced and laced, with gilt buttons, worn with waistcoat and breeches or trousers.

If based on the Windsor uniform it is probable that all the first civil uniforms had red facings, but if that is so, a change was soon made and the red collar and cuffs were confined to members of the Household, other entitled officials having black velvet facings. This was certainly so in 1831 when Thomas Creevey went to Court in May: "Would you believe it? in about ten minutes I was detected as being in the wrong livery. It is the Household only that wear *red* collars and cuffs: the official ones are *black*". (*The Creevey Papers.*)

We do not know whether he made the same mistake when he first appeared in the civil uniform in March 1831. On this occasion he wrote:

Lord Grey [said] ... "you *must* go to Court, you are very wrong in not doing so."

"And am I," I said, "to pay £120 for my cloaths to go in?"

"No," said he, "it is only the dress of Privy Councillors etc. that costs so much."

And Lady Mary Wood added that Mr. Wood's dress (which is the same as mine is to be) cost £40, and so Grey is to take me ... to the King on Wednesday week and to the Queen the first Drawing room afterwards.

To the first I go in blue pantaloons, an immense broad gold lace stripe down the sides and BOOTS. To the Queen I go in white serrididles [breeches], white silk stockings, shoes and gilt buckles and a hat with feathers all round the edges. Thank God! Mrs. Durham [Creevey's landlady] lends me the hat, sword, shoes and knee buckles – they belong to a lodger of hers now out of Town ..."

(Creevey's Life and Times)

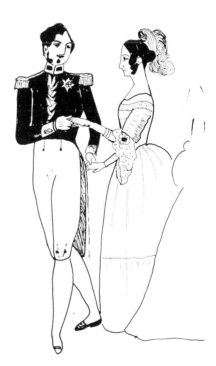

95. Civil uniform in a romantic setting. The épaulettes are artistic
licence. *c* 1840. (From music cover,
The Queen's Country Dances)

The civil uniform seems to have been established with five classes, with a full dress and levee dress versions in some of the classes: first and second in the case of the Civil Service and first, second and third of the Household (that of the scarlet facings). In full dress the chest, back, coat tails back and front, collar, cuffs and pocket flaps were decorated with gold "oak-leaf" embroidery: for levee dress, collar, cuffs and pocket flaps alone were so decorated. Fourth and fifth class of the Household and third, fourth and fifth class of other officials had only the levee dress coat for all occasions. As the Household uniform had scarlet cloth facings, so the others had black velvet collar and cuffs.

96. Civil uniform with trousers (levee dress). First class. See text. 1867. (After *Illustrated London News*, 16 February 1867)

Such is the basic uniform throughout Victoria's reign; in 1890 it was pictured, but not described, in *Civil Uniforms in the Queen's Household*, and in 1898 it was briefly detailed in *Dress Worn at Court* – "Her Majesty's Household and Civil Service. Revised, Lord Chamberlain's Office 1875 . . . . There are Five Classes of which the First and Second only have a Full Dress Coat, excepting in the Queen's Household where it is extended to the Third Class. Full Dress is worn at Drawing

Rooms, State Balls, State Concerts etc. Levee Dress is worn at Levees and other ceremonies where Full Dress is not worn". (This corresponds with Creevey's variations for drawing room and levee.)

The full dress is described as:

Coat – Blue Cloth, lined with Black Silk, Blue Velvet Collar and Cuffs, Gold Oak-leaf Embroidery. (Household, Scarlet cloth Collar and Cuffs.)

	Civil Service			Household	
	1st Class	5 in. wide		1st Class	5 in. wide
	2nd	4		2nd	4
Same	3rd	3		3rd	3
coat	4th	2	Same coat	4th	2
both for			both for	5th	$\frac{3}{8}$
full &	5th	$\frac{3}{8}$	full &		
undress			undress		

Breeches   : White kerseymere with covered Buttons at the Knees and Gilt Buckles.

Stockings   : White silk

Shoes   : With gilt Buckles

Hat   : 1st Class. Black Beaver Cocked Hat, Black silk Cockade, *White* ostrich Border Feather, Treble Gold Bullion Loop, with Tassel and Hangers.
2nd Class. Same, but with Double Gold Bullion Loop, Plain gold Tassels without Hangers.
3rd, 4th, 5th Class: Same, but with *Black* Ostrich Border Feather and Plaited Gold Bullion Loop – no Tassels.

Sword   : Black Scabbard with Gilt mountings, the Sword Knot Gold Lace, Bullion Tassel

Sword Belt : Silk shoulder, with White Cloth Frog for Sword.

Stock   : White

Buttons   : 1st & 2nd Class – With Supporters
3rd, 4th & 5th Class – Without Supporters

For the Ambassadors, the Full Dress have [sic] the addition of embroidered Sleeves, and also the back seams.

Levee Dress is: Coat, – Same width Embroidery as Full Dress, but only on Collar, Cuffs and Pocket Flaps.

Trousers – Blue cloth with Gold Oak Lace
1st & 2nd Class, $2\frac{1}{2}$ inches wide
3rd & 4th Class, 2 inches wide
5th Class   1 inch wide

Boots are worn with Undress.
Sword Belt – Silk Shoulder with Blue Cloth Frog.

97. Full dress civil uniform; first class. 1890s. (After T. H. Holding, *Uniforms of the British Army, Navy and Court*, 1894)

The full dress coat was fastened by hooks and eyes, with dummy buttons; the levee coat had practical buttons and button holes. In addition, a scarlet lined blue cloth cloak, double breasted, black velvet collar and two rows of six buttons each, with a detachable cape, was described for outdoor wear, and a soft cloth forage cap, with a blue peak and scarlet welts around the crown and gold braid on top for the household, and gold braid instead of scarlet in the case of other officials. There is a strange addition also: "Cap for Consular use, same, with silver welts, in place of Gold Braid". Several pages on details of orders of dress for the Consular service make no mention of caps, and no reference to this entry. At the foot of the description is the note: "The Civil Uniform is worn only during tenure of office".

The various editions of *Dress Worn at Court* issued during the present century do not differ substantially from 1898 detail above. The bulk of the description originally comes under the heading "His Majesty's Household" or "Royal Household Uniform" and "Civil Uniform" is referred back to the Household for most of the detail, and the Foreign and Diplomatic Service referred in turn to the civil uniform, the Foreign Office and Embassy appointments being equated with the five civil classes. Later editions detail civil uniform in full without reference to the household.

In the earlier editions it is noted that the Lord Chamberlain's and Lord Steward's departments wear a different uniform and in the 1912 edition these are described as much the same as the Household

98. Jubilee reception. 1897. Household uniform, first class, worn by official holding White Rod. Other civil and military uniforms also shown include Indian officer. Ladies wearing ribands of orders. (*Illustrated London News*, 26 June 1897)

generally, but with different patterns of gold lace, one and a half inches wide on collar, cuffs, pocket flap and back. White breeches or blue trousers with one and three-quarter inches gold lace stripe are available for courts or levees. In 1912 we are also told that the Lord Great Chamberlain's uniform is the same in every respect as that of the first class household "except that the Coat is scarlet instead of blue".

Later descriptions are more detailed than in the original edition; for instance boots and shoes are to be of patent leather, and in 1912 the knee and shoe buckles are described as "Gilt, Rose, Shamrock and Thistle pattern". A great coat with a cape is an alternative to the cloak, now without the cape. The cap is described as "Military Staff Shape". In 1908 white gloves are mentioned; in 1912 they are not, and in 1937 it is stated that "gloves are not worn". From 1912 against the hat is the note that "hangars . . . no longer hang."

Also, after the First World War, a sixth class, that of Privy Councillor, was added. The details of gold lace were now: Privy Councillor 5 inches, 1st Class $4\frac{1}{2}$ inches, 2nd Class 4 inches, 3rd Class 3 inches, for household full dress. (These figures, by the way, referred in all cases to the width at the base of each front of the coat, as well as the depth of embroidery on the cuffs.) For levee dress the Privy Councillor, first, second and third classes have embroidery as for full dress on collar, cuffs, pockets and back waist. The 4th and 5th classes have similar lace but one inch wide. This last replaces the former two inch lace of the fourth class and three eighths of an inch edging for the fifth. The stripes on the trousers are now, Privy Councillor, 1st and 2nd Class $2\frac{1}{2}$ inches wide, 3rd Class 2 inches, 4th and 5th Classes $1\frac{3}{4}$ inches.

From the early twentieth century the levee coatee was also embroidered at the centre back waist. On both full dress and levee coatees the embroidery has a purl edging (a twisted cord finish) for the Privy Councillors, a wavy edging for the first class and a saw-edge for the lower classes. For full dress the buttons are the royal arms with supporters, for levee dress, without supporters, but with a crown.

Civil uniform was, and is, distinguished by its black velvet facing instead of the scarlet cloth of the household uniform: by the restriction of full dress to Privy Councillors, first and second classes, and in the case of levee dress, gold braid instead of scarlet welts on the forage cap.

The wearing of household and civil uniform is confined to those appointments specifically detailed, and cannot be varied without the monarch's permission. Similarly it is worn by the Foreign and Diplomatic Service: ambassadors wear first class uniform and are entitled to extra embroidery on the sleeves and the seams of the coat.

99. (a) Privy Councillor's full dress civil uniform coat. 1920–30 (Colchester Borough Council). (b) Second class levee coat. 1920–30. (Author's collection)

Chargés d'Affaires and secretaries wear appropriate uniform of inferior grade. Up to 1947 the old Government of India and Indian Civil Service were also entitled to wear civil uniform according to their rank.

Full dress is worn at courts, state balls, and evening state parties. The full dress coat is also worn with trousers on special occasions. Levee dress is worn at levees and other ceremonies when full dress is not worn. Uniform is only worn during tenure of office, or by special permission when retired. In the case of the Household, members who were senior service officers have the option of wearing naval or military or air force uniforms.

100. Ambassador in full dress.
c 1840. (From contemporary
print)

101. Diplomatic undress or half
dress. 1890s. (After Holding, *Uniforms
of the British Army, Navy and Court*,
1894)

102. Privy Councillors'
uniforms. Full and levee
dress. 1937. (After *Dress
Worn at Court*, 1937)

An addition to the 1898 book is that of household evening dress. It consists of dark blue cloth evening dress coat (tails) with a black velvet collar: there are three flat gilt buttons, engraved with the royal cipher and crown, on each side, two at the back waist and two at the bottom of the tails and three on the cuffs. In 1908 a double breasted white marcella waistcoat, changed to a single breasted one in 1912, which was forbidden to have long pointed fronts. Plain black evening dress trousers or breeches and boots or shoes with the trousers are specified. Court shoes with bows and black silk stockings are to be worn with breeches. A white necktie is required; and gloves are referred to in 1908, but not mentioned later. For members of the Queen's and Royal Dukes' households special buttons were worn.

103. Privy Councillor in full civil uniform at the Coronation of H.M. the Queen, 1953. (Painting by Elisabeth Grant)

Among other occasions, the civil uniform was worn at Accession Councils, and at some meetings of the Privy Council. Indeed Edward VII decreed that all meetings of the Privy Council should be attended in uniform, a decision said to have been prompted by the glittering entourage of the Kaiser, seen during a brief visit to Berlin. In view of the antipathy between uncle and nephew, there may have been an element of one-upmanship on both sides.

Apart from those who were entitled to the civil uniform as described above, there were, and are, at court, a number of officials who have acquired for themselves over the years special uniforms for state occasions. Many appointments in the Royal Household have been abolished or fallen into desuetude: some are only activated at coronations. Among these last is the Queen's Champion, who originally rode on a horse into the coronation banquet clad in full armour, but who now appears in the Abbey in military uniform (assuming he is, like the present holder of the hereditary office, a soldier) and carries a silken flag.

One can only lament the disappearance of the King's Cock and Cryer whose duty it was during Lent to "crow" the hours instead of

104. Her Majesty's Rat Catcher. 1850s. (After illustration in H. Mayhew, *London Labour and the London Poor*, 1851)

105. The King's Herb
Woman. 1821. (After
Naylor, *Coronation of
George IV*, 1824–39)

crying them in the usual manner of the watchmen. He last performed
for George I, but the office survived until 1822 at £60 per annum: at
George IV's coronation he appeared in a silver gilt badge, although he
"had no duties to perform". And what of the Royal Rat Catcher, clad
in 1758 in a "crimson cloth coat guarded with blue velvet and embroidery, richly on back and breast, with His Majesty's Letters and
Crowns, and on the arms with Rats and Wheatsheaf" (Sheppard,
St James's Palace)? A century later the ratcatcher used to wear "a
costume of white leather breeches, and a green coat and a scarlet waistcoat, and a gold band round my hat, and a belt across my shoulder . . .
the uniform of the Queen's rat-catcher" (Mayhew, *London Labour and
the London Poor*). We are surely the poorer for the demise of the
Herbwoman and her Maids: these ladies appeared at Coronations,
strewing sweet herbs and flowers about the floor of Westminster Hall.
They seem to have worn ordinary dress of the day though for James II
they also wore hoods. The herbwoman herself had an allowance annually of scarlet cloth and at George IV's coronation, her last
appearance, she is shown wearing a scarlet mantle over her fashionable
high-waisted gown.

Of these appointments carrying a special uniform that have survived
economies, egalitarianism and expediency, it is proposed briefly to
deal with those most frequently seen and which are not described in
other chapters.

CONSULAR OFFICIALS

As well as the Diplomatic, the Consular Service is also in possession of full dress and levee dress (half dress in 1898). The coatee for both is blue cloth, prussian collar, single breasted buttoning with nine frosted gilt buttons of royal arms; there are two more buttons on the back waist and two more on the coat tails. Consul-generals and consuls have embroidered gold and silver lace on the collar, cuffs, pocket flaps and back; two and a half inches wide for the consul-generals and two inches for consuls. Vice-consuls have one and a half inches of embroidery on cuffs and front half of the collar only. All wear white breeches and stockings and patent court shoes with gilt buckles for full dress, and trousers with silver lace stripes and patent military boots for levee dress. Consul-generals' stripes are two and a quarter inches, inferior ranks one and three quarter inches wide. Hats are black beaver cocked, with a black cockade silver bullion loops and gold tassels. Consul-generals have treble loops and also a border of black ostrich feathers: others have double or single loops and no feathers. A blue great coat or cloak and a blue detachable cape for outdoor wear are available. Full dress is for court wear in England: levee dress may be worn abroad as well as at home. It should be noted that British subjects who are employed as consular officials of foreign countries may attend court and levees in their official capacity in the consular uniform of the country they represent.

MASTER OF THE HORSE

The Master of the Horse, one of the three principal officers in the household hierarchy, was originally responsible for all matters relating to the monarch's horses and stables, and also of his travels. These duties are nowadays carried out by the Royal Mews Department. George Monk, Duke of Albemarle, was Master of the Horse to King Charles II on the Restoration, and on the day before the coronation "rode bare after the King, and led in his hand a spare horse, as being Master of the Horse". From contemporary prints it appears that "bare" meant that his head was uncovered. He is shown mounted, in half-armour, with a periwig and a broad lace falling band or collar coming down over his breast-plate. He is hatless, with a cloak, and he carries a short staff or wand of office.

By the nineteenth century a cavalry-like uniform of scarlet tunic with blue velvet collar and cuffs, gold embroidery, shoulder cords, breeches or pantaloons, had evolved. In 1908 and 1912 the uniform is much the same: the detail of embroidery is given as seventeen double bows of gold plait, arranged on the front in an hour glass pattern, wide at the shoulders, narrow at waist, and widening again on the tunic skirts; four double chevrons of gold plait, with four buttons on each cuff; embroidery on the collar and back skirts; nine buttons, but actual fastening by hooks and eyes; a general's cocked hat with white and red swan's feather plumes; white leather pantaloons; Life Guard jack boots. For levees a tunic without the front embroidery and made to button was worn with red striped overalls and Wellington boots. By 1937, white leather breeches, Life Guard's pattern, were substituted for the pantaloons.

PAGES OF HONOUR AND PAGES IN WAITING

Pages in the Middle Ages were boys of good family who served the king or a great lord in return for an aristocratic upbringing, food and clothes. Under Henry VIII the royal pages had to do a certain amount of menial housework, as well as performing personal service to the King, and running errands for the Lord Chamberlain. Later their duties became less onerous and more decorative. In modern days the Royal Pages of Honour appear at state functions such as the Opening of Parliament, and those of the nobility are apparently only recruited for coronations.

In earlier days the pages' clothes were the normal fashionable dress: Henry VIII's page had velvet and satin doublets, and a century or so later the Earl of Bedford was providing his page in the 1670s and 1680s with periwigs, stockings, hats, shoe buckles, among other items of clothing. Like other ceremonial dress the page's uniform diverged from the fashion in the eighteenth century: the status also changed in part; the page of honour remaining as a gentleman appendage to royalty, and the page in waiting to the nobility. The page became a domestic servant, albeit of a superior kind, but eventually descending to the staff of hotels and the like.

Although the pages' clothes were originally of the fashionable cut, they would be in the livery colours of the family they served. One result of this in time was the alteration of livery colours at coronations if they

106. Page of Honour. 1821. (After
Naylor, *Coronation of George IV,*
1824–39)

were similar to the royal livery of scarlet. In 1937 the Earl Marshal's
Regulations included:

> Pages: waiting on Peers are to wear the same pattern of clothes as the
> Pages of Honour wear, but of the Livery colour of the Lords ... they
> attend ... The Royal liveries being scarlet and gold, the use of this
> combination of colours is restricted to the Pages of Honour, and in the
> case of a Peer whose colours are scarlet and gold, for scarlet some
> variant, such as Murrey or Claret should be used.

At King George IV's coronation in 1821 the Pages of Honour, like
all the other participants, wore "Elizabethan" dress; paned trunk hose,
doublet, cape, ruff and plumed hat, in red and white and gold. The
pages of the nobility wore similar clothes in their respective livery
colours.

Ten years later at King William IV's coronation the Pages of
Honour had "a scarlet tunic with standing collar and black stock, no
waistcoat, white breeches and silk stockings, gilt buckles both knees
and shoes, and a blue sash – expense under £20". (Gore, *Creevey's Life
and Times*.)

At the beginning of the twentieth century the dress of a Page of Honour was a scarlet single-breasted "frock", knee length, full skirted, frogged and edged with gold lace, blue velvet cuffs, gold laced, as were the pocket flaps. There were white ribbons and cords on the right shoulder, descended from the late seventeenth-century "shoulder knot", originally worn by fashionable gentlemen, but after 1700 remaining as a part of livery only. With the frock were worn white kerseymere breeches, as for household uniform, white silk stockings and black court shoes with red heels and gilt buckles matching similar buckles on the breeches, of household pattern. There was now a long white satin, gold laced waistcoat worn beneath the frock. Lace cravat

107. Page of Honour, carrying coronet of a Royal Duke at the Coronation of H.M. the Queen. 1953. (Painting by Elisabeth Grant)

and ruffles, short cross hilted sword, a three cornered hat, gold laced and edged with scarlet feathers and white gloves completed the outfit. This is the same dress as worn today. A complete outfit, dating from about 1912 is to be seen at Claydon House, seat of the Verney family.

The Museum of London has the livery of the Page of the Master of the Horse, worn at coronations of both King George V and King George VI: this is an eighteenth-century style dark blue coat, with light blue cuffs and silver laced edges and frogging, the rest much the same as for the Royal Pages of Honour.

GOVERNORS GENERAL, HIGH COMMISSIONERS,
etc.

If these posts were held by naval or military officers, service uniform was worn on all occasions. For civilians, civil uniform was laid down in the early twentieth century with the addition of lord lieutenants' uniforms for wear, by special permission, at reviews and inspections in the colonies. The 1912 edition of *Dress Worn at Court*, however, details a special uniform for governors general, service uniform being restricted to admirals and generals only, subsequently extended to major-generals and equivalent ranks in the navy and air force.

The uniform consisted of a dark blue cloth coatee with cutaway skirts, turned back and edged with white, double breasted with two rows of nine silver buttons. Collar, cuffs, and pocket flaps were scarlet and trimmed with silver lace, as was the bottom of the coat-tails. The epaulettes and sword belt were silver. Dark blue overalls with a two and a half inch silver lace stripe were worn with Wellington boots. Black silk cocked hat with crimson and silver decoration and white and red swan's feather plume.

This uniform was modified in 1959, with less silver lace on the coat and red stripes instead of silver on overalls or trousers. Lieutenant governors and below were entitled to second or third class civil uniform.

INDIAN DRESS

Instead of civil uniform, Indian gentlemen holding positions in the Indian Civil Service were entitled to wear either "the national dress which they are accustomed to wear on ceremonial occasions", or merely to substitute the turban or pagre (or puggree) for the cocked hat. They could also wear a blue coat buttoning from the neck to below the waist, worn with white trousers or pyjamas and the native head-dress. (*Dress Worn at Court* – various editions.)

KING'S MESSENGERS

King's (queen's) Foreign Service messengers were entitled to fifth class civil uniform: with it was worn the distinctive greyhound badge. In 1929 they were upgraded to fourth class uniform, with no mention of their greyhounds.

FOREIGN DIPLOMATS

Both Pepys and Evelyn saw the arrival of the Russian ambassadors accredited to King Charles II in 1662. According to Evelyn they were accompanied by attendants "clad in their vests after the Eastern manner". (Among other gifts for the King they brought a Pelican, "a melancholy water-fowl.") Pepys recorded that the son of one of the ambassadors (he says there were three) "was in the richest suit for pearl and tissue, that ever I did see, or shall, I believe".

Another embassy, in 1667, were also finely dressed: "their vests sumptuous, much embroider'd with pearls", according to Evelyn. Pepys states that the clothes of this embassy were not their own, but provided by the Czar, "which they dare not bring back dirty or spotted, but clean, or are in danger of being beaten .... Sir Charles Cotterell [the Master of the Ceremonies] says, when they are to have an audience they never venture to put on their clothes till he appears to come to fetch them ...." In 1795 the Turkish Ambassador appeared at St James's in native dress, including a jewel-studded turban; and in 1803 the ambassador from the French Republic wore the general's uniform of the consular guard.

The aim and object of such magnificence was of course to impress the monarch and court with the importance and wealth of those coun-tries represented by the envoys and embassies. During the nineteenth century this was toned down and a fairly uniform standard of diplomatic dress achieved, at least among European nations.

Mr Stevenson, the American Ambassador appointed in 1836 dressed, according to his wife, "buttoned up to the throat and his clothes fitted him to a charm – cocked hat very rich and handsome sword ... gold lace enough about him to adorn at least a dozen well dressed footmen . . . ." But, this splendour from across the Atlantic was not to last, and according to the Rev. Edgar Sheppard (*Memorials of St James's Palace*) "about the year 1858, plain black was adopted as the official dress at court ceremonials in this country". Another theory holds that the change occurred when James Buchanan, later President, was Ambassador in London from 1853 to 1856.

According to the 1898 *Dress Worn by Gentlemen at Her Majesty's Court*: "Foreign Ambassadors, Ministers, Attaches, etc., are expected to appear in the Uniforms or Dress according to the Regulation of their own Court, with white Breeches on Full Dress Occasions." By 1912 this had been altered to "Foreign Ambassadors, Ministers, etc. . . . are expected to appear at Court and on State occasions in the Uniforms or Dress prescribed by regulations of their own Court for functions of corresponding character". The 1912 edition added, "The Ambassador and Diplomatic Staff from the United States, Switzerland, and Cuba, wear Frock Dress at Courts, State Balls and Evening State Parties, but they wear Evening Dress with Trousers when Levee Dress is worn." The 1929 and the 1937 editions of *Dress Worn at Court* said: "Ambassador and personnel of the Embassy from the United States, and of some other Embassies and Legations . . . wear Evening Dress with breeches and stockings at Courts, State Balls and Evening State Parties . . ." or trousers as above. Since the last war the tendency all round is to plain evening dress with decorations.

Yeoman of the Guard

Officer
Gentleman at Arms

Ensign
Yeoman of the Guard

PLATE II

Royal Bodyguards. See text. (*Dress and Insignia Worn at Court*, 1929. Copyright of The Lord Chamberlain.)

CHAPTER VI

The Officers of Arms and the Earl Marshal: Gentlemen at Arms, Yeomen of the Guard and Yeoman Warders

The office of herald dates from the Age of Chivalry, and as early as the 1200s heralds wore coats showing their master's arms, both royal and private families employing these servants at first. Down to the middle of the sixteenth century it seems to have been customary for the heralds to be provided with the appropriate livery, and the last recorded issue was crimson velvet to a Garter King of Arms in 1640. For mourning, payments for black cloth were made up to the time of Nelson's funeral in 1806.

The original function of the herald seems to have been as an organiser of entertainments and ceremonies and especially of such affairs as the military tournament. They also carried important messages between men of high degree, were employed in delicate negotiations and diplomatic missions. With the rise of the science of arms and blazonry, they became experts in and authorities on all matters heraldic and in England they finally became incorporated as a "College of Arms" in 1483 by charter of Richard III. The college was re-established in 1555 under what is almost its present constitution. The supreme authority over the heralds was the Earl Marshal and the heralds were established in three grades, the chief being three Kings of Arms, Garter, Clarenceux and Norroy, then Windsor, Richmond, Somerset, Lancaster, York and Chester Heralds, and Rouge Croix, Blue Mantle, Rouge Dragon and Portcullis Pursuivants, or assistant heralds. Kings of Arms are also appointed, with limited functions, to the other orders of chivalry.

108. Tabard of Royal Arms worn by
William Bruge, *c* 1430. (British
Museum. Redrawn from Stowe MS.
594)

Garter King of Arms was established in 1415 by Henry V and given
the responsibility for the genealogy of the order: he was also senior to
the other Kings of Arms and Heralds. Clarenceux King of Arms was
responsible for heraldic affairs south of the River Trent and Norroy
King of Arms north of it. Heralds and pursuivants assisted.

From the thirteenth century heralds were wearing "coats of arms"
and at the end of the fourteenth and beginning of the fifteenth century
this took the shape of a "tabard", a contemporary over-garment from
the thirteenth century, which was sleeveless, with a front and back
panel, open sides fastened or sewn at the waist and perhaps below. It
eventually died out of general use and remained the costume of the
heralds alone, where it became their distinguishing characteristic.
Although regarded as sleeveless some illustrations show short "cape"
sleeves – as in the picture of *c*. 1430 of William Bruge, first Garter King
of Arms. In the herald's tabard the sleeves became mere flaps attached
only at the point of the shoulder, so the garment appears to consist of
two large panels front and back and two small side panels.

The material of which the tabards were made differed according to
the wearer's rank: in 1544 Kings of Arms had satin ones, heralds
damask and pursuivants sarsanet. At King James I's coronation velvet
tabards were worn by Kings of Arms, and satin by heralds. These were
all laced or embroidered. The pursuivants, however, had to make do

with mere painted damask. The embroidery or painting took the form of the royal arms of the period on the back, front and sleeves.

In addition to the tabard the Kings of Arms and heralds wore collars of Ss – the livery collar of the house of Lancaster. Kings of Arms and Garters had crowns of gold, and Norroy and Clarenceux crowns of silver gilt. Since 1904, however, Garter has only got a silver gilt one like the others. The present pattern of crowns, of sixteen acanthus leaves, alternately tall and short, was introduced in Charles I's reign, with a slight variation in 1720 from an engrailed to a straight rim. The crowns are inscribed with words from Psalm 51; "Miserare mei Deus secundum magnam tuam misericordiam" (Have mercy upon me, O God, after thy great goodness). Garter has also carried a silver or gold rod since 1522. It has been noted that in his capacity of an Officer of the Order, Garter has a special mantle. By 1624 the pursuivants' tabards were also embroidered and the three grades of material, velvet, satin and damask as used at James I's coronation, were still in use and still are today.

Down to the 1880s tabards and insignia were provided by the government for newly created officers of arms, but from that time

109. A herald, late seventeenth century. Tabard of Royal Arms over normal contemporary dress. (Redrawn after Lely. See British Museum, *Catalogue of British Drawings*)

onwards the issue has stopped. A stock is now held by the Lord Chamberlain from which loans are made "during the tenure of office".

The tabard of Sir William Dugdale, Norroy King of Arms 1660, is in possession of the family still and is the oldest known surviving English specimen. The Victoria and Albert Museum have that worn by the two John Anstis, father and son, in the early and mid eighteenth century, and the Museum of London has a silk damask pursuivant's tabard of the reign of George III.

It should be noted that up until about 1672 the pursuivants wore their tabards "athwartships" – with the sleeve panels hanging back and front and the back and front panels over the shoulder and hanging down the sides. This is a reminder of the Elizabethan habit of wearing the mandilion, another open-sided tabard-like garment with false sleeves, "colley-westonward", i.e. sleeves hanging down back and front. The Garter procession pictured in 1672 shows this practice: but in the processions of 1670 and 1687 they wear them in the normal manner, as they did at the coronation in 1689.

Despite his golden (or silver-gilt) crown, Garter is represented bareheaded in the procession shown in Ogilby's "Coronation of

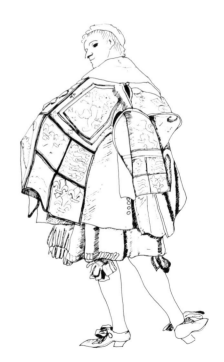

110. A Pursuivant, late seventeenth century, wearing his tabard "colley-westonward", i.e. sleeves hanging down back and front. (Redrawn after Lely. See British Museum, *Catalogue of British Drawings*)

111. John Warburton, Somerset Herald 1720–59. Tabard with Royal Arms of Hanoverian period and collar of Ss. 1746. (From mezzotint by Andrew Miller after a painting by Vandergucht)

Charles II". In the 1672 Garter procession the heralds and pursuivants are shown bareheaded, but carrying normal wide-brimmed, medium crowned hats. In the early eighteenth century the three-cornered hat was worn, as shown by Joseph Highman's drawings of the Bath procession of 1725; though in one of his preliminary sketches of the banqueting hall they are again bareheaded. Wigs were, of course, used at this period. A rather fancy representation of heralds proclaiming the Peace of Versailles and Recognition of American Independence in 1783 has them on horseback, hatless, but be-wigged. Up to 1805 the heralds had claimed exception from the hair powder tax on the grounds that they were Royal "menial servants".

In 1902 a black velvet hat or bonnet with a soft crown and turned-up brim, with a Tudor rose and crown badge was introduced for wear on certain state occasions. At other times black cocked hats are worn, as with household dress. Garter's hat has a white ostrich feather border, the other Kings of Arms, heralds and pursuivants have black feathers.

The uniform worn under the tabard is a scarlet cloth tailed coatee with blue-velvet collar and cuffs, hook and eye front fastening, but

112. The Earl Marshal (centre in coatee and trousers) next to Garter King of Arms bearing his gold sceptre or rod. Kings of Arms, Heralds and Pursuivants, the latter without collars of Ss. Left foreground, Household Cavalry trumpeters in state dress. Gentlemen at Arms and Yeomen of the Guard in rear. 1897. (*Illustrated London News*, 16 October 1897)

with nine dummy buttons on the front and four more on the skirts behind. The front, edges, back, tails, collar, cuffs and pockets are embroidered in gold varying with rank: Garter is the most resplendent. Breeches, stockings, shoes, buckles, sword and sword knot are as for household dress, except that on certain occasions, as the Opening of Parliament, black breeches and stockings are worn. A levee dress with blue trousers with gold stripes is also provided.

This pattern of uniform for the heralds was introduced and approved by Queen Victoria in 1849, before that a dark blue uniform was authorised by William IV in 1831. Before 1831 the under dress of the officers of arms was the normal contemporary gentleman's clothes. Up to the late seventeenth century mourning gowns with hoods were worn by heralds attending funerals: this again was common form for mourners. It may be noted that until this time, and even, in a few instances, during the eighteenth century, the heralds would attend and even organise private funerals. Pictures of the officers of arms at the funeral of the Duke of Albemarle in 1670 seem to indicate that at these solemnities collars of Ss were not worn, as private, not state, functions. But even at state funerals the heralds did not always wear their full habits – at the Prince Consort's funeral in December 1861, "Garter King at Arms was indeed present and took his customary part . . . but . . . wore no splendid tabard, no gewgaw crown. Like every other assistant at this sad solemnity, he was in plain evening dress, wearing only his golden collar and badge and carrying his golden sceptre or baton of command." (*Daily Telegraph*, 24 December 1861.)

113. Provincial King of Arms, tabard over levee dress with trousers: black velvet hat of 1902 pattern. 1937. (Redrawn from contemporary photograph)

114. Heralds at the funeral
of the Duke of Albemarle in
mourning gowns and hoods
under their tabards and
carrying spurs and gloves of
the deceased. 1670.
(Redrawn from engraving in
Francis Sandford, ... *Inter-
ment of George, Duke of
Albemarle*, 1670)

At least up to the Civil War it was customary for the officers of arms
to attend royal christenings carrying their tabards over their arms, and
not putting them on until the actual moment of baptism. The Calender
of State Papers records the christening of the Duke of York on
24 November 1633, and says, "the Officers of Arms put on their coats
which before they bare on their arms" at the instant the Archbishop of
Canterbury named the Prince.

115. Herald at christening of a Royal
Child carrying a tabard over his arm
and wearing gown with hanging
sleeves and flat cap. Late sixteenth
century. (Redrawn from British
Museum MS. Stowe 583)

The collars of Ss were gilt for Kings of Arms and silver for heralds. In addition Garter wears a triple gold chain carrying the Garter badge and Clarenceux and Norroy Kings of Arms have a similar chain bearing their appropriate badge, which, in the case of the Provincial Kings, was worn at courts and levees, without the collar. Heralds had no chain or badge, and only wore the collar at state ceremonies.

In 1906 the Provincial Kings, heralds and pursuivants, were given a short ebony baton, gilt mounted and carrying their badge of office. In 1953 these were replaced by white staves with gilt metal handles and at the top a gilt coroneted blue dove. A blue cloth caped greatcoat, similar to those of the household, is also worn. The buttons on the uniforms of officers of arms bear the royal cipher and imperial crown.

The Earl Marshal of England, one of the great officers of state, is, as mentioned above, the supreme authority of the College of Arms and the Court of Chivalry (a court to determine cases of precedence, armorial disputes), and is, today, responsible for all state ceremonial.

116. Garter King of Arms wearing tabard over full dress uniform and wearing crown, collar of Ss and gold Garter chain. Carrying gold rod. 1953. (Painting by Elisabeth Grant)

117. Earl Marshal wearing Duke's
coronation mantle over scarlet and
gold uniform of his office. Collar,
star and garter of the Garter are worn
and baton carried. 1953. (Painting by
Elisabeth Grant)

For many centuries the office has been hereditary to the Dukes of
Norfolk, an inheritance confirmed to the Howard family by King
Charles II in 1672.

The first duke, John Howard, killed at Bosworth in 1485, is depicted
in armour wearing a short coat of arms. His sixteenth-century
successor wore normal dress, sometimes with a fur lined gown, Tudor
flat cap, garter collar, and carried the white rod and black-tipped
baton which were the Earl Marshal's insignia. Seventeenth-century
engravings show the Earl Marshal at coronations in his peer's robes,
worn over coat and breeches, periwig and Garter insignia, carrying his
baton. When a uniform was established in the early nineteenth century
it was a scarlet coatee, single breasted, with gold embroidery,
aiguillette, and blue-black velvet collar and cuffs. Breeches, hose, shoes
and a cocked hat.

Dress Worn at Court details a scarlet coatee, collar and cuffs of blue-
black velvet; nine false buttons and hooks and eyes; gold embroidery

on edges, front, collar, cuffs, pockets, back, skirts, all as first class household uniform; gold aiguillette and scarlet silk linings; breeches, stockings, and shoes, all as for the first class household, as was the hat, cocked, with white ostrich feather border. For mounted duties white cord breeches and patent leather jackboots were worn; and special horse furniture was also prescribed. After the First World War the embroidery and hat were altered to conform with the new class of Privy Councillor's household uniform.

A levee dress with less gold lace on the coatee, worn with blue trousers with a two and a half inch gold oak leaf lace stripe is also worn; the late Duke of Norfolk wearing it for some of the pre-coronation conferences in 1953 and 1937. On occasions such as a coronation the full dress is worn under the ducal robes. Whenever the Earl Marshal is on duty he carries his insignia, a gold baton, tipped at each end with ebony.

THE HONOURABLE CORPS OF GENTLEMEN OF ARMS

This royal bodyguard was raised by King Henry VIII in 1539/40. They were as originally Gentlemen Pensioners, and are recorded as "appareled in velvet and chains of gold," in Hall's *Chronicle*.

They are said to have worn black cloaks and gold chains in 1580 under Elizabeth I (Curling, *Some Accounts of the Ancient Corps of Gentlemen at Arms*). They do not ever seem to have been regarded as part of the military establishment, but of the Royal Household, and this was confirmed in 1874 in a letter from the Lord Chamberlain, to the Captain of the Corps: "I have received Her Majesty's commands to make it distinctly understood that the Corps is a Houshold Corps in the department of the Lord Chamberlain". Quoted in Sanderman, *The Spears of Honour and the Gentlemen Pensioners*. An exception to the above seems to have been at the coronation of James II when the Corps wore their hats in Westminster Hall on His Majesty's orders as they were a military body but this is an isolated case.

During the Commonwealth Cromwell either retained them or raised a similar bodyguard and, upon the Restoration, the Corps was almost immediately re-embodied by Charles II. During the seventeenth century the dress seems to have been buff coats and perhaps breastplates. (The latter certainly had to be provided, among other equipment, by the pensioners.)

Ashmole's plates of 1672 show the Band of Pensioners at the Garter celebrations. They are in procession wearing coats, waistcoats and full breeches, the coats open from the neck down, plain falling bands, long hair or periwigs, a sword supported by a baldrick, and round hats carried under the left arm: they carry ceremonial long axes. Indoors at the Garter Feast the Pensioners are wearing short capes.

The early eighteenth century saw the pensioners in crimson uniform, and in 1711 or 1712 they approached the Lord High Treasurer and asked for the payment of their allowances which had fallen into arrears. One reason they advanced for payment of their money was that "to maintain the honour of their posts they must be at great expense to new clothe themselves on Her Majesty's [Queen Anne] happy birthday". In 1714 they were mourning in April and again in August for the Queen herself. Again they complained of the cost of their clothes, for the Queen's birthday, funeral, and then "rich clothes" for George I's coronation.

Mourning seems to have been "a regimental coat", black waistcoat, breeches and stockings, and a mourning sword with a plain hilt. In 1727 they were again in mourning for the monarch "a scarlet coat trimmed with black, with a black cloth waistcoat and breeches . . . you must also put your axe into mourning". The axe, a long handled, ceremonial pole axe type with, from Charles II's day, a pike-head, had the shaft covered with crimson velvet and gilt nails; for mourning these were replaced by black velvet and nails.

The Band of Pensioners in the early eighteenth century seemed to limit their attendance to Sundays, Christmas, Easter and the sovereign's birthday. Originally fifty, their number was reduced to forty in 1670, and for most ordinary appearances only twenty were on duty. George II required their presence at the, apparently, daily levees held by him, and also at the Queen's drawing rooms. The year 1737 saw them in mourning for Queen Caroline, more elaborately than before, with crape hat-bands, black swords, buttons and buckles, shammy gloves and cambric weepers (that is, loose white cuffs worn over the coat sleeve which could be used in lieu of a pocket handkerchief).

In 1741 the "Brigadier" wig was ordered to be worn, and four years later light grey stockings were introduced, replacing the red ones said to have been brought in under George I. Headwear was the usual eighteenth-century three-cornered hat, edged with gold. In all, the uniform was much the same as that of the contemporary infantry officer.

When George III died the order of mourning for the Pensioners was only a crape band on the left arm. George IV's coronation, of course, saw the Pensioners in "Elizabethan" dress. The Museum of London has the costume worn by the Harbinger of the Band, an office filled in 1821

118. His Majesty's Band of Gentlemen Pensioners. Red coat heavily gold laced with deep turned back cuffs, breeches (not visible) and stockings with buckled shoes, Ceremonial Pole-Axe, sword and three-cornered cocked hat. 1742. (*A Representation of the clothing of his Majesty's Household etc.*, 1742. British Library)

by a Colonel Samuel Wilson. He had a red and blue velvet doublet, with puffed and paned sleeves and wings, matching breeches with silk ribbon and gold lace trimming, a mini-cape of gold laced red velvet, white satin shoes with red heels and red, white and blue rosettes, and a gold laced belt.

In the early days, Gentlemen Pensioners were recruited from younger men and it was considered a step towards a commission in the regular army: by the time of George IV and William IV this order of things was reversed and serving or retired officers were appointed to the Band, which was renamed by King William IV "The Honourable Corps of Gentlemen at Arms". At this time the uniform was similar to that of the Foot Guards: red coatee, blue trousers with gold stripe in the winter and white trousers in the summer, and a shako. At the coronation of Queen Victoria in 1838 the Gentlemen at Arms wore the above coatee and trousers, a shako with the VR cipher, a white belt and a cavalry pouch.

In 1849 the Gentlemen asked for, and were granted, a cavalry helmet, described by the *Illustrated London News* of 3 March as of "classic design", gilt, highly embossed and ornamented with the royal arms, a silver star in front and a white plume. Curling (*Some Accounts of*

119. Gentleman at Arms wearing
early nineteenth century uniform and
helmet of pattern introduced 1849.
(After *Illustrated London News*,
8 March 1849)

the Ancient Corps of Gentlemen at Arms) says that at this time they wore a
scarlet coatee faced with blue velvet, collar and cuffs gold embroidered, gold embroidered belt and pouch, blue trousers with a gold
oak-leaf lace stripe, a heavy cavalry sash, sword and gold sling-belt,
boots and spurs.

Dress Worn at Court for 1908 and 1912 details the uniform as:

> "scarlet cloth single breasted [coatee]. Blue velvet collar, cuffs and turn-
> back on skirts. Gold embroidery on collar and cuffs, with portcullis in
> silver on collar. Gold embroidered wreath and crown and portcullis in
> silver on back skirts. Nine buttons down front and two at waist behind.
> Skirts lined blue silk .... Trousers, blue cloth with gold lace ... 2 inch
> stripes, black leather footstraps. For Officers: oakleaf lace 2½ inches wide.
>
> Helmet – gilt metal, with scroll and leaf ornaments. Front ornament
> gilt Royal Arms quartering within the Garter, mounted on a silver cut
> star. Gilt chin-scales, with lion head bosses.

The helmet plume was eighteen inches long, in white swan feathers.
The epaulettes were of boxed gold bullion, gilt, and gold lace with a
Tudor portcullis in silver embroidery. The officers also wear gold gimp

cord aiguillettes on the right shoulder. All buttons show garter and star and portcullis.

The sword is a steel, cavalry pattern sword, with a steel scabbard, and a gold knot, on one inch gold lace slings from a web waist belt worn under a gold and red waist sash, with tasselled end hanging down eighteen inches. The shoulder belt is of two and a quarter inch gold lace while the officers have two and a half inches of oakleaf pattern lace. The blue velvet pouch bears the royal cipher and crown in gold, and gold lace edge: the officers have an oak leaf wreath and lace. They wear wellington boots with straight, gilt spurs, and white gauntlet gloves.

A scarlet-banded blue forage cap with gold embroidered black patent leather peak is also provided, as is a double breasted blue cloak with a detachable cape; collar, cuffs and lining in scarlet. The officers have a gold and blue collar patch. On the coatee epaulettes and the shoulder straps of the cloak are embroidered the badges of rank that the Gentlemen held in the army.

On appointment the captain is given a gold stick by the sovereign: the lieutenant, standard bearer and clerk of the cheque and adjutant have silver sticks. These sticks are of black ebony with gold or silver mounts. The sub-officer, the old harbinger, receives an ivory headed stick from the captain on appointment. For mess dress, household evening dress is worn.

THE QUEEN'S BODYGUARD OF THE YEOMEN OF THE GUARD AND THE YEOMEN WARDS OF THE TOWER

There exists a persistent belief that the Yeoman of today is dressed in clothes which have not altered since his early Tudor forebears, but this is a myth. We do not know what livery was worn in 1485 when Henry VII founded the bodyguard, but at the wedding of Prince Arthur in 1501 they are said to have worn jackets of white and green damask (similar garments in the same colours are also recorded as being worn by seamen, or soldiers, fighting in the royal ships, at about the same time). White and green were favourite colours of the Tudors, and as late as 1556 under Queen Mary the Gentlemen Pensioners had each to provide three men-at-arms in green and white livery. According to Charles Beard, the historian of the early dress and arms of the Yeomen, there is no evidence that they wore any kind of red uniform before 1514. (*Archaeological Journal* Vol. LXXXVII, 1928.)

120. Yeoman of the Guard. Long skirted doublet with Tudor Crown and Rose on chest, neckruff. 1585. (Effigy of Robert Rampston said to have been formerly at Chingford, Essex, after engraving in Clinch, *English Costume*, 1909)

Sandeman in his *Spears of Honour* quotes an account of the Field of the Cloth of Gold in 1520, when Henry VIII was accompanied by a guard wearing red coats with a rose and crown on the breast; and another which mentions archers of the King's Guard in red cloth jackets with a gold rose before and behind. From this date until about the mid seventeenth century it seems that the guard possessed three or more livery doublets or coats of various colours and degrees of richness.

Hollar's engraving of the coronation procession of Charles II in 1661 shows the Yeomen of the Guard in very short, but full, skirted, fitted coats or doublets with sleeves very full to the elbow and thence close-fitting to the wrist. For collars they wear a plain deep falling band after the fashion of the day. Wide breeches, open at the knee were worn with "canons", wide frills on the stocking tops turned down over the garters to fall as flounces below the knees, and shoes. The breeches, also in the fashion, were trimmed with bunches of ribbons. The doublets or coats were guarded with black velvet and narrow lace, and had the rose and crown embroidered at front and back. The Yeomen carried high crowned, wide flat-brimmed hats decorated with knots of ribbon.

Sandford's *Coronation of James II* describes the Yeomen at the coronation in 1685 as having coats of red broad cloth with full skirts gathered at the waist, and large sleeves gathered at shoulder and wrist.

The breeches, he says, were of similar material and "large". The rose and crown, royal cipher and "Dieu et mon droit" were embroidered back and front. Black velvet bonnets with crimson and blue ribbon, grey worsted stockings and buff waist belts were worn. The change to this new style of long-skirted doublet or coat seems to have taken place about 1670, for the *Angliae Notitia* edition of that year talks of scarlet coats, "down to the knee" and black velvet round caps, "according to the mode used in the reign of Henry VIII". An engraving by Van Hove of 1679 shows similar length coats, full sleeves, full breeches and black velvet "bonnets", and cravats or neckcloths.

A similar dress is shown in the engraving of King William III and Queen Mary's coronation procession in 1689, but no cipher or motto accompanies the rose and crown. On the other hand a woodcut of the same year illustrating a popular patriotic song shows the joint monarchs, enthroned, and with two Yeoman in attendance. The Yeomen's dress is as described above, but on their chests are the letters WR alone with no motto, or rose and crown. In both cases, however, the artist's observation may be at fault. In all the above cases the coats and breeches are guarded with black velvet.

The style of dress introduced about 1670 seems to have been a conscious effort to clothe the Yeomen of the Guard in what was then considered the correct Tudor style. The knee length coats with gathered skirts certainly resembled the sixteenth-century "base coat", with its knee length skirts falling in tubular pleats or folds from the waist (these skirts were sometimes without a body and worn like a kilt over armour by military men) as seen in various portraits of King Henry VIII. The black "bonnet" is based upon the flat cap introduced by Henry VIII. The breeches and stockings are of a later date. But throughout the period under survey the front of the doublet or coat, where the varying devices were embroidered, has presented an unbroken surface across the body; this panel is the "plackard" of fifteenth- and sixteenth-century fashion, when it was a chest-piece to cover up the gap in the front of the low, wide necked, doublet or jacket. It has been retained, outlined by guards of velvet and gold lace, and to this day, the doublet buttons on the left shoulder and down the left side. Shoes, cravats, and in some cases apparently, periwigs, are, however, firmly of the late seventeenth-century style.

The styles as described above remained fairly constant throughout the eighteenth century although under Queen Anne the cravat seems to have been abandoned. In the painting by Peter Angelis of the Queen and the Knights of the Garter in 1713 two Yeomen reveal a small amount of shirt collar only above the neckline of the coat.

121. Yeoman of the Guard at Knights of the Garter ceremony. Royal cipher, motto, rose and thistle and Tudor crown. 1713. (Queen Anne and Knights of the Garter, by Peter Angelis, National Portrait Gallery)

From the early seventeenth century the crown shown on the coat was that known as "St Edward's"; Queen Anne restored the Tudor design and also, at the Union of England and Scotland in 1707, added a thistle to the rose.

Later in the eighteenth century the crown was changed back to the St Edward design, although a picture of a Yeoman dated 1813 in *Picturesque Reproductions of the Dress and Manners of the English* by William Alexander shows the Tudor crown. In this picture the yeoman also wears a small white collar and a baldrick or shoulder belt, another eighteenth century innovation (it can be seen in a drawing of the Royal Maundy ceremony in 1733), as was the wearing of white stockings for a time.

In 1801, on the Union with Ireland, the shamrock was added to the rose and thistle, and in 1821, at his coronation, King George IV re-introduced the Elizabethan ruff to accord with the general character of that event. The last previous appearance of the ruff was about 1630.

122. Yeoman of the Guard of George II, St Edward's Crown surmounting insignia. No shoulder belt is shown, although earlier drawings show it. 1742. (*A Representation of the Clothing of his Majesty's Household etc.*, 1742. British Library)

123. Yeoman of the Guard at Coronation of George IV showing the re-introduced ruff. He is described as the Lieutenant, but though carrying a silver-headed stick his dress is that of a Yeoman, except for the plumed hat. 1821. (From a contemporary drawing, unreferenced, reproduced in J. Perkins, *The Coronation Book*, 1902)

At the beginning of the present century King Edward VII again changed the crown back to the Tudor one; apart from that the uniform has remained unaltered except for the necessary amendments to the royal cipher.

In 1912 *Dress Worn at Court* details the dress of the "King's Bodyguard of the Yeomen of the Guard" as

> a scarlet cloth Tudor doublet, embroidered, back and front cut whole. Full sleeves gathered into wrist band with one hole and small button. Four skirts pleated into waist. Three small buttons and holes on left shoulder, and five small buttons and holes on left side seam. Blue velvet and gold lace shoulder strap on left shoulder with one large button.

(This shoulder strap is not in evidence in photographs and other representations of the Yeomen.)

The doublet is embroidered with the rose, thistle, shamrock, with a scroll underneath (no wording mentioned) and a Tudor crown above. The letters GR, are at each side of the flowers. The guards are described as blue velvet and gold lace. The skirts of the doublet are lined with blue, the rest with white.

Sergeant majors have four three-quarter-inch gold lace chevrons with a crown over, on the right arm. This badge goes back to the nineteenth century at least. The breeches are scarlet cloth, not guarded, with gold lace garters and gilt buckles, and red, white and blue rosettes at the knees. Scarlet merino stockings, patent leather Oxford shoes with buckles and red, white and blue ribbon rosettes are worn. A white muslin four-row ruff three inches deep, is goffered into a neck band with a drawstring. White buckskin gloves and a scarlet lined blue, hooded, Inverness cloak with a gilt rose clasp and eight gilt buttons are worn. The hat is of black velvet, flat brimmed, "Tudor" style, with a five inch crown and two-and-three-quarter inch brim, with "red white and blue ribbons in bows all round close above brim". The weapons carried are a sword and a partizan, an infantry weapon described by Kelly and Schwabe as "a short pike with a board blade with symmetrical side-flukes" (*Short History of Costume and Armour*). In place of the partizans the sergeant majors carry a silver topped, tasselled, black walking-stick.

The sword is suspended from a narrow leather waist belt three and a quarter inches wide decorated with scarlet cloth, blue velvet and gold lace with gilt fittings and a similarly decorated sword-frog. The sword itself is straight with a half-basket hilt, white grip and black leather scabbard, all with gilt fittings. The shoulder belt matches the sword belt but is of scarlet cloth without the leather backing of the sword belt.

It is secured by a blue ribbon tie and has a gilt swivel at the end. It is worn over the left shoulder.

The officers of the Yeomen are the captain, lieutenant, ensign, clerk-of-the-cheque and adjutant, and exons (from the French "exempt", that is, an officer taking over in the absence of senior officers). The officers have apparently always worn a different dress or uniform from the Yeomen: this was in line with general military practice and the officers of the guard in the seventeenth century are shown in fashionable coats, hats, cravats and periwigs. In the William and Mary coronation engraving of 1689 they look much the same as the captains of the Gentlemen Pensioners and of the Horse Guards.

Officers dress of the seventeenth and early eighteenth centuries in general was similar to fashionable civilian dress. Uniform emerged during the latter period, and the officers of the guard seemed to follow suit. During the century epaulettes appeared; at first on one shoulder only in the case of junior ranks, later, on both shoulders for all. Pictures of the early nineteenth century show the officers of the Yeomen of the Guard wearing military uniform. At the coronation of Queen Victoria in 1838 the officers are in red coatees, blue trousers and cocked hats, much the same as today, except that only a single epaulette is shown.

The twentieth-century editions of *Dress Worn at Court* describe the dress for the captain and officers as a scarlet cloth double breasted coatee with dark blue velvet collar and cuffs. Two rows of nine buttons on the front and two at the waist behind. Buttons on slashes of the mariner cuffs and on the pocket flaps are here called "sword flaps". The buttons have rose, shamrock and thistle on them, and the embroidery on collar, cuffs, pocket flaps and bottom of the coat tails uses the same device. Gold epaulettes are worn on the shoulders and gold aiguillettes on the right shoulder by the captain, lieutenant, ensign and adjutant, but not by the exons.

The trousers are blue with two and a half inch stripes of gold lace, and the hat is a black silk cocked hat with a General's plume of eleven inch white swan's feather, with red feather underneath. A straight sword, black scabbard, gilt mountings, is held by a blue velvet frog on a shoulder belt worn under the coatee. There is a gold and crimson waist belt or sash and white gloves, gilt spurs and black patent military boots are worn. For outdoor wear there is a blue caped cloak. Household evening dress is worn as mess dress.

The captain carries a gold mounted and tasselled ebony walking stick, and the other officers have similar sticks but mounted and tasselled with silver. These, known as Gold and Silver Stick, are presented by the Sovereign on the Officer's appointment.

YEOMEN WARDERS OF THE TOWER

The Yeomen Warders are an off-shoot of the Yeomen of the Guard, having originally been formed from a dozen or fifteen Yeomen left behind for duties when King Henry VIII vacated the Tower as a residence.

124. Her Majesty arriving for dinner at the Royal Artillery Mess, Woolwich, wearing riband and star of Garter with evening dress. The Master Gunner with riband and badge of the Bath. Yeoman Warders, ex-Gunners, on duty. (*Gunner* Magazine, January 1977)

125. Yeoman Warders of the Tower: full dress doublets worn with blue trousers. Sergeant Major on left. 1890s. (Cascell's *The Queen's London*, 1897)

The uniform of the Yeomen Warders is in all respects similar to that of the Yeomen of the Guard except that no shoulder belt is worn. It is said that the warders did not, however, catch up with the early changes in dress until the reign of King Edward VI. The story is that the Duke of Somerset, the Lord Protector, when imprisoned in the Tower in the years 1549–50, was so impressed by the Warders' excellence that he promised that when he was released he would see that they were granted the right "to weare the King's clothe as the yeomen of the guarde did". Somerset obtained his release, and caused the Warders of the Tower to be "sworn extraordinary of the guarde, and to weare the same livery they do; which had the beginning by this meanes" (Thomas Astle quoted in Pennant, *Some Account of London*).

Yeomen of the Guard do duties at royal functions on a rota basis: the Yeomen Warders are continually on duty at the Tower, where they act as both guards and guides. For these daily duties an undress blue uniform is worn with trousers: the coat is embroidered with the royal cipher only, and is cut on the lines of the scarlet dress coat. With the blue undress a blue and red hat with a blue and red cockade is worn.

Blue trousers have also, from some time in the nineteenth century, been worn on occasions with the scarlet dress coat. Officers wear a scarlet single-breasted tunic, blue trousers with red stripe, gold waist sash with tassels, and cocked hat with white and red ostrich plumes.

CHAPTER VII

Lord Warden and Barons of the Cinque Ports; Lords Lieutenant; Sheriffs; Chief Constables; Highland Dress; Brethren of Trinity House; The Order of St John

THE LORD WARDEN AND BARONS OF THE CINQUE PORTS

As late as 1912 it was the rule that "if the Lord Warden is entitled to wear uniform of a Lieutenant of a County, Deputy Lieutenant, the Royal Naval Reserve, or that of the Corporation of the Trinity House, one of these should be worn at Court functions, otherwise ordinary Court Dress . . . .

No official dress is prescribed for the Captains of the Port Castles or other Officers of the Cinque Ports".

The office of Warden was established by William I, it is suggested on the lines of the Roman *comes littoris Saxonii*, to control the narrow seas and the Kent and Sussex coastline. He combined, in early days, the offices of admiral, sheriff and lord lieutenant and the five ports of Dover, Sandwich, Hastings, Romney and Hythe enjoyed special rights in exchange for equally special duties. Other towns, notably Winchelsea and Rye were later added to the original five, but the ancient designation of Cinque Ports was retained.

After the First World War, however, an official dress for the Lord Warden is described, both in full dress and undress versions. Full dress was a naval pattern blue cloth tailed coatee, double breasted, with two

126. Lord Warden of the Cinque Ports. Sir Winston Churchill, K.G. wearing full dress uniform inspecting troops. The right épaulette had unfortunately become detached just before this photograph was taken. "Orders and decorations" in the form of riband, stars, neck badge and medals are worn. 1946. (Press Association)

rows of nine buttons each, two buttons back waist and two on coat tails, which were edged and turned back in scarlet. The collar, cuffs and pockets were scarlet with gold lace. The epaulettes were of naval pattern and bore the arms of the Cinque Ports, as did the buttons, the coat tails, where the arms are embroidered at the points, and the collar badges. Blue trousers had a one and three quarter inch gold stripe. The sword belt was gold and crimson. The sword was of naval pattern and cocked hat was worn.

The levee dress had a double breasted naval frock coat, red turn-down collar and cuffs, two rows of five buttons each, and four on the back of the coat and tails, a buff "cassimere" waistcoat, plain blue trousers, no stripe, and a cap with one row of gold lace on the peak. The cuffs on the coats were of the "mariner's" pattern, that is a round cuff with a vertical flap or slash with a scalloped edge and three buttons in a vertical line at the front.

The full dress uniform was worn by Sir Winston Churchill when, in 1946, he was installed as Lord Warden. On this occasion he wore only one epaulette, the other having fallen off *en route*.

The full dress and undress coats, and a pair of undress trousers, with the sword that belonged to the late Marquis of Reading (Lord Warden 1934–36) are in the collection of the Museum of London.

"Barons" of the Cinque Ports, one of the ancient offices, formerly appeared at coronations to carry a canopy over the monarch in his

127. Baron of the Cinque Ports as dressed at the coronation of King George IV, 1821. Surcoat of blue, lined and faced white, doublet and hose slashed scarlet, red stockings. (From contemporary illustration reproduced in Perkins, *The Coronation Book*, 1902)

progress to and from Westminster Hall. In the seventeenth century the dress was normal coat and breeches, with a gown complete with hanging sleeves and a flat, brimmed soft round hat or cap. The cap, apparently to enable both hands to grasp the supports of the canopy, was worn suspended on the left arm of the gown. With the abandonment of the procession the barons lost their jobs, but continued to claim their right to be present at coronations. In 1953 they appeared dressed in old style velvet court suits, cloaks, cross-hilted swords, and wearing a large, flat, beret-type cap.

LORDS LIEUTENANT: LORD-LIEUTENANTS

Lords lieutenant of counties would seem to have originated during the reign of Henry VIII, and were increased in number under Edward VI. They were originally military officers introduced "as standing representatives of the Crown to keep the Counties in military order" (Blackstone, *Laws of England*). Over the years they acquired civil functions, including that of appointing county magistrates and in 1908 King Edward VII granted them precedence over the high sheriffs. Within his county the lord lieutenant is the permanent representative of the Crown.

Originally the lieutenancy was not granted to every county: in the Tudor period there appear to have been only seventeen. Some of these held power in more than one county; for instance, under Philip and Mary, the Earl of Bedford was appointed "their Highness Lieutenant of the Counties of Dorset, Devon, Cornwall and their citie of Exeter".

In former days the lord lieutenant was responsible for the militia and up to 1871 he appointed its officers. With the creation of the Territorial Army in 1907, and later of the Auxiliary Airforce, its counterpart for the R.A.F., the Lord Lieutenant headed the county Territorial Association (later Territorial Army and Auxiliary Air Force Association). With the replacement of the T.A. by the Territorial and Volunteer Reserve in 1968, the county associations have disappeared and the lord lieutenant's responsibility thereby decreased, although they are all members of the new District T.A. and V.R. Associations and hold the presidency in turn. The original military status of the lord lieutenant is thus maintained, vis-a-vis the volunteer forces of the Crown.

Although popularly known for many years as "lord lieutenant" the title had properly been "Her (or His) Majesty's Lieutenant of and in the County of – " until the Local Government Act of 1972 (operative from 1 April 1974) when the style lord-lieutenant was for the first time officially used, and in hyphenated form. The plural has become "lord-lieutenants."

The same Act authorises also the appointment (a new one) of "lieutenants", if necessary, to be senior deputies and assistants to the lord-lieutenant. Both lord-lieutenants and lieutenants of counties are selected by the monarch and appointed under the Great Seal. Lord-lieutenants may appoint deputy lieutenants, and from the lieutenants or deputy lieutenants may appoint a vice lord-lieutenant (previously vice-lieutenant) to take over in case of absence or sickness.

Today the lord-lieutenancy is an honorary position demanding dedication, public spirit and hard work. Apart from duties connected with the volunteer forces the lord-lieutenant is responsible for preparing and co-ordinating visits of members of the royal family within his county, meeting and escorting them. He attends Regular Army parades and ceremonies if required; presents medals to individuals, awards to industry, civil charters etc.; attends parades of the St John's Ambulance, Royal British Legion and such organisations, memorial, civic and military church services; he heads various county and local organisations, convenes conferences and meetings and plays a leading part in charitable concerns, among many other activities.

As befitted their original military responsibilities, when a uniform, in today's sense, was introduced in about the year 1831, it closely resembled that of an army general, and for deputy and vice-lieutenants it was based on staff officers' pattern.

Previous to the introduction of this uniform lords lieutenant probably wore on official occasions a dress approximating to that of a

128. Lord Fairfax "General" of Yorkshire, mid seventeenth century. (After engraving from Fairholt after W. D. Fellowes, *Historical Sketches of Charles I*)

contemporary general officer – in the seventeenth century perhaps a buff coat, sash and cuirass or gorget (the throat-piece of armour retained as a badge of military rank long after armour ceased to be worn in the field of battle) and a baton. Ferdinand, Lord Fairfax, appointed Parliamentary "General" for Yorkshire was so dressed. Also during the Commonwealth we find Cromwell's Major-General Harrison arrayed in scarlet with a profusion of silver lace. Later in the century, after the introduction of coat and waistcoat, these garments, generally in scarlet or red were adopted by the army and cut on civilian lines. Generals no doubt wore more lace, gold or silver, than other officers, and perhaps more plumes in the broad-brimmed three cornered hat. The sash and baton remained.

Charles II, on his Restoration, confirmed the functions of the old militia and these county volunteers again came under the jurisdiction of the King's lieutenants of counties. Military uniform, which had really started during the Civil War, gradually crystallised, and the first official "Clothing Book" dates from 1742. I think it most likely that during this period, and up to the introduction of the early 1830s pattern of uniform, the lords lieutenant, as commanders of the county militia, wore a uniform based upon that of their militia regiments, suitably embellished to indicate their position.

In 1829 the officer's scarlet coatee, a short waisted, double-breasted coat with skirts at the back only, forming tails, acquired a new look. It became very tight fitting, was worn buttoned to the neck, where it had a high collar, and had "mariner" cuffs, with a vertical slash. The amount of gold or silver lace was considerably reduced and in 1830 gold lace was standardised for the Regular Army. Dark blue trousers came in with gold lace stripes. A variation of the trousers was overalls, tight fitting riding trousers worn strapped down over Wellington boots. This was the uniform for general officers, and in 1831 the lieutenants uniforms were like this, but with silver buttons and lace and with an ornament or badge on the back of the "tails" in the form of national heraldic devices; a rose, the Prince of Wales feathers, a thistle or shamrock. The deputy and vice-lieutenants had similar but less decorated coatees. We learn from Mary Frampton's Journal that when royalty visited the Duke of Devonshire at Chatsworth in 1843, "Mr Mundy and the four County Members were in a deputy-lieutenant's uniform and the Duke wore his handsome lord lieutenant's dress".

In 1855, at the end of the Crimean War, the coatee was replaced in the army generally by a rather long and loose fitting tunic with a collar much lower than the old coatee. Generals took to the tunic with the rest. Twenty years later, in 1875, deputy and vice-lieutenants of coun-

129. Viscount Maynard, Lord Lieutenant of Essex, 1825–65, wearing style of uniform introduced about 1831. The épaulettes bear a baton, sword and crown. The Rose of England appears on sword slings. The sword is not of the mameluke pattern. (Portrait by courtesy of C. H. Bullivant Esq., Essex Record Office)

ties changed to the tunic, to be followed in 1876 by the lieutenancy of the City of London, but county lords lieutenant had to wait until 1889 to catch up.

The new dress was a scarlet tunic, single breasted, with nine buttons and two at the waist behind and three smaller ones on the slashed mariner cuffs. The collar, cuffs, and slashes on the cuffs were of blue cloth and the slashes on the back skirts were of scarlet; all were embroidered with silver of oak, thistle, or shamrock pattern for English and Welsh, Scottish or Irish counties respectively. Although this description particularises cuff slashes of blue cloth, contemporary coloured illustrations show scarlet slashes, as on the skirt.

Blue cloth trousers, with two and a half inch silver lace of the appropriate floral design in stripes down the side seams were worn with the tunic. The hat was the black cocked pattern with a ten inch plume of white swan's feather with red under. A ''Mameluke'' sword (a sword with a plain cross-guard and a curved blade) of the type worn by general officers, and a brass scabbard were worn. The waist belt is described as one and a half inch Russian leather, with sword sling, and one inch square plate with a wreath encircling a VR and crown. The belt was ''embroidered same pattern as on tunic''. However, again, a coloured illustration issued by *The West End Gazette* shows a belt with

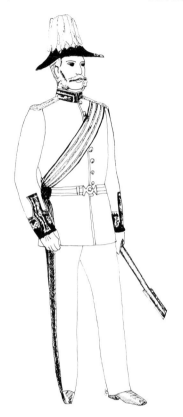

130. Lord Lieutenant's uniform,
1889 pattern. (After *West End
Gazette of Fashion*)

two narrow and one wide central horizontal stripes of plain gold embroidery and a round clasp, not a square one. Again, a later written
description gives the plate as two inches by two and a half inches.
There was also a gold and crimson net, six inch wide, sash worn over
the left shoulder, and gilt spurs. The buttons carried the device of a
crossed sword and baton – as for general officers.

The deputy-lieutenants' and vice-lieutenants' uniforms, authorised
in 1875, were similar but with no slashes on the cuffs and with a badge
in the form of a rose, thistle or shamrock embroidered on the front
edges of the collar. (The repetition of the description in 1912 says these
are embroidered in gold.) Lace of appropriate pattern in silver was on
the collar, cuffs and skirt slashes. The lace stripe on the trousers was
only one and three quarter inches wide: and the cocked hat carried a
seven inch drooping plume of white swan's feathers. Spurs and sashes
were not worn.

The deputy and vice-lieutenants' swords were straight with a black scabbard and the sword belt was scarlet leather and silver lace one and three quarter inches wide with a square silver plate showing a rose, the Prince of Wales feathers, and a thistle or shamrock, within a wreath. The buttons had a similar wreath surrounding a crown.

In 1902 the uniforms reverted to a coatee in place of the tunic and with modifications in 1908 this continued until 1920 when the last pattern of full dress was introduced, once again with a tunic. This last pattern persisted until at least the 1950s in some places, but since the last war rapidly gave place to the present No. 1 dress, ceremonial. The 1902 coatee was much the same as the earlier one, but easier fitting, with a lower collar.

In 1908 the coatee is described as double-breasted, two rows of nine buttons each and with two more buttons at the waist at the back; the skirts turned back with white both at the leading edges and at the centre back vent, from the waist; where the white turn-back edges met at the bottom of the tails a gold embroidered device of a rose, the Prince of Wales feathers, and a thistle or shamrock holding them in place. The

131. Lord Lieutenant's uniform, 1902 pattern. (After *Dress Worn at Court*, 1908)

collar and cuffs were blue; the cuff slashes and pocket-flaps scarlet, all embroidered in silver. There were silver epaulettes bearing the appropriate national device, as did the buttons, which had also changed in 1902 from the previous general officer's pattern. The trousers were unaltered. The cocked-hat had been modified over the years, but was basically the same, as was its ten inch red and white drooping swan's plume. The Mameluke sword went into a black and gilt scabbard, and had the appropriate national device on the hilt, instead of crossed batons as before, up to 1902. The sword belt became gold lace on crimson morocco, one and three quarter inches wide with a gilt rectangular plate with the royal cipher and crown in silver within a wreath, but this time with the motto "Dieu et mon droit" below. There is no sash now, but a blue caped cloak for outdoor wear is added. Wellington boots and brass swan-neck spurs are worn.

Deputy and vice-lieutenants wore a similar coatee but with no slashes to the cuffs and no lace on the pocket flaps. The lace on the blue collar and cuffs is less than that of the lieutenants, and there is no embroidered badge on the collar now, although it appears on the back skirts as for lieutenants, and on the epaulettes. The trousers, sword-belt, sword and scabbard remained much the same, but the cocked hat acquired a red and white upright plume of swan's feathers, rather resembling a feather duster.

The final 1920 version of full dress with the re-introduced tunic closely resembled the earlier pattern but with less elaborate slashes to the cuffs and back of the tunic, and with simpler silver lacing in place of the former silver embroidery to the blue collar and cuffs and the scarlet slashes on cuffs and tunic. The single-breasted tunic had eight buttons down the front, three on each of the back slashes, and three on each cuff slash. Deputy and vice-lieutenants had similar tunics, including slashes on the cuffs, which, however, were not so deep, and had less silver lace. Silver plaited (for lords lieutenant) or twisted (for deputy and vice-lieutenants) silver shoulder cords bore the national emblems.

The lord lieutenant's trousers were replaced by overalls strapped under the Wellington boots which had steel box-spurs (that is, the spurs pushed into a spring-clip device housed in a small steel "box" inset at the back of the heels). The overalls had two and a half inch scarlet stripes in place of the former silver lace. The Mameluke swords went into steel scabbards. Deputy and vice-lieutenants retained their trousers, but with one and three quarter inch scarlet stripes, and still no spurs. However, they lost their feather dusters and went back to drooping swan's feather plumes, this time of red and white, eight in-

132. Deputy Lieutenant's uniform, 1920 pattern, worn under mayoral gown.
c 1953. (Portrait of Alderman Sir Percy Sanders by Frank Daniel; Colchester
Borough Council)

ches long, in the cocked hat. Lieutenants still had their ten inch plume which they had clung on to throughout all the changes of the past. The deputy and vice-lieutenants' swords were changed to the standard infantry pattern.

At the formation of the Territorial Army and the consequent involvement of the lords lieutenant in 1908, provision had been made for them to wear an undress uniform of blue frock coat, pantaloons or overalls, a sword and a military style blue and scarlet peaked forage cap or the cocked hat for military occasions. After the First World War, khaki service dress was added to the lieutenant's wardrobe. Both undress and service dress had buttons and badges of lieutenancy instead of military insignia, but a footnote in 1929 allowed retired military men to wear army service dress with military badges of rank, a privilege later extended to retired naval and R.A.F. officers who were allowed, on the appropriate occasions, to wear the uniform of their services and corresponding badges. These two latter orders of dress, being specifically "non-ceremonial" do not really come within the scope of this book and are therefore not described in any detail: illustrations of contemporary service uniforms will go to indicate their appearance.

Full and undress uniform were to disappear after the Second World War, when the decision was made to clothe the lieutenancy in the army No. 1 dress, of single-breasted blue tunic and scarlet gorget patches carrying the appropriate design of silver lace, five lieutenancy buttons with two more to the flaps of the breast pockets, no buttons to hip-line pocket flaps, and two on each of the cuffs and silver plaited cord shoulder cords with regional badges; blue overalls with a two and a half inch scarlet stripe, Wellington boots and spurs, or trousers; silver and crimson sword belt and Mameluke sword and scabbard as before. The headwear is the blue, scarlet-banded forage cap, with the lieutenancy badge and two rows of silver lace on the patent leather peak. The same dress, with Sam Browne belt and leather scabbard but without shoulder cords, becomes "non-ceremonial" uniform. The new "lieutenants" of counties wear the same dress. Deputy lord-lieutenants have blue gimp instead of silver lace on the gorget patches, one row of silver lace on the cap peak, a one and three quarter inch stripe on the overalls or trousers and infantry pattern swords. Khaki service dress may be worn when with troops by all members of the lieutenancy.

The Woman's Movement has not so far made much impact on the lieutenancy, although the Lord-Lieutenant of Sussex is the Dowager Duchess of Norfolk and more than one county has a lady deputy. No official dress is laid down for such cases, although it is understood that if any lady so appointed had held a regular commission in one of the women's services she would be entitled to wear the uniform, presumably with the lieutenancy insignia. In the case of the Duchess of

133. Lord Lieutenant of Essex, Colonel Sir John Ruggles-Brise, Bt. (left) accompanying H.R.H. Princess Margaret at Colchester Tattoo, 1968. Number one dress ceremonial as introduced after 1946. The similarity to the General Officer's uniform (right) is obvious. (Ministry of Defence, Army Dept., Public Relations Branch)

Norfolk a badge or jewel is worn on formal occasions. This badge is unofficial, but it is to be hoped that some official mark of distinction in recognition of the services these ladies perform and of the honourable office that they hold will eventually be forthcoming.

THE LIEUTENANCY OF THE CITY OF LONDON

This office is held in commission by the Lord Mayor, and, inter alia, aldermen, the Governor of the Bank of England, and the Recorder of the City. It derives from an Act of 1662.

Generally the dress is that of a lord-lieutenant, but there have been a few minor differences in the past. The City lieutenants have always worn buttons with the City arms and not the general's sword-and-baton design, and the City badge appeared on the shoulder cords before the corresponding national badges did so on those of lord-lieutenants. A little less silver lace was allowed for the coatees and tunics. Swords were straight and not of the Mameluke pattern.

In the 1876 Regulations the sword belts of the city lieutenants were only edged with gold, not embroidered as for lords lieutenant, and early this century they changed to silver lace on the belt though the lords lieutenant did not do so until 1928. Cocked hats with ten inch white and red swan's feather falling plumes were worn as for lords lieutenant until the First World War, after which they were reduced to eight inches, the same as deputy and vice-lieutenants. Overalls with two and a half inch scarlet stripes replaced the former silver laced trousers.

Subsequent changes in the county lieutenancy uniforms generally applied also to the city lieutenancy. Today lieutenants of the City of London wear No. 1 dress as for deputy lieutenants of counties, but with a two and a half inch scarlet stripe on overalls or trousers.

ASSISTANT LIEUTENANTS OF GREATER LONDON

Upon the creation of Greater London and the appointment of a lord-lieutenant, provision was made for up to four assistant lieutenants whose uniform is to be the same as a lord-lieutenant's.

SHERIFFS

The office of sheriff in England goes back to Saxon times and sheriffs were originally county officers appointed by the Crown responsible to the central authority in Norman times, and later for civil and military matters in the shire, including, up to 1788, collection of certain taxes. Their prestige began to decline from the mid-thirteenth century, with the rise of municipal and borough administrations, and finally the creation in the sixteenth century of lords lieutenant as the military representatives of the Crown stripped them of military power.

Sheriff was an annual office, the county sheriff being appointed by the monarch for a year, and designated "high sheriff". With the rise of civic responsibilities, cities and boroughs were empowered to elect sheriffs, their term of office also being one year. London was granted the right in 1130, and in 1270 the privilege was extended to elect two sheriffs. By the eighteenth century twenty-one boroughs and cities had the right of election. In these cases the term "high sheriff" was not used, they were merely "sheriffs".

King James I made the office obligatory for the knights of the shires (that is county Members of Parliament) in 1636. Two years before this the father of John Evelyn was appointed High Sheriff for Surrey and Sussex, "before they were disjoyned".

> He had one hundred and sixteen servants in liverys, every one livery'd in greene sattin doublets; divers gentlemen and persons of quality waited on him in the same guard and habit, which at that time (when thirty or forty was the usual retinue of the High Sheriff) was esteem'd a great matter. Nor this was out of the least vanity that my Father exceeded (who was one of the greatest decliners of it), but because he could not refuse the civility of his friends and relations, who voluntarily came themselves or sent in their servants.

A lavish display of servants and guards was required of the high sheriff, mainly, in later times, as an escort for the judges of assize, and to assist in entertaining the judges adequately; all of which, with the cost of maintaining and clothing the retinue, was at the charge of the sheriff. It is not surprising, then, that many tried to dodge the honour. Hence James I, and others, orders for the appointment of county high sheriffs. Gradually the entertainment of the judges was rationalised by the local and central authorites, and the escort whittled down to a couple of policemen, sometimes, in memory of the older order when "javelin-men" armed with pikes or spears carried out the duty, carrying wands or staves. In 1634 Humphrey Cheetham as High

Sheriff of Lancaster provided an escort of twenty gentlemen in livery and forty javelin-men for the opening of the assizes; and himself indulged in a new velvet suit, gold laced, and a new hat.

134. Sheriff's Javelin Man,
Devonshire, early nineteenth century.
After "*Old England for ever*", 1819.
Reproduced in *Hone's Table Book*,
1830)

During the Civil Wars and the Interregnum the appointment of sheriffs was taken over by Parliament; from the Restoration the office again declined in importance, becoming in the eighteenth century merely an expensive honour. In 1787 the *Manchester Mercury* recorded that Sir Richard Arkwright, Sheriff of Derbyshire, had thirty javelin-men dressed in a livery of military pattern. "Their coats were dark blue elegantly trimmed with gold lace: scarlet waistcoats laced with gold and buff coloured velvet breeches: they also had blue greatcoats buckled behind after the manner of H.M. Regiment of Horse Guards: their hats were smartly cocked with gold button, cap [sic], and tassels . . . ."

In 1913 the *Tailor and Cutter Year Book* published a photograph of a "County Sheriff's Livery", showing a coach with coachman, two footmen and two trumpeters. Trumpeters and footmen in sloped-back, eighteenth-century style coats, white breeches and stockings and fore-and-aft cocked hats: the footmen carry long, elaborately-headed canes. There was no description of the high sheriffs themselves. As with Humphrey Cheetham a new suit was all that was required: no uniform nor prescribed dress was needed. The city and borough sheriffs wore

135. Livery of County Sheriff's Javelin men. 1913. (*Tailor and Cutter Year Book,* 1913)

the gowns associated with civic dignity which will be described in a later chapter.

The county high sheriff's display was confined to his followers and servants, a rather more onerous task than just providing a ceremonial outfit for oneself. Court dress, or if entitled, service uniform, has been the normal wear on ceremonial occasions for high sheriffs in recent years. Mr Liberty when Sheriff of Bucks at the end of the last century wore court dress, as did Mr F. E. Burton, High Sheriff of Nottinghamshire, in 1938 and his velvet court suit is today in the Museum of Costume and Textiles in Nottingham. Court dress was worn in 1977 by the High Sheriff of Essex. In 1969, Captain Elwes, High Sheriff of Lincolnshire, wore the full dress of his old regiment, the 60th Rifles, and seven years later the High Sheriff of Essex, Lt. Col. R. W. G. Charlton, wore his uniform as deputy lieutenant. Colonel Charlton tells me that the order of dress worn is generally "in agreement with the wishes of the High Court Judges", as the greater part of the county sheriff's duties today consist of receiving and attending the judges at the crown courts. Colonel Charlton's father, also High Sheriff for Essex, in his day wore the blue frock, gold sash and cocked hat of a brigadier-general.

CHIEF CONSTABLES

The acceptance of the new police, the increasing importance of them, especially in London on state occasions during the nineteenth century, led to the requirement of a full dress or state uniform for special functions in connection with the sovereign, and appearance at court, for the Metropolitan and City of London police commissioners and their immediate subordinates. County chief constables were also given a full dress uniform, as, later, were those of cities and boroughs.

The city commissioner in the early twentieth century was to wear a dark blue tunic, embroidered on the fronts, collar, cuffs and back skirts in gold, hook and eye fastenings, not buttons, and gold lace striped trousers or pantaloons. He had a general's sword, gold sword belt and sling and a black silk cocked hat bordered with black feathers. The assistant commissioner was less conspicuous in a tunic trimmed with black cord "as for Rifle Regiments" with gold embroidery on the collar. He had black stripes on his nether garments, a steel sword and no feathers on his hat. Various changes are evident in the details in the 1937 edition of *Dress Worn at Court* no gold on the commissioner's tunic fronts, overalls instead of trousers, a gold and black sash instead of a gold sword belt, and a ten inch plume of black and white swan's feathers in the hat. The assistant commissioner's tunic was like the commissioner's, and he acquired an eight inch plume for his hat.

The full dress of the metropolitan commissioner and his assistant commissioner at the beginning of this century was much the same as for the city, but without the distinction of rank. The lace on the tunic and trousers was silver instead of gold and they wore regulation army cocked hats with ostrich feathers of black, and infantry pattern swords with silver lace sword belts and slings. In addition to the commissioner and assistant commissioners the Metropolitan Police had for many years a rank known as "chief constables of districts". – These officers wore a uniform similar to the assistant commissioner of the City of London, but with silver collar embroidery.

By 1937 modification had also taken place: overalls were substituted for trousers, a silver and black waist sash instead of a sword belt, the commissioner received a general's pattern of sword and the assistants cavalry ones, and again swan's plumes were added to the cocked hat. The district chief constables do not appear.

136. Commissioner of Metropolitan
Police, full dress uniform. 1886.
(*Punch*, 1886)

County chief constables had a dark blue single breasted tunic made to button with eight buttons and with collar and cuffs and back skirt embroidered in silver, silver laced overalls or pantaloons, silver and black waist sash ("as Lancer girdle"), a general's sword, steel scabbard, cocked hat with no feathers.

137. Provincial Chief Constable, full dress. Lieutenant Colonel Stockwell, Chief Constable of Colchester. *c* 1930. (Courtesy of the Chief Constable of Essex)

In the 1937 Regulations the overall or pantaloon stripes were black laced, the sword altered to a Rifle Regiment pattern and the waist sash replaced by a black patent leather sword belt. "City and Borough" chief constables had been given a similar full dress by 1929.

With all the varieties of dress summarised above the officers concerned wore spurs, white gloves, and a cloak if necessary. In the case of the county chief constables the cloak had a cape, and in 1937 a great coat was listed as an alternative for them. Somewhat similar, but less elaborate, full dress was provided for subordinate ranks.

138. Provincial Police Inspector full dress. *c* 1930. Colchester Borough Police. (Courtesy of the Chief Constable of Essex)

SCOTTISH DRESS

The ceremonial costume of most Scots visiting the court in London seems to have been in accordance with our native customs. That the Highland dress was proscribed after the rebellion in 1745 is known to all: however, an exception was that military officers could wear it. What the full Highland dress was like in the late eighteenth and early nineteenth centuries is well portrayed in Raeburn's painting "The Macnab".

With the lifting of the ban, the popularity of Sir Walter Scott and Queen Victoria's love affair with the Highlands, the nineteenth century created a romanticised version of things Scottish, and black velvet doublets and frilly lace jabots appeared on canvas, and on the stage. (Winterhalter painted the three-year old Princess Helena in gold embroidered doublet, kilt, belt and an enormous hairy sporran in 1849.) Respectability drove out rebellion and Highland dress was allowed at court for those who chose to wear it. In 1898 *Dress Worn at Court* stated tersely, under the heading, "The Highland Kilt", that "The Highland Kilt may be worn at Court, as a military uniform, i.e. with sword and dirk etc., but only by Chiefs and Petty Chiefs".

By 1908 this had expanded to "Highland Dress", "The Highland Kilt and sporran with doublet of cloth or velvet; Highland belts, claymore, dirk, and long plaid may be worn at Court, but only by Highland Gentlemen".

In 1912 "Highland Dress" lists

> Black silk velvet full dress doublet, set of silver celtic or crest buttons . . . superfine tartan full dress kilt, short trews, . . . tartan stockings . . . . Full dress long shoulder plaid . . . white hair sporran, silver mounted and tassels . . . dirk with knife and fork . . . skean dhu with knife . . . patent leather shoulder belt, silver mounted [and] waist belt, silver clasp. Silver mounted shoulder brooch, silver gilt pin, lace jabot, one pair buckles for instep of shoes, one pair small ankle buckles for shoes. Full dress brogues. Highland claymore. Glengarry or Balmoral, crest or ornament.

No mention is made of chiefs or Highland gentlemen.

In 1937 this was amplified, for instance the "shoulder plaid" became "shoulder plaid or belted plaid", the dress sporran could be of "hair, fur, or skin, any pattern". Footwear was "dress shoes and brogues" and for the head the "Highland Bonnet; feather or feathers if entitled". Also in the 1937 list "Highland pistols and powder horn may be worn"; there is also the stern admonition "Gloves are NOT worn".

139. A Highland Gentleman. (From coloured engraving in R. McIan, *Costume of the Clans, c* 1843)

THE ROYAL COMPANY OF ARCHERS, THE MONARCH'S BODYGUARD FOR SCOTLAND

This is the personal bodyguard of the monarch in Scotland, and is an appendage of the Scottish court. A court dress is prescribed, and this no doubt was worn, and could be worn, when attending court in England. It is a dark green double-breasted coatee of cloth, faced with green velvet collar, cuffs, skirt edges and turn-backs, all embroidered in gold; gilt buttoned; gold epaulettes; gold lace striped green trousers; black silk cocked hat with green cock tail feather plume, crimson silk waist sash; sword; Wellington boots and white kid gloves. Previous to this nineteenth-century uniform the royal company of archers had, soon after the Act of Union of 1707, clothed itself in a tartan dress, reputedly the first tartan-uniformed corporate body.

This uniform is seen in various contemporary portraits: King George III as a child was painted in it. It consists of a predominantly red tartan coat of more or less contemporary cut, but with slashes in the sleeves after the manner of the earlier doublets. The coat is faced with blue, and trimmed with much silver lace and embroidery. The rest comprises breeches, stockings and shoes and a blue and silver feathered bonnet or hat. The Earl of Wemyss in 1715 wears a similar tartan, but the coat is much more doublet-like and has more and bigger sleeve-slashes. Again blue facings and much silver lace predominate. Matching tartan breeches and a very elaborate plumed blue bonnet complete the outfit. A quiver of arrows is apparently supported by a waist-belt under a silver sash.

By 1791, when Raeburn painted Dr Nathaniel Spens in the uniform of the royal company, the dress is a dark green tartan coat of contemporary style, silver "frogging", white waistcoat and long white breeches or pantaloons with Hessian boots. White leather cross-belts are worn, one of which carries the quiver. A flat green bonnet with plume and badge is the headdress. This uniform is in essence very like the military officer's of the time (see the same artist's portrait of General Sir W. Maxwell, Bart). In the 1820's the dress appears to have been a rather baggy tunic with puffed and slashed sleeves, tartan trousers, and a flat plumed cap and a neck-ruff. Altogether there is a whiff of George IV's Coronation about it. Later in the nineteenth century the present dark Lincoln green was adopted.

THE MASTER AND BRETHREN OF TRINITY HOUSE

The "Fraternity of the most glorious and undividible Trinitie and of St. Clement in the Parish Church of Deptford Stronde", is first recorded in the early sixteenth century. It was over the centuries one of five such guilds for the assistance and relief of seamen, others being established at Kingston-upon-Hull, Newcastle-on-Tyne, Dundee and Leith. The London Guild, however, was the only one to acquire more than limited jurisdiction and authority, the other four being in time but charitable or benefit societies. The Trinity House of London became the national authority empowered to regulate all matters relating to sea marks and lighthouses for England and Wales and adjacent waters (including Gibraltar), and also to act as the principal pilotage authority for the United Kingdom. In addition works of charity and relief for master mariners and their families when in need are carried out through a variety of trusts.

By 1793 the headquarters of the Trinity House had moved by degrees westwards until it arrived at its present site on Tower Hill: the original building, by Wyatt, was destroyed by German bombs in 1940, and the present building by Professor Sir Albert Richardson was opened by Her Gracious Majesty on Trafalgar Day, 1953, the Coronation year.

During the seventeenth century both Samuel Pepys and John Evelyn were on numerous occasions entertained by the Corporation of Trinity House, and Pepys was indeed made Master of the Corporation.

The Corporation of Trinity House today consists of Master, Deputy Master, Secretary and nine active elder brethren: these are the administration. In addition there are some three hundred younger brethren and a limited number of honorary elder brethren: in our own times one of these was Sir Winston Churchill, who was always most proud of this distinction bestowed upon a "former Naval person" by the mariners of England; another was Lord Mountbatten of Burma.

Until 1790 no particular uniform was worn by the brethren, but in that year it was decided that the elder brothers should adopt a dress of a blue cloth coat with scarlet lapels and collar, white waistcoat, breeches and stockings, and a cocked hat; all with gilt buttons bearing the corporation's arms. The uniform was introduced, according to the corporation, as "many inconveniences had been experienced by the Elder Brethren on Trinity Monday and other public occasions from persons who were strangers and not connected with the Corporation mixing in the procession and otherwise giving interruption". In 1801 boots were permitted in the winter and on Trinity Monday in place of the shoes and white stockings as the latter were too easily "dirtied by mud".

The breeches and stockings ceased to be worn at any time of the year some thirty years later, when, in April 1831 under King William IV, blue cloth trousers were prescribed for winter wear and white ones for the summer. The cocked hat was replaced by a round black pattern. This style remained unaltered until 1866, when by Order dated 22 March, Queen Victoria authorised the wearing of a uniform based upon that of a Royal Navy captain, but with special badges and buttons.

By another Order of 5 February 1893, the Queen commanded that "from that date the uniform of the Elder Brethren of The Trinity House should be of the Royal Navy pattern for the time being, save as respects the colour of the collar and cuffs of the full dress coat, and the description of lace, buttons, badges, and other distinguishing marks specified in the Order dated 22 March 1866, which remain unaltered, and are as specified below". (*Dress Worn at Court*, 1912 edition.) The detail of full dress is –

Coat, ['coatee' in other editions] blue cloth, double breasted, with eight buttons in each row, and stand up collar. The collar, the cuffs and the slashes on the cuffs are of scarlet cloth. The collar has gold lace on top, bottom and ends. The slashes on the cuffs are laced with gold on the top,

140. Elder Brother of Trinity House. Sir Winston Churchill in the full dress uniform (Painting by Sir Oswald Birley, 1951. Courtesy of the Corporation of Trinity House, London)

round the points, and on the bottom, and there are three small gilt buttons on each slash. A band of gold lace (1 inch wide) round the top of the cuffs. Pocket flaps with three points on the waist seam, laced round with gold and a large gilt button under each point, two buttons behind at the waist, and two at the bottom of the skirts. Body linings, black silk. Skirt linings, white kerseymere.

The lace was R.N. pattern, buttons, epaulettes, sword and sword belt, and cocked hat were as for captains R.N., but with Trinity House badges or coat of arms when appropriate. Trousers were gold-lace striped blue cloth.

A year after the publication of this edition of *Dress Worn at Court*, in 1913, King George V gave to the master the distinction of a wider (one and three quarter inch) band of gold lace around the top of the cuffs and on the shoulder straps, and in 1952 her present Majesty approved the addition of another, nine sixteenths of an inch, band of gold lace above the existing one. In addition, the deputy master in 1952 was authorised to wear one and three quarter inch lace instead of the one inch of the other elder brethren. Apart from these distinctions of gold lace, master, deputy and other elder brethren have identical uniforms.

The secretary of the corporation wears a special uniform of a single breasted blue cloth full dress coatee with six buttons of special pattern, a stand up black velvet collar and velvet cuffs and slash with three buttons, blue cloth pocket flaps and three buttons, collar cuffs and flaps edged with half inch and five eighths of an inch gold lace. He has four buttons at the back, two at hip level, two at bottom of skirts, which are lined with white silk. The secretary has a waistcoat, blue trousers with three quarter inch gold lace stripe, a white cravat and a court dress pattern hat and sword, but with the Trinity House device on the hat button and sword hilt.

An undress uniform of a naval frock coat, blue cloth waistcoat and trousers, without any stripe, is also provided, to be worn with a black leather sword belt, and epaulettes, cocked hat and sword as for full dress. Alternatively no epaulettes and a navy captain's peaked cap with the Trinity House badge. The coat has round cuffs with gold lace as on the full dress but with three vertical bars of lace, half an inch wide, with a button at the top of each, also. The secretary has in addition a band of white cloth around the cuff, next to the gold lace. He wears his special buttons and a navy cap.

The master, deputy master, and elder brethren also have a mess dress and a dinner dress: the mess dress as for the Royal Navy, but with lace and buttons as on the frock coat: a blue cloth waistcoat and plain blue trousers. The secretary does not have a mess dress.

The dinner dress is of a blue evening dress coat (tails) with gold lace and buttons on the cuffs as for the frock coat. Trinity House buttons of gilt. The shoulders are fitted for epaulettes. Until the 1937 edition of *Dress Worn at Court*, the secretary had no gold lace, but a black velvet collar and cuffs. In 1937, however, he was deprived of the velvet and given his gold lace and white stripe on the cuffs. He wears his secretary's pattern buttons. With dinner dress a white waistcoat and blue trousers with gold stripe are worn. A black tie is worn with both mess and dinner dress.

The Trinity House buttons are the shield from the coat of arms of the corporation within a belt inscribed "Trinitas in Unitate" all round the circumference. The secretary's buttons are without the belt and the inscription occupies the lower part of the circumference only.

The full dress is worn on occasions of state or ceremony, when swearing in the masters or honorary elder brethren and at other times if specially ordered: otherwise undress uniform, with or without sword is worn. All dress is subject to the Admiralty dress regulations. There is no official uniform for the younger brethren.

THE MOST VENERABLE ORDER OF THE HOSPITAL OF ST JOHN OF JERUSALEM

This charitable and medical order differs in many respects from the native orders dealt with in Chapter II. It is of medieval origin from outside England, and although Her Majesty is the sovereign head of the re-constituted British order, membership of it does not carry any rank or title, nor give any precedence as do the other orders of chivalry.

The foundation of the order seems to have been in the eleventh century as a hospice for the relief of Christian pilgrims to Jerusalem. In the twelfth century they became militarised and raised to an order of knighthood. According to Ashmole "the Knights of this Order then took the black habit of Hermits of St Augustine, and lived under his rule . . . and on the Breast of this habit wore, at first, a plain cross of white cloth, since changed to one with eight points . . . ."

When driven out of the Holy Land the Hospitallers went first to Cyprus, then to Rhodes, then in 1530 to Malta until 1798, when they were expelled by Napoleon and eventually set up their headquarters in Rome. During the Middle Ages the order spread throughout Europe in the form of priories, all owing allegiance to the grand master, the international head of the order.

In England the prior was known as "Prior Hospitalis Sancti Johannis Jerusalem in Anglia" and held the rank of baron. He was centred at the priory of Clerkenwell. The priory was dissolved with all the other like institutions during the 1530s and 1540s, and the Order of St John was dormant in England until the first half of the nineteenth century when a revival took place which resulted in a new constitution of the order as a Protestant institution.

In 1888 the modern order of St John was granted a royal charter by Queen Victoria who then became the sovereign head. As an Anglican foundation it is not, of course, in communion with the grand master and the priories of Roman Catholic origination. It is however appropriate that the headquarters at St John's Gate, Clerkenwell, occupy what is the surviving part of the old priory confiscated in 1540. The title "Venerable" was bestowed on the British order in 1926 by royal charter of King George V.

141. Order of St John. Sixteenth century examples of surcoat and mantle. The right-hand figure represents symbolically the Martyrdom of Adrian Fortescue, beheaded 1539. (After paintings in the College of St Paul, Rabat, Malta G.C., reproduced in E. J. King, *Knights of St John*)

The black habit embellished with a white eight-pointed cross, generally known as a Maltese cross was inherited by the modern order. For the star this badge was surmounted by a crown and between the arms were figures of lions and unicorns alternating. These embellishments were removed in 1871. In 1888 the lions and unicorns were restored to the badge and added to the star, and the grand prior's star was surmounted by an imperial crown.

The robes of the order are at present, for the sovereign and grand prior, a black velvet mantle lined with white silk and bearing a gold embellished white silk badge twelve inches in diameter on the left breast; the mantle of the soverign is distinguished by having a train and the imperial crown.

Members of the highest ranks are bailiffs and dames grand cross,

142. Order of St John. Robes of Bailiff Grand Cross. (After photograph of H.R.H. the Duke of Windsor at St John's Gate. Courtesy of The Order of St John)

ranking with whom are knights and dames of justice appointed before 1936: these officers wear black silk mantle, lined with black silk and again with a twelve inch badge, of linen with the embellishments in gold coloured silk, the tongues of the animals being in red. Lesser ranks of knights and dames of justice and of grace wear black merino mantles faced with black silk; for knights and dames of justice the badges as for a bailiff grand cross; the knights and dames of grace have a similar badge but with white silk embellishments. Commanders and officers holding certain appointments have similar mantles with nine or six inch badges. The secretary also bears two crossed quill pens with a six inch badge superimposed.

The mantles are in the form of a cloak with organ pleating at the neck, fastened in front at the neck by a large hook and eye and a cord. There are cordons and tassels at the same place, and from 1930 there has been a single stand collar. Beneath the mantle the men also wear a surcoat or under mantle known as a sopra vest. This is a cassock like garment, buttoning down the side, and in the case of bailiffs grand cross having a twelve inch plain white Maltese cross on the chest, and is reminiscent of the "habit" mentioned by Ashmole. It is, in fact, the medieval surcoat or "supra vestis".

For outdoor wear there is a plain black velvet hat of the shape of the Tudor flat cap; this is rarely worn today. Chaplains are entitled to a silk gown with a six inch linen badge on the left breast: parsons who are members of the order, when officiating at ceremonies of the order may wear a red lined and edged black tippet with red buttons and a three inch badge. The clerical headwear is a square black velvet cap with red edges and buttons. The wearing of mantles by ladies, with the exception of the sovereign of the order, dates from 1974. The riband is black watered silk with a white and gold enamelled badge.

| Lord Mayors | Mayors | Town Clerks |
| Councillors | Aldermen | Aldermen or Councillors |

PLATE III

Civic Robes: examples of gowns suitable for Lord Mayors (black and gold), Mayors (scarlet faced with fur), Town Clerks (black tufted silk), Councillors (blue faced black silk or velvet), Aldermen (scarlet faced black and gold), Aldermen or Councillors (blue or black faced gold). 20th century (Copyright Messrs. Ede and Ravenscroft Ltd).

CHAPTER VIII

Civic and Municipal Robes and Dress

THE LIVERY COMPANIES

For those of us who do not live in the capital or its vicinity perhaps the most commonly seen examples of English ceremonial costume are the traditional robes and uniforms associated with the dignitories and officials of municipal and local government bodies; the mayors, councillors (alas, except for the City of London, no more aldermen), town clerks, mace bearers, beadles and a wealth of other officials, some peculiar to individual localities, such as the Ripon Horn-blower, of ancient and honourable lineage.

The inhabitants of London have, in the City, an unique civic establishment which is intimately connected throughout the year with state and royal occasions. Many provincial cities and municipalities, especially those created within the last century, have modelled the robes and insignia of their chief magistrates and others on those of the City of London. So it is chiefly at London that we shall be looking to see civic costume since the Restoration, but without neglecting entirely other cities and boroughs of the kingdom.

The title of mayor is apparently of Norman origin, supplanting or incorporating in most instances the earlier Saxon officials such as reeves and aldermen. London's mayor is first mentioned in 1191, and in 1414 he is designated as "Lord Mayor". By the seventeenth century the mayor's office had become one of great importance and influence: as the first citizen he was, inter alia, chief magistrate, chairman of the council and coroner: he had powers, also, of appointment to various borough offices.

Reorganisation of local government by the Municipal Corporations Act of 1835 created many new mayoralties and in some cases substituted the title "mayor" for that of "bailiff" or "warden" in places where such officials had survived. The more recent local government shake-up of 1974 resulted in the loss of many ancient charters and consequent loss of the office of mayor, and also the creation of a host of new mayors out of former chairman of urban district councils. These latter dignitaries do not, to date, show many signs of acquiring robes, making do with the chains of office inherited from the former chairmen.

The municipal corporations of boroughs consisted of mayor, aldermen and burgesses, or freemen. Later the burgesses comprised most of the townspeople, and councillors or counselmen were elected to represent them: the council then electing its mayor and aldermen. In the case of the ancient boroughs it would seem that the municipal corporation arose out of the merchant and craft guilds of the towns, as these guilds possessed both wealth and property and had organizational and administrative ability and potential.

The guilds were presided over by an official generally known as an alderman, a title which was also being applied to the head of a civic district or ward, and during the reign of Edward III the London guilds, at least, were reorganised and became known as livery companies, each by now having assumed a distinctive uniform type of contemporary dress, or "livery". At the same time the title alderman was replaced by master or warden to designate the head of the company or livery. Aldermen were restricted to a territorial administration, for which they had become increasingly popular from the twelfth century.

As the livery companies succeeded to the guilds so they succeeded to the close connection with local government, and it is this connection and the dominance of livery-members in local affairs and administration that the familiar mayoral and counciliar robes owe their origin. By wearing a distinctive livery of a particular colour, or combination of colours, the companies were in line with the great lords who clad their followers in their family livery and with the knightly orders whose fellowship was proclaimed by their ceremonial dress.

Little is known of these liveries of city companies until the fifteenth century, at the beginning of which sumptuary laws were enacted controlling the use of liveries generally. As befitted the gravity of those men of affairs who constituted the livery companies, their dress was sober in design and usually included a houppelande, a full garment with long and loose sleeves worn over the gipon or doublet and hose. The fifteenth century houppelande for formal wear was ground length,

143. Livery Men of the
Grocers' Company in gowns
and hoods. The hoods held
over the shoulder by the
liripipe or "tippet". 1588.
(After engraving by de Bry:
Thomas Lant, *Funeral of Sir
Philip Sidney*, 1588)

and by 1540 became known as a "gown", often with hanging sleeves. A
hood was worn, first as headwear, and later as an appendage to the
gown, worn on the shoulders. The gowns and hoods were, as they
became obsolete as daily dress, relegated to purely ceremonial wear.
By the end of the sixteenth century the gown became more or less standardised, with hanging sleeves, that is long, wide sleeves with a slit at
the elbow for the hand and lower arm, the rest of the sleeve hanging
down, sometimes to an exaggerated degree. For winter wear gowns
could be fur-lined, and could always have a fur trimming to the front
edges, and sleeves. This standardised gown persisted and survives
today in civic, legal, academic and ecclesiastical dress, having
"fossilised" in these strata of society in the early seventeenth century.

Worn in their distinctive colours gowns and hoods were the
prescribed wear for members of the livery companies when meeting
formally or attending fraternity feasts, civic gatherings, religious services, and other solemn celebrations. The differing colours of gowns
and hoods distinguished the companies, originally, of course, composed of masters of a craft or trade or "mystery", but from quite early
times also having "honorary" members chosen from those outside – knights, lords, even monarchs – whom the company wished to
honour, or from whom it perhaps hoped for favours. Gradually the
companies lost most trade or craft connections, except in name, and
the livery became open to all.

During the sixteenth century gowns and hoods became more
standardised in colour; scarlet, violet, crimson, black, being popular,

black gradually prevailing. Stowe wrote in 1598, of the city companies, ". . . but of late time they have used their gownes to be all of one colour and that of the saddest". And nearly a century later, in 1673, the Carpenters' Company had a "livery gowne of black cloth lined and faced with Budge and a whod [hood] of black and red cloth" (Jupp, *Historical Account of the Worshipful Company of Carpenters*). Today most livery gowns are black. Fur facing or edging was common from the seventeenth century to the fronts, hems and hanging sleeves of the gowns. Masters, wardens and "assistants" (that is, the governing body, of a company) had their gowns edged with foins or foynes, the fur of the pole-cat, the liverymen generally were confined to budge or boge, that is lambskin, as a trimming. The Mercers, no doubt in view of their trade, had their liverymen's gowns faced with satin, instead of budge. The tendency during the last forty years or so, since about the mid 1930s, has been for the various companies to incorporate their heraldic colours in their gowns by having narrower fur and adding coloured silk borders.

During the late sixteenth century and in the reign of King James I flat caps were in general wear by the liverymen: ". . . every person . . . in the livery of the Company of Butchers whensoever he shall wear his livery gown and whood [hood], shall wear therewith a rounde cap and not a hatt . . . ." (Ordinances, 1607.) After James I's reign the caps were generally replaced by hats, as these became fashionable and the sumptuary laws and regulations were repealed or lapsed.

Masters and wardens of most companies were also invested on election with ceremonial caps or "garlands"; the Ironmongers' Company in 1565 had "garlands . . . like the heraldic wreath except that they are made of red velvet, and have pieces of silver fastened on them, engraved with the company's arms" (quoted in Herbert, *History of the Twelve Great Livery Companies*). A very similar garland in the possession of the Carpenters' Company, together with others of the seventeenth century, is described by Nevinson in Appendix J of *A History of the Carpenters' Company*.

In 1671 John Evelyn dined with the Ironmongers' Company, when the four stewards were chosen for the coming year, "with a solemn procession, garlands upon their heads and musiq playing . . . ." (*Diary*, 21 September 1671).

The city companies really went to town in all senses on the occasions when one of their livery was elected lord mayor and the company put on its finery to celebrate Lord Mayor's Day and provided colourful contingents and "pageants" for the procession. For instance in 1686, when Sir John Peake, a Mercer, was inaugurated, the Mercers' Com-

144. Early seventeenth century gown of purple silk
trimmed with gold lace.
Undersleeves and hanging
sleeves. (Crown copyright,
Victoria & Albert Museum)

pany provided for the Procession together with drummers, trumpeter, marshals,:

> Master, Wardens and Assistants in gowns faced with foins, in their hoods.
>   The Livery, in their gowns, faced with satin, in their hoods.
> Threescore poor men [the company's almsmen] in gown and caps . . . . each bearing a banner.
> Fifty gentlemen ushers, in velvet coats, follow next, each a chain of gold about his shoulders, and in his right hand a white staff.
> A splendid train of bachelors [junior members of the Livery] invested in gowns and scarlet satin hoods, etc.
>   (Herbert, *History of the Twelve Great Livery Companies*)

The close connection in London between the livery companies and the local government dates back almost to "time out of mind". In the last years of Edward III's reign the companies were given the exclusive right of electing all the City dignitaries as well as the Member of Parliament, which right they exercised until the Reform Act of 1832 and subsequent Local Government Acts of 1849 vested these privileges and duties in the rated householders, who need not be freemen or "citizens" of the City. Again, for many centuries the lord mayor was exclusively chosen from one of the twelve great companies, no one else being deemed eligible. (The twelve companies were the Mercers, Grocers, Drapers, Fishmongers, Goldsmiths, Skinners, Merchant Tailors, Haberdashers, Salters, Ironmongers, Vintners and Clothworkers.) If a member of a minor company were to be elected, or nominated, as lord mayor, he had to be "translated" to one of the twelve. In the period we are chiefly considering, Sir John Frederick, a Barber-Surgeon, was translated to the Grocers' Company in 1661 on being elected lord mayor. This tradition was apparently broken in 1742 when Sir Robert Wilmot, a Cooper, was sworn in as lord mayor, counsels' opinion being that there was no law requiring translation.

It is not surprising that this intimate relationship between companies and local government should influence the official dress of the latter. Men from different companies sitting down together as aldermen or common councillors each in his own livery are likely, as municipal rather than guild business came to predominate in local government, to have desired and adopted a dress which, founded on their livery gowns, reflected their primary concern and *esprit de corps* in the council chamber and proclaimed their disinterest, as men of affairs and guild members, when legislating for the common good. Tradition holds that as early as the thirteenth century certain citizens of London at the marriage of Henry III dressed alike in an ordered manner, although drawn from various guilds.

Particulars of civic dress before the fifteenth century are very scanty, but from the early 1400s we get more and more detail, not only from London but from many provincial cities also; York, Hull, Bristol, Nottingham among others. All these municipal records show that the mayors, and also their wives in most cases, were provided with some form of distinguishing dress. Also we find express mention of mayors' dress as exempt from certain provisions of the Sumptuary Laws.

For instance, Letters Patent of Henry VI issued in July 1440 to the City of Kingston-upon-Hull authorised ". . . the Mayor . . . and the rest of the Aldermen of the same town . . . to make use of robes, capes and tunics, of one suit and one livery, together with furs and fringes suitable to those capes, in the same manner and form as the Mayor and Aldermen in our City of London use; the Statutes of Liveries of Cloths and Hoods or any other statute or ordinance heretofore enacted notwithstanding". (*18 Henry VI* (*2*), Hull Record Office.)

And again in 1463 ". . . the maires and baliffs of Colchester and Lynne . . . and the aldermen of the same, and their wyfes . . . may use and were such array as is before limited to Squires and gentlemen . . . having possession of the yearly value of XL li". (*Ordinance against Excessive Apparel*, 3 Edward IV.)

In 1539 the sheriffs and ex-sheriffs of Southampton were enjoined to "provide, and use for their owne personage one right honest gowne of crimson or scarlette cloth . . . and the same gowne shall be made after suche fashyn as all Mayors, Aldermen and other Shreves have heretofore used . . . ." (*Book of Remembrance of Southampton 1514–1602*, f.83v.) It was also laid down in the same document that with the crimson gowns, black velvet tippets should be worn, but if the gown was made of scarlet cloth, no tippet was worn unless the sheriff was eventually elected mayor. If the sheriffs failed to wear their gowns on those days, such as the festival days of the Church calendar, they were liable to a fine of ten pounds.

Thirty years later, in 1569, it was decreed that as "tyme out of mynde yt hath byn an aunchiant order and use that every aldermans wyffe w'th'n the Towne of Suthampton should and ought to have and ware a gowne of scarlot at certain dayes and tyme", the aldermen were to buy their wives "scarlot gownes." This order also reminded the aldermen that they, as well as their "wyffes" were to wear scarlet gowns "at all dayes and times here before accustomid". The ladies were also to wear a "frentche whodde" (French hood, a close fitting bonnet made on a stiffened base or frame worn towards the back of the head, with the lower border curving forwards to cover the ears, and with a pleated "curtain" or a stiff flap falling down the back of the neck). Anyone not complying with the order and failing to provide the gown was liable to a ten pound fine; an amount reduced to five pounds in 1573, though in both cases an additional ten shillings for each day the gown was not worn was also levied. (*Southampton Remembrance Book*, ff. 101v and 120r.)

By the seventeenth century the pattern of dress for mayors, aldermen and councillors was established much in the same style as it remains today.

During the Commonwealth there were instances, Salisbury is one, of the use of civic robes being discontinued in deference to Puritan ideas, but this was by no means universal, and upon the Restoration the robes reappeared as of old. Salisbury, incidentally, although giving up its robes (or perhaps because it did) was granted a sword of state and a Swordbearer by Cromwell; the Swordbearer to "weare a cap of maintenance before the Mayor". When the old robes were reassumed in 1660 the Cromwellian sword was abandoned.

THE CITY OF LONDON

When King Charles II entered London at his Restoration Evelyn noted the "Maior, Aldermen and all the Companies in their liveries, chains of gold and banners . . . . ." and James Heath, gent., in his *Chronicle of the Late Intestine War* published in 1676 records the same event and notes "the two Sheriffs, and all the Aldermen of London (among whome, much wondering there was at Alderman Ireton) in their Scarlet Gowns and rich Trappings . . . ."

As early as 1568 the City of London had printed its first *Ceremonial Book* detailing the dress and ceremonies in connection with City occasions and on certain feast and fast days the lord mayor and aldermen had black, scarlet and violet gowns and violet and scarlet cloaks. In addition "at such times as a King is Crouned, the Lord Mayor weareth a crimson velvet goune, a collar of Esses and Sceptre but no cloak". (John Stowe *Survey of London*, 1633 edition, obviously quoting from the Official Handbook.)

A century later, at the Restoration, the rules were contained in *The Order of My Lord Mayor, the Aldermen and Sheriffs for their Meetings and wearing of their Apparal throughout the whole Year*. Printed by J. Flesher, Printer to the Hon. City of London in 1656. This details the ceremonies and dress from the election of sheriffs of London on Midsummer Day to attendance at St Paul's at Whitsun, Christmas and Twelfth Day; and also such annual occasions as election of governors of Christ's Hospital, election of City officers, and the like. The more

145. Lord Mayor of London wearing gown, collar of Ss and wide brimmed hat. 1657. (From Lady Alice Frances Archer Houblon, *The Houblon Family*, 1907)

unusual occasions such as coronations, funerals and elections to parliament are also fully covered.

Gowns for lord mayors and aldermen, and sheriffs, were still violet, scarlet and black, with violet or scarlet cloaks on certain days. According to Stowe from Michaelmas to Whitsuntide violet cloaks, furred, were worn, and from Whitsuntide to Michaelmas, scarlet, lined.

The lord Mayor and past lord Mayors "ought to have their clokes furred with Grey Amis" or lined with "changeable Taffeta". Those aldermen who had not passed the chair "to have their cloakes furred with Calabre" or lined with "greene taffeta." Amis or amice was the fur of the marten or of a grey squirrel: calabar or calabre that of a squirrel also, possibly grey. So some confusion reigns as to the exact distinction. "Changeable taffeta" is "shot", showing a different shade or colour as the fabric changes position to the light due to different coloured warp and weft threads used. In addition to the gowns and cloaks, tippets were also worn: "All the Aldermen except the Mayor and those that have passed the chair and the two Sherriffes are to wear a black velvet tippet when wearing either Scarlet, violet or black Gowns" (*The Order of My Lord Mayor etc.* 1656). Normal clothes were worn under these civic robes and headwear was the usual wide brimmed round hat of the seventeenth century.

Various editions of *The Order of My Lord Mayor etc.* were published during the eighteenth century with little variation from the 1656 issue. Typical details are, for instance, "Upon Michaelmas Day for the Election of My Lord Mayor", the aldermen and sheriffs meet "at Guildhall, in their Scarlet Gowns and their cloaks furred", and on the day after Michaelmas "for the Sheriffs going to Westminster" [to be presented to the Exchequer] and aldermen wear "their violet gowns furred . . . without cloaks; but my Lord [Mayor], Master Recorder, and the two Sheriffs must be in their scarlet gowns furred, and their cloaks born to Westminster with them . . . and in the Hall [Westminster] put on their cloaks, and so go up to the Exchequer . . . ."

An interesting copy of the 1715 edition of *The Order of My Lord Mayor etc.* in the Guildhall Library, has manuscript interleaving giving some minor alterations and variations to the printed ceremonies and dress on the alternate pages: also a note on the fly-leaf records that in 1700 the lord mayor and aldermen discontinued wearing cloaks on Midsummer Day, and thereafter only the lord mayor and sheriffs wore them at all "provided at the expense of the City" until about 1735 when they were "wholly laid aside".

The seventeenth- and eighteenth-century books contain two puzzling references to "gray cloaks": on Michaelmas Eve the new sheriffs are escorted to Guildhall "between two of the Gray Cloaks" and "For the Election of Knights and Burgesses of Parliament" at whatever date this occurs, the lord mayor, sheriffs and aldermen wearing their violet gowns and cloaks furred or lined according to the season, "must chuse Master Recorder for one of their Knights, and one Gray Cloak for the other; . . . ." I think that these may be references to the past lord mayors (referred to in the book as "those Knights that have borne the office of mayoralty") whose cloaks are specifically to be furred with "grey amice," but there may be another explanation waiting to be discovered.

A black velvet hood was worn by the lord mayor and ex-lord mayor on certain days: 29 October, when the new one was sworn in at the Exchequer at Westminster Hall, and on Christmas Day, Twelfth Day, Candlemas and All Saints Day to services at St Paul's, and on Monday and Tuesday in Easter week. On Holy Innocents Day and also on the Wednesday in Easter week the lord mayor and aldermen's ladies were to wear black: on the Monday and Tuesday of Easter week, in the seventeenth century, according to Stowe's report, the ladies wore scarlet. This last requirement was dropped in the eighteenth century.

In 1751 the New Calendar was introduced, and as one consequence the swearing-in of the new lord mayor at Westminster on "the morrow after Simon and Jude's day (29 October) was transferred to 9 November, and that date became known as Lord Mayor's Day. Traditionally the trip to Westminster and back had been a time of merry-making and pageantry, but during the eighteenth and nineteenth centuries this largely lapsed, and was revived in its modern form of procession to and from the Royal Courts of Justice in the Strand when that building superseded Westminster Hall in 1873. The lord mayor is now presented to the Lord Chief Justice, to make his final declaration of office. Up to the middle 1850s part of the journey to Westminster was by river; and previous to 1712 the land part of the journey had been made on horseback. In 1712 a coach was introduced, and in 1757 the lord mayor's state coach, now still in use, was first seen in the procession.

Although lord mayor, sheriffs and aldermen are described in their official gowns and cloaks, nothing so far has been said of the "Commons" or "Counsellors of the City" or Common Councilmen as they are now known. In *The Order of My Lord Mayor etc.*, various editions, we read of the election of sheriffs, that, when going to be sworn in, "if the Sheriff be no Alderman, then to come between two of the Aldermen without cloaks, and the Sheriff in his Livery-Gown and his hood [i.e. of his Company]. And after, when he is sworn, then to put on his violet gown and cloak, and his chain thereon . . . ." which seems to indicate no civic gowns for those who were not aldermen; at least until the second half of the eighteenth century, from which time we hear of blue gowns for the common council.

As early as 1680 a change had occurred in the wearing of the black velvet tippet: in that year the rule stated: "It hath been usual when the Lord Mayor and Aldermen wear scarlet and violet gouns also to wear their velvet tippets" with no mention of exclusion of lord mayor, ex-lord mayor and sheriffs, or of wearing it with the black gown. In 1715, and subsequently until discontinued later in the century, or early in the nineteenth, the entry reads: "It hath been usual, when the Lord Mayor and Aldermen wear Scarlet and Violet Gouns, also to wear their Violet tippets." Whether "violet" in the second instance is a continuing misprint for "velvet", or whether a change of colour actually occurred I do not know.

The black gowns were not worn very frequently – instances during the seventeenth and eighteenth centuries were on "working days" during the twelve days of Christmas; when the lords of the council came to assess the City subsidies, nominations of aldermen; at elections of governors of Christ's Hospital, and certain other charities, and at Quarter Sessions (except the first days when violet was worn).

146. Lord Mayor of London wearing his coronation gown and carrying the crystal sceptre. 1821. (After Naylor, *Coronation of King George IV*, 1824–39)

To summarise, during the seventeenth and eighteenth centuries the lord mayor wore on occasions, a scarlet, violet or black gown, scarlet or violet cloak (until *c.* 1735), on certain days a tippet, and on others a hood and collar of Ss. For coronations he had a special crimson velvet gown and a sceptre.

The sheriffs and aldermen had likewise the three gowns and two cloaks and the tippet. For certain days the immediate past lord mayor wore a hood and a chain. The sheriffs also wore chains of office, and there is some indication that the aldermen did so; the order for Good Friday says: "My Lord and the Aldermen meet at St Paul's Cross at one of the clock, to hear the Sermon, in their Pewk Gowns, and without their chains and tippets". This is the only time "Pewk" gowns are noted and the word may mean either the fabric or colour. Puke, or pewk is listed by Willett Cunnington as imported woollen cloth, dyed in the wool to an almost black colour, or, as a colour alone, "a dirty brown" (*Dictionary of English Costume*, 1960). *The Shorter Oxford Dictionary* defines the word as a superior woollen cloth of which gowns were made, or as a colour formerly used for woollen goods, apparently a "bluish black or inky colour." The word, in both senses, is of fifteenth- and sixteenth-century usage, and I am inclined to think it is a hang-over from an earlier description and means the black gown: probably originally made of puke. During the eighteenth century, as earlier, contemporary headwear was worn.

By the early nineteenth century we find the lord mayor equipped with two more robes: the state robe of crimson velvet, said in 1834 (*Ceremonies Connected with the Office of Lord Mayor*, Corporation of London, 1834) to be worn when presenting an address to His Majesty, and the entertaining gown, of gold embroidered black silk, worn as an alternative on the same occasions, and at the Lord Mayor's Dinner and other appropriate times. Ten years later, in 1844, the *Illustrated London News*, writing of the lord mayor, reports that this gold and black gown is his wear "In public or ordinary state occasions," with his collar and jewel in addition. Of the state robe the *Illustrated London News* (9 November 1844) says: "The crimson robe worn in conducting the Sovereign through the City is so rarely used and differs in form so much, according to the taste of the wearer, that it can hardly be considered to form part of the official costume of the Lord Mayor". This last seems to indicate that each holder of the office provided his own State robe, or had it adapted to his individual fancy.

The *Ceremonies Connected with the Office of Lord Mayor* replaced the earlier *The Order of My Lord Mayor etc.* and is more in keeping with the new age of the nineteenth century. Some of the ancient ceremonies and feasts are omitted and some new ones added: Plow Monday and first Sunday after Epiphany, for instance. Also "Public Fast Days", when black gowns were worn, were mentioned, although the custom of Public Fasts was, of course, older. Black gowns, not pewk, are also enjoined for Good Friday, retaining the proviso "no chains". For lord mayor and aldermen violet gowns seem to be the usual wear for council and corporation meetings and some outside events, but mostly for

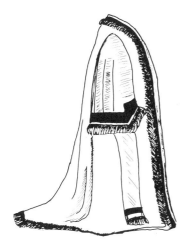 

147. Lord Mayor of London: (a) Violet Robe, trained for mayorality; (b) Scarlet Robe but shown untrained. (After *Illustrated London News*, 1844)

public display the scarlet gown was worn by them and by the sheriffs. At the Old Bailey and when accompanying the judges to service at St Paul's on the first Sunday of the Easter and Hilary Terms scarlet was worn by all.

Regulations are now made for what is to be worn underneath the gowns. For dinner with the Merchant Tailors in May, "the Aldermen have places at the same table, being in full Court Dress with their scarlet gowns": and again, in the same month for the service in Bow Church of the Society for the Propagation of the Gospel, the lord mayor, aldermen and sheriffs wear "violet gowns over full dress Black Court suit". An interesting change occurs at the swearing-in of the sheriffs: now both sheriffs elect appear in the livery gowns of their company with no remarks about "not being an Alderman", which they change for violet gowns after taking the oath.

Some attention is given to the dress of aldermen attending the Old Bailey (they do so during sessions of the Central Criminal Court, in rota) or dining with the judges:

> It is most particularly recommended [to] wear under their Violet Gowns full-dress black coats: black pantaloons and boots may be permitted as the feet are hid . . . and as gentlemen come from business the change of boots to shoes and stockings may be inconvenient: but there cannot be pretence for neglecting the change of coat and waistcoat, as convenient dressing rooms are provided . . . . When the Scarlet gown is worn boots cannot be permitted, but the full court-dress must be considered as the only decent dress that can be worn under an Alderman's State robe.

It is during the nineteenth century that the common councillors' blue gowns came more into the picture. They were of a violet-blue, known as "mazarine", a name first applied about 1760. There is a specimen of 1820 in the Museum of London and it is very like its modern successors, as indeed, are all the City's robes.

Although there is no fur trimming on the sleeves, as on the modern version, there are traces which indicate that it was originally so decorated.

Various editions of *Ceremonies etc.* appeared during the century and in 1906 a *Handbook of Ceremonial* was issued. In this much the same detail is given and some old rules restated. For the election of the lord mayor on 29 September (Michaelmas Day) all the members of the livery companies are summoned to Guildhall "that they came habited in their Livery gowns and hoods": although this was an ancient custom it is not specifically mentioned in the earlier books. Also the aldermen were to wear black court suits with scarlet gowns; the ex-lord mayor and lord mayor with hoods and chains. The common councilmen were to wear their mazarine gowns.

The *Handbook of Ceremonial* lists the various types of dress required by an alderman:

An Alderman's Costume is:
    Scarlet Gown
    Violet Gown
    Lieutenancy Uniform
    Black velvet Court Suit, sword, etc.
    Black cloth court suit with trousers in addition

and goes on to say "it is etiquette for an Alderman in the discharge of his duties when special costume is not prescribed, to appear in dark morning dress, with white or black tie". There were amendments in 1910 and 1913 making minor simplifications to procedures and dress.

The lord mayor and sheriffs had now got into the pages of *Dress Worn at Court*, and the 1912 edition states that when attending courts, levees and evening state parties the lord mayor shall wear old velvet court dress with his chain and jewel: if presenting new lieutenants at a levee, lieutenancy uniform is to be worn. When in the presence of the sovereign within the City:

The Crimson Velvet Robe of State, as for an Earl except that the Miniver edgings are powdered with black fur and fastened together with Gold Cordons and tassels, is worn over the Old Style of Velvet Court Dress or over the uniform for a Lieutenant of the City. The Chain and Jewel. Hat – Black Velvet Three-cornered, with border of black ostrich feathers, and a steel loop at side.

148. Lord Mayor of London. Crimson velvet robe of state. 1874.
(After *Illustrated London News*, 30 May 1874)

149. Lord Mayor of London. Black damask robe worn over old style black velvet Court suit. Collar and jewel and sceptre. 1913. (*Tailor and Cutter Year Book*, 1913)

On other ceremonial occasions: "The Black Robe of State, trimmed with gold, over the Old Style of Velvet Court Dress. The chain and jewel. Hat – three-cornered as described above".

This description of the crimson robe worn in the monarch's presence contrasts with the *Illustrated London News's* remarks of seventy years before: it is today known as the reception robe. The black and gold gown is the "entertaining robe".

The chain or collar is a gold collar of Ss, given by Sir John Alen in 1545. It was probably a livery or knightly collar originally bestowed on Sir John by the King. It comprises Ss, Tudor roses and knots as the links, and is reputed to be made of Welsh gold. The Jewel was at first a pendant jewelled cross added in 1558, but replacements were made at various times and as it is now the present cameo City badge and motto surrounded by a gold and diamond border dates from 1866. A story current in the 1890s told that a certain lord mayor lost the jewel, and accidentally found it three months later, when he had become resigned to replacing it out of his own pocket, under a chair in his library. (*The Notebooks of a Spinster Lady.*)

The 1933 edition of *Handbook of Ceremonials* lists for an Alderman:

A Scarlet Gown
A Violet Gown
Lieutenancy Uniform
Court Dress
"Old Bailey Dress" [i.e. black cloth suit with trousers]
Full evening dress: black knee breeches and silk stockings.

"Old Bailey dress" is later expanded into "Old Bailey Trousers" and "Old Bailey Breeches", under which titles it appears in the current *Ceremonials of the Corporation of London* published in 1962, where the "trousers" is defined as black cloth court coat and waistcoat, black trousers, lace jabot and ruffles, no sword. This description of "Old Bailey Trousers" is reminiscent of the early nineteenth century dispensation to keep on your pantaloons when changing to "full dress black coats" when attending the Old Bailey: an instance, perhaps, of an informal habit of one generation being the hallowed tradition of the next-but-one and becoming part of the Law of the Medes and Persians. And the "breeches" version is detailed as "for evening wear," with black cloth knee breeches, silk stockings and patent shoes with steel buckles, with or without a sword. In 1962, however, "Old Bailey Dress" is restricted to the lord mayor and sheriffs, and for wear by the Swordbearer and Common Cryer. Aldermen are to have a velvet court suit and "full evening dress" of black cloth with knee breeches. Lieutenancy uniform is now no longer detailed in these instructions.

A type-written insert to a copy of the 1933 *Handbook of Ceremonials* in the Guildhall Library gives the following details about the "fur trimming on Robes":

Common Council – Fitch [pole cat, or "foynes"]
Alderman's Scarlet – Sable
Alderman's Violet – Bear
Lord Mayor's Crimson Velvet – Ermine
Lord Mayor's Coronation – Ermine

The city chamberlain is also to have sable. There is a note to the effect that when sable cannot be obtained, marten may be substituted for it.

Although black gowns are not listed, the 1933 book gives them as wear for Fast Days when attending St Paul's, and similarly, for Thanksgivings, the lord mayor in his crimson velvet, the aldermen in scarlet. These occasions are omitted from the 1962 edition. In 1933 the note about "dark morning dress" is still included.

Today the lord mayor has a scarlet and a violet gown, both of the same design as the alderman's, but for the mayoral year both with the addition of a train, and the scarlet worn with a scarlet hood from the occasion of his presentation to the judges (Lord Mayor's Day). The black and gold robe is trained of silk brocade and guarded with gold lace: the crimson velvet reception robe is also trained, with an ermine cape powdered with three rows of black fur (as for an earl) as are the ermine edges, with gold cordon and tassels and a white satin ribbon bow on each shoulder to secure the collar of Ss; the lining is white satin.

The coronation robe is seen only rarely and is of crimson velvet, with four bars of miniver on each front, these bars and the fronts being guarded with gold lace. There are two white satin bows on the shoulders and the robe is lined with white corded silk.

The lord mayor wears a black three cornered cocked hat of eighteenth-century style with three black ostrich feathers and a burnished steel ornament. The hat is nowadays made of best black velvet, and since 1968 a new hat has been ceremoniously presented each year to the new lord mayor at the Mansion House by the master of the Worshipful Company of Feltmakers of London. For the presentation the master is accompanied by the wardens and clerk of the company. For underdress there is the choice of velvet court dress or Old Bailey Trousers or Old Bailey Breeches for evening wear.

The aldermen's scarlet gowns are cloth, with hanging sleeves under wide upper sleeves; guarded with black velvet and sable on the sleeves, collar and revers. The hanging sleeves and bottom of the gown are

150. Lord Mayor of London. Scarlet gown, collar and jewel, three-cornered cocked hat; flanked by the two sheriffs wearing chains and badges and accompanied by the Sword Bearer in black damask tufted gown and wearing a cap of maintenance; and by the Common Cryer and Sergeant-at-Arms wearing similar gown and a short legal wig. Beneath all these gowns Old Bailey Trousers are the correct underdress. 1947. (Radio Times Hulton Picture Library)

guarded with black velvet alone. Fore parts and sleeves lined in white satin, and scarlet ribbon bows on shoulders to hold chain. Ex-lord mayors are entitled to add a scarlet hood to the right shoulder. The violet gown is much the same in design, but of ribbed silk and with bear fur.

A plain cocked hat with burnished steel ornament and loop is worn; underneath the gown can be worn velvet court dress or "full evening dress" with breeches as noted above.

The sheriffs are gowned and hatted like the aldermen, but are allowed Old Bailey kits as for the lord Mayor, in addition to velvet court dress. The common councilmen wear their mazarine blue silk gowns with fitch fur guards on the sleeves, a cocked hat ornamented with black braid and a silver City badge and underneath the gown whatever they like, for nobody seems to have laid anything down for them.

Over the centuries the numbers of officers of the corporation have declined considerably: Stowe gives about forty in the earlier seventeenth century; Fairholt (*Lord Mayor's Pageants*) lists twenty-eight, and sixteen appear in 1962. Among those fallen by the wayside are the three Sergeant Carvers, the Yeomen of the Waterside and the Water Bailiff's Second Young Man. On the other hand a medical officer of health, solicitor and an engineer have been added. These officials all seemed to have some livery or clothing with the job: some provided by the lord mayor and the others by the City Corporation.

Of the corporation officers three are household officers of the lord mayor: The Swordbearer, the Common Cryer and Sergeant-at-Arms and the City Marshal. These ancient officials are connected with the administration of justice and the law. The swordbearer carries in front of the lord mayor the sword granted by the monarch to indicate powers of criminal jurisdiction. The Common Cryer and Sergeant-at-Arms bears the mace, representing authority to arrest offenders and bring them before the Mayor's Court, serve processes, and make official proclamations. The City Marshal (there were two up to 1862, when the number was reduced to one) and six assistants, did general police work until a regular police force was established in 1829. Today his main tasks are marshalling processions and challenging troops wishing to march through the City.

The Swordbearer has worn a black damask gown from the sixteenth century: it is today described as black satin damask with tufts. The gown is guarded with black velvet and silk lace. "Tufts" indicate a pattern of raised pile on the surface of the fabric or a decoration of small added tassels. Also worn, and probably pre-dating the gown, is the Cap of Maintenance, probably granted with the sword some time in the fourteenth century. The cap is a round brimless hat of sable, widening towards the crown which is of crimson velvet. Originally there was also a silk cap for summer wear, but this was abandoned some time after the sixteenth century. There is also a chain of office, and at one time the Swordbearer also wore a tippet, for the 1656 Order states that when the new Lord Mayor is elected "the Swordbearer taketh off his tippet, and has it for his labour, and putteth on his chain." This instruction is repeated in the eighteenth-century books. Presumably the new Lord Mayor provided a replacement tippet for official wear. When an alderman died the Swordbearer received a black gown.

The Common Cryer and Sergeant-at-Arms wears a gown similar to the Swordbearer's: he has no hat or chain but wears a legal wig. Both Swordbearer and Common Cryer wear Old Bailey Trousers for day appearances and Old Bailey Breeches for evenings.

The City Marshall differs from all the other members and officials of the City Corporation in having no gown but a military style uniform. This, from at least the beginning of this century, is a scarlet coatee, single-breasted, laced in gold on the fronts, lower sleeves and back waist and skirts, with blue cloth stand collar and cuffs. There are heavy gold epaulettes and a gold laced word belt. The sword has a gilt hilt and brass scabbard. The overalls are dark blue with two inch gold lace stripe. Wellington boots, gilt spurs and a cocked hat with a white and red swan's feather plume complete the uniform today. Earlier in the century trousers were specified instead of overalls, with pantaloons "for mounted duties".

There is an undress uniform of blue coatee originally laced in gold, but slightly less on the back, as the full dress. The collars and cuffs are of scarlet cloth, without epaulettes but with scales on cloth shoulder straps. The trousers had a two inch scarlet stripe. Today the undress coatee is gold laced only on the collar and cuffs. All other items are as for full dress. An evening or "informal" dress based on army mess dress consists of a blue shell jacket (that is, ending at the waist at the back, with no tails) with scarlet and gold faced collar and cuffs, scarlet waistcoat and overalls as above, red or gold stripes and a blue patrol cap. The buttons, badges, and waist belt clasp are of the City arms in all cases.

Of the other officials the Recorder who is one of the City's own judges (today the Common Sergeant is the only other) has a scarlet gown and a violet gown, not furred, over court dress, and a short legal wig – on ceremonial occasions he wears a full-bottomed wig – and white bands at the collar. The Common Sergeant wears a black silk tufted gown, short wig and bands, or a full bottomed wig for ceremonial.

The Remembrancer dresses in a similar manner, but his gown is plain black silk. The Chamberlain's black gown is black silk guarded with black velvet and with sable on the fronts. The Town Clerk has two gowns, a plain black silk and a tufted silk guarded with black velvet: he wears the short legal wig and bands. The remaining officials all wear black silk gowns. The normal wear underneath is laid down as black cloth court suit, or court coat and waistcoat with trousers, or, in some cases, is not specified.

SOME PROVINCIAL CITIES AND TOWNS

As we have said many municipalities, old and new, based their official civic dress on that of the City of London, but in most cases less lavishly, contenting themselves with one gown only. Scarlet seems to have been the most popular colour from early days: in 1554 the Mayor of Oxford wore a scarlet gown, cloak and velvet tippet "as formerly", and at Leicester in 1585 the Mayor wore scarlet "as of auncient tyme". In 1686 the charter granted to Stamford by James II enjoined that the mayor and aldermen "in and upon all feast days and the Lord's days be dressed in scarlet vestments or gowns". At Sudbury, Suffolk, in the early sixteenth century, mayors and ex-mayors wore scarlet gowns and velvet tippets and capital burgesses (or councillors) had murrey gowns.

In 1721 the mayor was to have a scarlet gown, the aldermen black faced with scarlet velvet or fur and the capital burgesses black gowns faced with black velvet. These were to be provided by the wearers, but five years later they were subsidised by the corporation. Sadly in 1813 the Corporation of Sudbury was involved in expensive litigation which resulted in corporation property being sold to raise some cash: the items included a scarlet robe said to have been bought by a neighbouring fox-hunter to wear as a hunting overcoat.

As in most places fines were levied upon those not wearing their robes on appropriate occasions. A few blue or black gowns are mentioned instead of scarlet for some of the ancient boroughs: in Bristol the lord mayor wears scarlet on special occasions, such as when the new lord mayor is chosen, and attending on the judges: at other times he wears a black gown for council meetings. Court dress is worn under the scarlet robe on civic occasions, and there is a pair of gold-laced gauntlet gloves the origin of which is unknown but presumably lies in the sixteenth or seventeenth century.

From the Restoration until the first half of the nineteenth century municipal authority had been in the hands of the rich and powerful merchants, lawyers, landowners and nominees of the local aristocracy and squirarchy. With the Municipal Reform Act of 1835 all this was radically changed and local elections were open to all rate-payers as candidates and voters. As a result much more democratic corporations and councils appeared, many of which during the succeeding few years, in an excess of reforming zeal, either changed the ancient colourful robes for a sober black, or in some cases, abolished them altogether. For instance, in Hull in 1836 the corporation voted to dispense with "gowns and the other paraphenalia of office".

In Cambridge, Romilly, a local diarist, noted in 1840 that at a University function "the Mayor attended but wore no robes (nor has done during any part of his office)." (Diary, 23 November 1840.)

Happily however the ancient customs were in general resumed later in the century. Today Hull wears not only mayoral and until 1974 aldermanic robes, as of ancient times, but blue gowns for councillors have been added.

Other local government acts were brought in during the nineteenth century and new cities and corporations created: most, but not all, of these adopted robes for at least the mayor, and in some cases for the aldermen and councillors also. Of those that did not do much about it Birmingham and Sheffield can be quoted as examples. Birmingham, incorporated as a borough in 1838, had no robes until 1858 when Queen Victoria and Prince Albert visited the City and the then Mayor "intimated to the Council that he intended to provide himself with a robe to wear on receiving the Queen". (*Official History of Birmingham Corporation.*) This lead to the proposal that all the Council should have robes, but the motion was defeated. In the event the mayor was robed in scarlet guarded with black velvet and fur, but also with narrow gold lace bars set across the upper sleeves in three rows of four bars each. According to his portrait he wore court dress under his gown. One or two councillors also appeared in court dress and it is recorded that a few did wear gowns, apparently bought themselves. But, to quote the

151. The first Lord Mayor of Birmingham to wear an official robe, "Similar to that worn by other Civic Heads". 1858. (Courtesy of the City of Birmingham)

official historian, "the great majority, true to the simplicity of Birmingham's inherent habits, simply wore ordinary morning dress". Apparently the Queen was quite satisfied with these varieties of dress for she later expressed "entire approval of the arrangements . . . ." The Lord Mayor of Birmingham retained his fur-faced red gown and wears one to this day; however the city's inherent simplicity still prevails among the rest of the council, all of whom are gownless.

The Council of Sheffield, created a borough in 1843, authorised the mayor to have an official robe of sable trimmed scarlet in 1874 to wear at all general meetings of the council and upon public and ceremonial occasions. Aldermen and councillors did not get any robes, and today only the lord mayor (the mayor was so elevated in 1897, four years after Sheffield attained city status) wears the gown on a few important ceremonial occasions each year.

Southampton has been previously mentioned: further details of this city's "apparell in tymes past used comenlie to be worne by the maiors, aldermen, shreffes and baylifes, and there wyves" was given in a Court Leet Record of 1576. The mayor and aldermen had scarlet gowns with marten's or polecat's fur (foynes) for the winter and black or russett silk facings for the summer. There is also mention of a fur or silk crimson gown and "about there necke a chayne of golde and dothe wear braslettes and rings": this latter may have applied to the mayor only. "Shreves and Bayliefes" (sheriffs and their deputies) had violet gowns, again fur or silk faced according to the season, also "other gownes furred with budge foxe and lame [lamb]". Underneath, but whether this is for all, or for sheriffs and bailiffs only is uncertain, were decreed

jackettes or coats [jerkin is the more usual name] of satten chamlett [probably mohair originally, then of mixed fibres] or worsted garded with velvett; dublettes of satten or wosted; hats of silk throme [thrum hats were made of materials with a very long pile, giving a somewhat shaggy appearance]; hosse [hose, male garments from the waist down: breeches and stockings] of fyne clothe playne: girdills and garters of silke.

The wives of the "shreves and bayliffes" had crimson cloth gowns, lined with grey amys (amice) for winter and silk for summer, trimmed with velvet.

Today the Mayor of Southampton wears a scarlet gown, the deputy Mayor one of purple and the Sheriff a dark blue one. The ladies probably abandoned their special dresses in the late seventeenth or early eighteenth century.

Hats when worn were of the usual style of the day, very often made of "beaver", originally of the imported fur, then of a felt made from the fur and later still, of any fine felt. The eighteenth-century hat with three cocks in the brim, or tricorne (a modern name), the edge of the brim decorated with gold lace or a feather border gave way to the hat with two cocks (bicorne) which could be folded flat. The latter is the most common wear with civic dress today, although a few tricornes are worn by mayors (for example, the Lord Mayor of London) by civic officials and often by lady mayors.

Chains, commonly worn by mayors, sheriffs and some aldermen, and ex-mayors were, like the gown, originally marks of dignity and affluence, with no special significance such as the collar of Ss had. London, indeed, has a collar of Ss bequeathed in the sixteenth century as a chain, and some places have collar-like chains. In London and York, where the lord mayor's chain dates from 1612, the transfer of office from the old lord mayor to the new is signified by the removal of the chain from the neck of the one and its ceremonial placing around the neck of the other.

There were few mayoral chains before the eighteenth century, and of these only a handful pre-dated the Restoration. In 1673 Guildford was given a "fayre chaine of gold, double linked with a medal of massy gold." Norwich was given a chain in 1716 and another in 1757. Yarmouth bought one by subscription in 1734. But most chains were acquired in the nineteenth century: generally in the latter half as a revival took place of those ancient costumes and customs suspended after the 1835 Act. It was estimated in 1895 that between 1860 and 1880 some one hundred and ten cities and towns provided chains for their mayors. Today most, if not all, lord mayors and mayors wear them as well as some deputy and past mayors and sheriffs. The chains were sometimes given by the charter mayors, sometimes by public subscription and sometimes by individuals or by societies. For instance, in 1873 the Royal Archaeological Institute held its annual meeting at Exeter, and the following year, 1874, the institute, to show its appreciation of the welcome and entertainment provided by the people and city presented the corporation with a mayoral chain and badge. (*Illustrated London News* 24 October 1874.) The account further stated that it was a replacement for a chain and badge lost during the Civil War; "sacrificed in old days to the Royalist Cause", as the *Illustrated London News* put it.

The commonest form for modern chains is a series of linked tablets or plaques, each one engraved in turn with the name of the current mayor: in some cases it is customary for retiring mayors to present a tablet for the chain, or a medallion to be suspended from a link of the chain, as a memorial of their year of office.

Since the time when chains of office became so popular, rules and customs to govern their use have arisen. Robes and chain are worn generally at civic receptions, for visits of members of the royal family, church parades and some council meetings. On other formal occasions the chain only is worn. However, the wearing of robes and insignia varies from place to place and additions to or omissions from this list can and do occur. Neither robes nor chain are worn in any other borough, or town, unless the visiting mayor is invited to do so by the mayor of the place being visited.

Dress Worn at Court, 1912 edition, states that attending court in their official capacity lord mayors (except London, who is given his own paragraph) and mayors should wear their chain and badge over new velvet court dress, without frill and ruffles, or old velvet court dress, with frill and ruffles. After the First World War "alternative dress" was added as a third choice. If a clergyman, then he may wear his chain over "full canonicals" ("clerical dress" in the 1937 edition). At royal garden parties today chains and badges are not worn with the formal dress prescribed for such occasions. A note in the 1929 edition of *Dress Worn at Court* mentions "ladies who are mayors" and states that they may wear chain and badge, "but not robes".

Some confusion has also occurred in connection with wearing the mayoral chain with uniform. The 1912 edition of *Dress Worn at Court* states that "The Mayoral Chain should never be worn with a Military Iniform". The 1929 edition says that if a mayor is entitled to service uniform it may be worn with chain and badge, and the Metropolitan Mayors' Association in 1931 said the mayoral chain and badge may be worn with army or R.A.F. uniform, but not with naval uniform (quoted in Tweedy-Smith, *History etc. of Mayors, Aldermen and Councillors*). The 1937 *Dress Worn at Court* states that the chain and badge are never worn with naval uniform. In the 1950s *The Manual of the Mace* and *Civic Ceremonial* by J. F. Garner both laid down that the chain and badge should never be worn with naval, army or air force uniforms. Similarly, for lord lieutenants' uniform, both a War Office Order of 1934 and Tweedy-Smith in the same year state that chains and badges may be worn with it, whilst the *Manual of the Mace* says they should not, and Garner says they probably should not be worn with lieutenancy uniform.

A former Mayor of Colchester was painted about 1953 wearing a deputy lieutenant's pre-war full dress uniform with the mayoral gown and chain.

A chain or badge of some type is now generally provided for mayoresses. Although mostly of recent origin the practice dates back at least to the seventeenth century. Hull had a lady mayoress's chain in

1604, but it was apparently disposed of in 1835 or 1836 as part of the despised "paraphernalia of office" the newly elected Corporation so objected to.

The Lady Mayoress of York also has a seventeenth-century chain to wear. For many years this chain was weighed annually and the weight at the beginning and end of the year of office checked. Presumably some former lady mayoresses became too attached to at least part of the chain and I am glad to record that this practice was stopped a long time ago and that the honesty of the ladies of York is no longer impugned by the city fathers.

Among the insignia of office, rods, wands and staves occasionally figure – as well as the chain the Lady Mayoress of York is invested with a wand of office, a "staff of honour", presented to the city in 1726. The Sheriffs of York also had wands, as did those of Southampton, Nottingham and Chester. In 1860 staves were presented to Clitheroe for the use of the aldermen. London, of course, has a sceptre, carried on special occasions by the Lord Mayor. In 1662 King Charles II conferred a white rod upon the Mayor of Derby, but its use has been given up.

152. Sheriff of the City of York, fur faced scarlet gown worn over normal clothes. 1642. (Redrawn from Clinch, *English Costume*, 1909)

In some towns, Reading and Lincoln for example, the mayor is invested with an official ring. That worn by the Mayor of Lincoln is a gold "posy" ring which traditionally obtains a holiday for any school in the city to which it is sent.

Swords, denoting power of criminal jurisdiction, were granted to some boroughs and cities to be carried before the lord mayor or mayor. The scabbard was covered in crimson or scarlet velvet in most cases, but purple and blue occur, as does black in times of mourning.

In 1440 the Corporation of Hull spent "Item for j q°rter cloth gold to the swerde .... Item for j q°rter blewe velvet to the same ...." (Corporation of Hull: "Costage of the Charter of Henry Sixth ..." in *Liber Albas*).

There are about thirty-two towns and cities with swords today. Up to the eighteenth century they were granted by charter, after that they seem to have been presented by private individuals without any apparent authority. Some post-Reformation grants were to Wigan in 1662, Yarmouth in 1684, Liverpool in 1695. Worcester was granted a second sword in 1690. In 1752 Bristol acquired a fourth, bringing the city in line with London. Of later date can be quoted as examples Derby in 1870 and Ipswich in 1887.

With the early swords the charters also granted a cap of maintenance to be worn by the swordbearer. Not many are still in use: London, York, Bristol, Coventry, Lincoln, Newcastle-upon-Tyne, Norwich, Worcester and Hereford. Hull and Salisbury are examples of towns where they have fallen into disuse (Salisbury's was granted by Cromwell and its use discontinued at the Restoration). Some places, London, Hull and Norwich for example, had two. They could be made of fur, as London, or of silk or velvet. Some of the latter were really low-crowned hats, embroidered with gold. Some had cords and tassels. In Exeter the cap is carried before the mayor on a cushion.

Among the early municipal officials were the sergeants, appointed to wait upon the mayor or baliffs to serve processes, arrest offenders, make proclamations, attend the mayor's court etc. As a mark of authority they most likely carried a staff. Later, probably during the late fourteenth century, they were granted small maces and charters of incorporation mention them and also "serjaents at mace", generally to be elected.

The character of the mace changed and by about 1650 the sergeants' maces fell into disuse and the great mace, borne before the mayor or bailiffs came into prominence. The great or mayor's maces had been granted in small numbers from the end of the fourteenth century to symbolise the deputed powers of the crown, and were in a way an extension of the principle of the sergeants' maces. They became more numerous in the seventeenth and eighteenth centuries. After the 1835 Act municipal charters do not contain powers to appoint sergeants, nevertheless, most of the nineteenth-century and later cities and boroughs acquired maces.

Although sergeants and sergeants' maces lingered on in some places until the nineteenth century the office and the symbol became redundant as new legal processes and increasingly numerous and efficient police forces came on the scene. The great mace, however, continues to mark the official presence of the lord mayor or mayor and an official is appointed to carry it. Today these officials are generally known simply as "mace bearers", and are dressed in a variety of fashions: some in uniform, some in gowns, most of which are of nineteenth century design, although some are more ancient. In Hartlepool there was no mace bearer and on ceremonial occasions the mace was carried before the mayor by a police-sergeant, as it was in Barnsley until 1954 when a mace bearer was appointed. At Reading in 1688 the council resolved that "the Sergeants to have cloakes made of black cloth . . ." and in 1725 the accounts include:

Cloth for Sergaents and Bellman	£10.14.0.
for their trimmings	3.11.10.
for Hats and Bands	2. 5. 0.
for gould lace	6. 9. 2.

(quoted in Jewitt and Hope, *Corporation Place etc. of England and Wales* 1895.)

At Saffron Walden in the 1870s and 1880s the mace bearers wore blue uniforms with cocked hats.

153. Beadles: (a) City of London Beadle. Dressed in Gown with hanging sleeves, round hat with deep turned up brim, carrying silver headed Staff of Office. 1747. (After Hogarth, *Industry and Idleness* plate 8); (b) Parish Beadle, wearing caped coat, cocked hat, breeches, carrying stick. 1840. (After Sir John Gilbert, "*Feeding the Hungry*")

154. "Superior" West End Parish
Beadle. 1862. (After *London Society*,
1862)

Ede and Ravenscroft, the robe makers, say the mace bearer of today
can wear gown or uniform or both: the gown of any colour, trimmed
usually with gold or silver lace. In 1970 the Prime Warden of the Guild
of Mace Bearers concluded that "the majority [of Councils] favour a
frock coat, trimmed with gold braid [lace], dress shirt, wing collar,
white bow tie and top hat". Plain or laced trousers are generally worn
with the frock coat.

Like the mace bearers other municipal officials such as beadles, town
cryers, watchmen, bellmen, and others wear or wore a variety of livery
or uniform, or at times none at all, often with a silver badge, or a staff
of office, most commonly with a silver head and some five or six feet
long.

Reading again in 1688 provided "caps, coats and breeches" for the
"Belman", and in 1725 spent £9 10s 0d "Bellmans Stalves [sic] and
silver heads". (Ede and Ravenscroft.)

Of municipal officers the town clerk is the chief, and he is generally,
but not always, a solicitor. His dress is traditionally a gown, which is
today standardised as silk with "tufts" and guarded with black velvet
and black lace. He wears a short legal wig and robes himself on the occasions when the mayor wears his robes.

Badges of various designs and of modern origin in most cases are
often provided for mayoresses, deputy-mayors and ex-mayors, and
sometimes for borough sheriffs, the mayor's chaplain and honorary
freemen. These are only worn at civic functions within the town or
borough boundaries. Orders, decorations and medals can be worn
with civic robes, but not on them: they should be worn in the normal
places on the clothes worn underneath the robe. Unfortunately the

habit seems to have crept in since the last war of pinning medals on to the mayoral robe itself.

The purchase of robes for use by mayor, aldermen or councillors from public funds is forbidden, but in exceptional cases a dispensation from this embargo may be granted by the appropriate government department and a contribution made from the rates. Uniform for beadles, town cryers and other such officials may be charged to the rate account.

To conclude this chapter it may be of interest to look at an ancient town and borough which has, however, in the last couple of years made a radical change from tradition in its mayoral gown, followed by a reversion to a more conservative pattern.

Colchester proudly claims to be the country's oldest recorded town with a continuous history since pre-Roman days. The first of its post-Conquest charters was granted by Richard I in 1189 and this gave the right to appoint bailiffs and administrative and judicial officers, freedom from courts outside the borough and rights of hunting fox, hare and polecat (the source of "foynes" fur for facing gowns).

There were four more charters up to 1462; and local government was in the hands of the bailiffs, assisted by a high steward, clerk and sergeants and possibly with a town council of sorts. About 1443 we see the appearance of aldermen, to be chosen from the councillors, and the bailiffs to be chosen from aldermen. Later we also read of "assistants" between aldermen and common councillors.

Two centuries later, in 1663, the Charter of Charles II authorises eleven aldermen, eighteen assistants and eighteen common councillors. The two bailiffs had already, in 1635, been replaced by a mayor. Later, the aldermen, assistants and councillors were cut down to ten each. The sergeants varied in number between three and five. There are also recorded in the seventeenth century a town clerk, deputy town clerk, beadles, waits (to provide music at official functions) and a bottlemaker. This last appears to have been an official to make up "bottles" or bundles of hay, presumably for municipal use: however, he disappeared later in the century.

In 1620 liveries and badges for the above officials cost £28. 14s 0d. In 1666 common councilmen attending meetings without their gowns were fined 3s 4d. In 1681 "the waits given new cloaks: for 20 yds of blew cloath for 5 cloaks for the Towne Musicke ... £12.0.0." (*Colchester Chamberlain's Accounts.*) There was also bought silver and gold lace, scarlet serge, six yards, and "blew white and scarlett silk" (presumably for sewing) to trim them. The entry also includes blue cloth for coats, not apparently for the "musicke", and an entry for

155. Mayor of Colchester about the turn of the century wearing the black silk
damask and gold gown introduced at that time. (Portrait of Wilson Marriage
Esq. J.P. by Frank Daniel. Colchester Borough Council)

1729 records the purchase of "blew" cloth for the sergeants. Throughout the eighteenth century clothes are bought for the sergeants, and less frequently hats: "Sept. 18 1788 For Sjts Hats etc. £6.12.6." but they apparently get re-trimmed occasionally, "Aug. 8 1777 For lace for Sjts Hats £1.1.0."

The year 1724 saw blue gowns also provided for the sergeants to wear in court. In 1838 £18 was paid for three suits of clothes for the "town sergeants" and similar items occur throughout the first half of the century, as do items for clothing "the Police".

As a result of the institution of the police and of the new administration under the 1835 Act we find that the number of sergeants is reduced to two and later to one, the present number. Today's town sergeant dresses on ceremonial occasions in blue coat, waistcoat and breeches of late eighteenth-century style, with gilt buttons, a gold laced three-cornered hat, white stockings and buckled shoes. With this costume is worn a wing collar and white bow-tie. A similar uniform is seen in photographs of the town sergeant of the second half of the last century. Another recurring item in the eighteenth century was an annual allowance for the town clerk's "livery" of 15 shillings, which seems a small amount and is presumably an upkeep allowance rather than the purchase price of a gown.

Colchester was one of the boroughs whose mayor and aldermen and their ladies were exempt from the provisions of the 1463 Ordinance Against Excessive Apparel. The gowns of the medieval corporation were presumably scarlet, as were the majority of civic robes. Post-Restoration charters of Charles II and George III confirm the use of robes.

Early nineteenth century mayors are shown in red gowns, but as with many other towns robes seem to have been abandoned after the 1835 Act, which also laid down an establishment of mayor, six aldermen and eighteen councillors. Again in common with others the council reassumed gowns later in the century. In 1883 the mayor and others wear plain black gowns over ordinary clothes, and top hats. The aldermen seem to have fur facings and the Councillors silk.

About the turn of the century the council was getting back to its old robes: proclaiming the Accession of Edward VII in 1901, the then mayor wore a black gown heavily gold embroidered and guarded with gold lace over court dress and with a fore-and-aft cocked hat. Aldermen and councillors dressed much as in 1883, most with top hats, but one or two in cocked hats. The town clerk wore a plain black gown and top hat.

Nine years later King George V's Accession was proclaimed by the

156. Mrs Brooks, Mayor of Colchester, wearing the new robe of unorthodox design made by the Colchester Technical College. 1977. (Courtesy of Essex County Newspapers Ltd.)

mayor dressed in the same robes, but the aldermen and councillors had apparently red and blue gowns and all wore cocked hats. The town clerk now had his legal wig on.

During this century the black and gold mayoral gown, scarlet aldermanic gowns and blue councillors' gowns have been worn with cocked hats. In 1974, following the latest reorganisation of local government, Colchester became the seat of a district council, and the aldermen were abolished, as were all others, except in the City of London. So that the fine scarlet aldermanic gowns should continue to grace civic occasions and add colour to a dull enough world the council decided to allot them for wear by chairmen of committees, and they are now so used. The other councillors continue in their former blue gowns, and so did the mayor in his old black and gold until 1976. By 1975 the youngest and least worn of the two existing mayoral robes was about a quarter of a century old and it was felt that it should be replaced. Estimates for a new one were about £400, a cost unacceptable to the town and

157. Mr D. Holt displaying the Second Mayoral Gown on more traditional lines designed and produced by Colchester Technical College. 1978. (Courtesy of Essex County Newspapers Ltd.)

vociferously cried down, and the whole idea of civic robes attacked by certain predictable elements of the townsfolk. However the day was saved by the offer of the Colchester Technical College to design and make a new gown as a co-operative effort by students and staff of the dressmaking and clothing department. A local firm offered the material free and so even the most radical of the anti-robe faction could hardly complain on grounds of cost. Designs of an original nature based partly on the old gown and partly on a compromise suitable for wear by both men and women (the mayor-elect for 1976 was a lady) were produced and accepted. The material used was a black light weight mohair and the gown cut on the lines of a loose raglan coat with fairly wide sleeves but omitting the medieval hanging sleeve. Gold embroidery of oyster shells and wheat ears decorates the fronts and there is gold lacing to the wide revers, cuffs and at the bottom of the gown.

Although accepted and worn there was a certain amount of criticism and two years later the college produced a further gown based on the traditional style, but simpler and with considerably less gold embroidery and lace. Again the fabric, a black barathea, was given by a local manufacturer. Colchester in 1978 is probably unique in having two modern mayoral gowns both of local design and manufacture offering future holders of the office a choice denied to other municipalities.

Appendix I

(a) Regulations for Ladies attending Courts, 1908 and 1937
(b) Advice to Gentlemen wearing uniform 1908 (and unaltered in 1937).

The following directions are taken from the 1908 and 1937 editions of *Dress Worn at Court*, issued by the Lord Chamberlain's authority.

(a) *Ladies attending Courts* – 1908

Dress Regulations for Ladies attending Their Majesties' Courts

Ladies attending Their Majesties' Courts will appear in Full Dress, with Trains and Plumes. For Half Mourning Black and White, White, Mauve, or Grey should be worn.

FEATHERS should be worn so that they can be clearly seen on approaching the Presence, with White veils or lappets. Coloured feathers are inadmissible, but in deep mourning Black feathers may be worn.

WHITE GLOVES only are to be worn, excepting in case of mourning, when Black or Grey gloves are admissible.

HIGH COURT DRESS. The King has been pleased to permit that a High Court Dress, according to the following description, may be worn in future at Their Majesties' Courts, and on other State occasions, by Ladies, to whom, from illness, infirmity, or advancing age, the present low Court Dress is inappropriate, viz., Bodices in front, cut square or heart shape, which may be *filled in with white only, either transparent or lined*; at the back high or cut down three-quarter height. Sleeves to elbow, either thick or transparent. Trains, gloves, and feathers as usual.

It is necessary for Ladies who wish to appear in "HIGH COURT DRESS", to obtain permission through the Lord Chamberlain, unless they have already received it.

Ladies attending Courts – 1937

Ladies attending Their Majesties' Courts must wear Low Evening Dresses with Court Trains suspended from the shoulders, white veils with ostrich feathers will be worn on the head.

The Train, which should not exceed 2 yards in length, must not extend more than 18″ from the heel of the wearer when standing.

Three small white feathers mounted as a Prince of Wales Plume, the centre feather a little higher than the two side ones, to be worn slightly on the left side of the head, with the tulle veil of similar colour attached to the base of the feathers.

The veil should not be longer than 45″.

Coloured feathers are inadmissable, but in cases of deep mourning Black feathers may be worn.

Gloves *must* be worn.

There are no restrictions with regard to the colour of the dresses or gloves for either debutantes or those who have already been presented.

Bouquets and fans are optional.

Sketches of typical Court Dress are on view at the Lord Chamberlain's Office, St James's Palace.

(b) *Manner of Wearing Uniform* – 1908

A soft fronted shirt with white cuffs is best to wear with uniform.

When breeches are worn, pants should reach to the knees only, or a combination suit to reach to the knees.

With stockings it is advisable to wear a *thin* pair of cotton hose under the silk. This prevents the flesh being seen through the silk. Both pairs should be well pulled up over the knees and should fit closely.

Shoes should not have too thin a sole unless they are worn for dancing. Care should be taken to secure sword belts from showing below coats or waistcoats or above waistcoat openings. This end may be achieved by wearing the belt under the braces.

With Court suits plain Gold or Pearl studs should be in the shirt front, and watch chains should not be worn. The Black silk fob with seals, if worn, should hang from the fob pocket on the right side.

Appendix II

Court Mourning in the nineteenth century

*Mourning for the late Royal Highness
the Grand Duke of Hesse*

Lord Chamberlain's Office, 4 July 1848.

Ladies to wear black silk, fringed or plain linen, white gloves, necklaces and earrings, black or white shoes, fans and tippets.

Gentlemen, black suits, full trimmed, fringed or plain linen black swords and buckles.

Second Mourning   9 July 1848

Ladies to wear black silk or velvet, coloured ribbons, fans and tippets, or plain white or white and gold or white and silver stuffs with black ribbons.

Gentlemen, black coats, black, white, or white and gold or white and silver waistcoats full trimmed coloured swords and buckles.

And the Court to go out of mourning on the 13th.

Court Mourning for Prince Albert

The following three Orders were issued by the Lord Chamberlain's Office:

16 December 1861
Orders for the Court to go into mourning for His late Royal Highness the Prince Consort.

The Ladies attending Court to wear black woollen stuffs trimmed with crape, plain linen, black shoes and gloves and crape fans.

The Gentlemen attending Court to wear black cloth, plain linen, crape hatbands, and black swords and buckles.

27 January 1862

Change of Mourning for His late Royal Highness the Prince Consort.

Ladies to wear black silk dresses, trimmed with crape, and black shoes and gloves, black fans, feathers and ornaments.

The Gentlemen to wear Black Court dress with black swords and buckles and plain linen.

17 February 1862

Change of Mourning for His late Royal Highness the Prince Consort.

Ladies to wear black dresses with white gloves, black or white shoes, fan and feathers, and Pearls, Diamonds or plain Gold or Silver Ornaments.

The Gentlemen to wear Black Court dress, with black swords and buckles.

And on Monday 10th March next the Court to go out of Mourning.

Bibliography

Adburgham, Alison. *Shops and Shopping, 1800–1914*, 1964

Alexander, William. *Picturesque Reproductions of the Dress and Manners of the English*, 1813

Alford and Baker. *A History of the Carpenters' Company*, 1968

Anon.
  Etiquette of Good Society, 1900
  The Habits of Society: A Handbook of Etiquette, 1859
  Manners and Tone of Good Society by A Member of the Aristocracy, 1822
  Civil Uniforms in the Queen's Household (illustrations, no text), 1890
  A Representation of the Clothing of H.M: Household and of all the Forces . . . of Great Britain and Ireland (illustrations, no text), 1742
  Notebooks of a Spinster Lady, 1919
  Court Etiquette by A Man of the World, 1849

Anson, Elizabeth and Florence (eds.). *Mary Hamilton at Court and at Home 1756–1811*, 1925

Armytage, Mrs *Old Court Customs and Modern Court Rule*, 1883

Arnold, Janet "A Court Mantua of *c*1740", *Costume* No. 6, 1972
  "A Court Mantua of *c*1760–5", *Costume* No. 7, 1973

Ashmole, Elias. *The Institution, Laws and Ceremonies of the Most Noble Order of the Garter*, 1672 and 1715

Beard, Charles R. "The Clothing and Arming of the Yeoman of the Guard 1485–1685", *Archaeological Journal*, vol. 87, 1928
  "King James II's Wedding Suit", *Connoisseur*, July 1928

Beattie, J. M. *English Court Life in the Reign of George I*, 1967

Berry, Wm. *Encyclopaedia Heraldica*, 1828–36

Blackstone, Sir William. *Commentaries on the Laws of England*, 1769

Bloomfield, Lady. *Reminiscences of Court and Diplomatic Life*, 1883

Boykin, Edward (ed.). *Victoria, Albert and Mrs Stevenson*, 1957

Brackenbury, H. *The Nearest Guard*, 1892

Burney, Fanny see D'Arblay

Bury, Lady Charlotte. *Diary of a Lady in Waiting*, 1908

Butler, E. M. (ed.). *A Regency Visitor, Prince Puckler-Muskau*, 1957

Chamberlayne, Edward. *Anglicae Notitia*, 1670

Clephane, Irene. *Our Mothers, 1870–1900*, 1932

Clinch, George. *English Costume*, 1909

Creevey, Thomas. *The Creevey Papers* ed. Sir Herbert Maxwell, 1903 and 1905
  Creevey's Life and Times ed. John Gore, 1937

Cunnington, C. W. and P. *Handbook of English Costume in the 17th Century*, 1955
   Handbook of English Costume in the 18th Century, 1957
   Handbook of English Costume in the 19th Century, 1959

Cunnington, C. W. and P. and Beard, L. *A Dictionary of English Costume*, 1968

Cunnington, Phillis, and Lucas, Catherine. *Costume for Births Marriages and Deaths*, 1972

Curling, J. B. *Some Account of the Ancient Corps of Gentlemen at Arms*, 1850

D'Arblay, Charlotte Barett (ed.). *Diary and Letters of Madame D'Arblay 1778–1840*, 1904

Delany, Lady Llanover (ed.). *The Autobiography and Correspondence of Mary Granville, Mrs Delany*, 1862

Douglas, Mrs *The Gentlewoman's Book of Dress*

Dress Worn at Court see under Lord Chamberlain

Ellis, Jennifer (ed.). *Thatched with Gold: Memoirs of Mabell, Countess of Airlie*, 1962

Evelyn, John. *Diary*
   Tyranus or The Mode, 1661

Fairholt. *Lord Mayors' Pageants*, 1843

Fellows, E. H. *The Knights of the Garter*, 1939

Fiennes, Celia. *The Journeys of Celia Fiennes* ed. Christopher Morris, 1949

Forbes, Lady Angela. *How to Dress for all Ages and Occasions*, 1926

Fordyce, James. *Chronology*, 1823

Frampton, Mary. *Journal of Mary Frampton* ed. Harriet Mundy, 1885

Froissart *Chronicles*

Garner, J. F. *Civic Ceremonial*, 1957

Gladwin, Irene. *The Sheriff: the Man and his Office*, 1974

Gordon, Major L. L. *British Orders and Awards*, privately published, 1959

Grammont, Anthony Hamilton. *Memoirs of the Court of Charles II by Count Grammont*, 1846

Gunn, Fenja. *The Artificial Face*, 1973

Halls, Zillah see London Museum

Hamilton, Mary see Anson

Hartnell, Norman. *Silver and Gold*, 1955

Hay, D. R. *Nomenclature of Colours*, 1845

Heath, James. *A Chronicle of the Late Intestine War*, 1676

Hesketh, Lady Christian. *Tartans*, 1962

Herbert, William. *History of the Twelve Great Livery Companies*, 1834

Hibbert, Christopher. *The Court at Windsor*, 1964

Hoare, Richard. *A Journal of the Shrievalty of Richard Hoare*, Bath 1815

Holding, T. H. *Uniforms of the British Army, Navy and Court*, 1894

Holme, Randle. *Academy of Armory*, 1688

Hope-Nicolson, J. *Life Among the Troubridges*

Houblon, Lady Alice Frances Archer. *The Houblon Family*, 1907

Ilchester and Langford-Brooke. *The Life of Sir Charles Hanbury-Williams*, 1928

Jerrold, Clare. *The Early Court of Queen Victoria*, 1912

Jesse, J. H. *Memoirs of the Court of England during the Reign of the Stuarts*, 1901

Jewitt, Llewellyn and St John Hope, W. H. *The Coronation Plate and Insignia of Office of the Cities and Corporate Towns of England and Wales*, 1895

Jupp, E. B. *An Historical Account of the Worshipful Company of Carpenters*, 1848

Kelly and Schwabe. *A Short History of Costume and Armour*, 1931

King, Colonel E. J. *The Knights of St John in the British Empire*, 1934

Knight, Cornelia. *Autobiography*, 1861

Laird, Dorothy. *How the Queen Reigns*, 1959

Lang, Jennifer. *Pride without Prejudice*, 1975

Lieven, Princess. *The Private Letters of Princess Lieven* ed. P. Quennell, 1948

Legg, L. G. Wickham. *English Coronation Records*, 1901

Leslie, C. P. *Memorial of the Life of John Constable*, 1843

London, Corporation of. *The Order of My Lord Mayor . . . etc.*, 1656 et seq
    Ceremonies Connected with the Office of Lord Mayor, 1834 et seq
    Handbook of Ceremonials, 1906
    Handbook of Ceremonials, 1933
    Ceremonials of the Corporation of London, 1962

London Museum *Catalogue No. 5 Costume*, 1934
    Women's Costume 1750–1800 (Zillah Hall) 1972
    Men's Costume 1750–1800 (Zillah Hall) 1973
    Coronation Costume 1685–1953, 1973

Lord Chamberlain's Office, *Dress and Insignia Worn at H.M.'s Court* (Dress Worn at Court) various editions from 1898 to 1937 (see Chapter IV)

Manchester, Duke of (ed.). *Court and Society from Elizabeth to Anne from the papers at Kimbolton*, 1864

Mansfield, A. D. and Cunnington, P. *Handbook of English Costume of the 20th Century*, 1973
    John Masters' Expense Book ed. Mrs Dalison and Cannon Scott Robinson in *Archaeologica Cantiana*, vols 16, 17, 18

Maxwell, Sir Herbert. *Sixty Years a Queen*, 1897

Milton, Roger. *The English Ceremonial Book*, Newton Abbott, 1972

Molloy, J. Fitzgerald. *Court Life Below Stairs, in London under the First Georges, 1714–60*, 1882
    Court Life Below Stairs, in London under the Last Georges 1760–83, 1883

Morshead, Sir Owen. "Windsor Uniforms" *Connoisseur*, May 1935

Municipal Corporations (England and Wales) Commission, *Report*, 1835

Naylor, Sir George. *Coronation of King George IV*, 1824–39

Nevinson, J. L. "The Robes of the Order of the Garter", *Connoisseur*, May 1937
    "Crowns and Garlands of the Livery Companies" *Guildhall Studies in London History*, vol I, April 1974
    Appendix J of *The History of the Carpenters Company* by Alford and Baker, 1968

Nevinson, J. L. and Tanner, L. E. "Later Funeral Effigies in Westminster Abbey" *Archaeologica*, vol 85, 1935

Nicholas, Sir N. Harris. *A History of the Orders of Knighthood of the British Empire*, 4 vols, 1842
Northumberland, Duchess of. *The Diary of a Duchess* ed J. Greig, 1926
Nowell-Smith, S. *Edwardian England*, 1964

Packett, C. Neville. *A History and A to Z of H.M. Lieutenancy of Counties*, privately published, Bradford, 1972
Papendiek, Charlotte. *Court and Private Life in the Times of Queen Charlotte* ed. Mrs V. D. Broughton, 2 vols, 1887
Peerages: *Burke's Peerage*, various editions
    Debrett's Peerage, various editions
    The Pocket Peerage, 1788
Pennant, Thomas, *Account of London*, 1790
Pepys, Samuel, *Diary*
Perkins, Jocelyn H. T. *The Coronation Book*, 1902
Pine, John. *Processions and Ceremonies*, 1730
Pine, L. G. *The Story of the Peerage*, 1956
Planché, J. R. *The Cyclopeadia of Costume*, 2 vols 1876–79
Ponsonby Fane, S. "Shoe Buckles", *Connoisseur*, vol 11, 1905

Reid, Hazel. "A Collection of Thistle Robes from Drummond Castle" *Costume*, No 8, 1974
Riske, James C. *The History of the Order of the Bath and its Insignia*, 1972
Royal School of Needlework, Exhibition of Coronation Robes, Catalogue, 1937

Sandeman, J. G. *The Spears of Honour and the Gentlemen Pensioners*, 1912
Sandford, Francis. *The Coronation of James II*, 1685
Scanlan, Nellie M. *Road to Pencarrou*, 1963
Scott-Tomson, Gladys. *Life in a Noble Household*, 1965
Seldon, John. *Titles of Honour*, 1614
Shaw, W. A. *The Knights of England*, 1905
Sheppard, Edgar. *St James's Palace*, 1894
Sibbald, Susan. *Memoirs* ed. Francis Paget Hett, 1926
Simond, Louis. *An American in Regency England*, 1968
Spencer, Sarah Lady Lyttleton. *Correspondence* ed. the Hon. Mrs Hugh Wyndham, 1912
St John Hope, W. H. *Heraldry for Craftsmen and Designers*, 1913
    "The Cap of Maintenance" appendix to *English Coronation Records* L. G. Wickham Legg, 1901
Stothard, Charles. *Monumental Effigies of Great Britain*, 1876
Stowe, John. *Survey of London*, 1633 edition
Strong, Roy. *The Elizabethan Image*, Tate Gallery, 1969
Suffolk, Lady. *Letters*, 1824

Thoms, William J. *The Book of the Court*, 1838
Thorne, Lt. Col. Peter. *Official Dress Worn in the House of Commons*, HMSO, 1960
Tozer, C. W. *The Insignia and Medals of the Order of St John*, 1975
Troubridge, Laura see Hope-Nicholson
Turner, E. S. *The Court of St James*, 1959
Tweedy Smith R. *History Law and Practice and Procedure relating to Mayors*, 1934

Verney, Lady F. and Lady M. *Memoirs of the Verney Family 1642–96*, 4 vols, 1892–99
  The Letters of Queen Victoria ed. A. C. Benson and Viscount Esher, 1908

Villiers, the Hon. Catherine. *The Memoirs of a Maid of Honour*, 1932

Wagner, Sir Anthony. *The Heralds of England*, 1967
Windsor, *A King's Story: the Memoirs of H.R.H. the Duke of Windsor*, 1951

MS. Sources

Among many such are:

British Museum: Additional MSS 35324   Harleien MS 6166
               Harleien MS 3319   Lansdown MS 255
               Harleien MS 6064   Lansdown MS 261

College of Arms: Vincent MS 151

Guildhall Library: The Noble Collection of MSS and Press Cuttings

House of Lords: Black Rod's Letter Book

Lord Chamberlain's Papers to 1904

Public Record Office. Extracts from the Notebooks of Sir C. Cotterell, Master of the
           Ceremonies 1710–58, LC5/3
           Household Ordinances, Charles II and James II, LC 5/196

War Office Orders and Papers relating to Lord Lieutenants etc.

Periodicals

Ackermann's Repository
Annals of Westminster Abbey Vol. 35
 "P. and M.: 4 and 5 1557/8"
Archaeologia
La Belle Assemblée
The Bystander
The Connoisseur
Costume
Country Life
The Court Magazine
The Gentleman's Magazine of Fashion
The Gentlewoman
Girls Own Annual 1911
The Graphic

Illustrated London News
The Ladies Magazine
The Ladies Newspaper
London Society
Minster's Gazette of Fashion
Mirror of Fashion
Punch
The Queen
The Spectator
Sphere 1911
The Tailor & Cutter
The Tatler
West End Gazette of Fashion
The World

Newspapers

The Daily Telegraph
The Morning Post
The Times
The Ipswich Journal and other local papers

Index

Numbers in **heavy type** refer to illustrations